WHOLENESS

Toward a Biblical

IN

Theology of Holiness

CHRIST

William M.

GREATHOUSE

BEACON HILL PRESS
OF KANSAS CITY

Copyright 1998
by Beacon Hill Press of Kansas City

ISBN 978-0-8341-1786-0

Printed in the
United States of America

Cover Design: Ted Ferguson

All Scripture quotations not otherwise designated are from the *New Revised Standard Version* (NRSV) of the Bible, copyright 1989 by the Division of Christian Education of the National Council of the Churches of Christ in the USA. All rights reserved.

Permission to quote from the following additional copyrighted versions of the Bible is acknowledged with appreciation:

The Bible: A New Translation (MOFFATT). Copyright 1922, 1924, 1925, 1935 by Harper & Row, Publishers, Incorporated. Copyright 1950, 1952, 1953, 1954 by James A. R. Moffatt.

The *New American Standard Bible®* (NASB®), copyright The Lockman Foundation 1960, 1962, 1963, 1968, 1971, 1972, 1973, 1975, 1977, 1995.

The New English Bible (NEB). Copyright © by the Delegates of the Oxford University Press and the Syndics of the Cambridge University Press, 1961, 1970.

The *Holy Bible, New International Version®* (NIV®). Copyright © 1973, 1978, 1984 by International Bible Society. Used by permission of Zondervan Publishing House. All rights reserved.

The New Jerusalem Bible (NJB), copyright © 1985 by Darton, Longman & Todd, Ltd., and Doubleday, a division of Bantam Doubleday Dell Publishing Group, Inc.

The *New King James Version* (NKJV). Copyright © 1979, 1980, 1982 by Thomas Nelson, Inc.

The New Testament in Modern English (PHILLIPS), Revised Student Edition, by J. B. Phillips, translator. Copyright 1958, 1960, 1972 by J. B. Phillips. Reprinted with the permission of the Macmillan Publishing Company.

The Revised English Bible (REB). Copyright © by Oxford University Press and Cambridge University Press, 1989.

The *Revised Standard Version* (RSV) of the Bible, copyright 1946, 1952, 1971, by the Division of Christian Education of the National Council of the Churches of Christ in the USA.

The Living Bible (TLB), © 1971. Used by permission of Tyndale House Publishers, Inc., Wheaton, IL 60189. All rights reserved.

The New Testament in Modern Speech (WEYMOUTH). Copyright 1929 by Harper and Brothers, New York.

Scripture quotations marked KJV are from the King James Version.

The Library of Congress has already catalogued the hardcover edition as follows:
Library of Congress Cataloging-in-Publication Data

Greathouse, William M.
    Wholeness in Christ : toward a biblical theology of holiness / William M. Greathouse.
        p.   cm.
    ISBN 0-8341-1702-9
    1. Holiness—Biblical teaching. 2. Bible.   O.T.—Theology.
I. Title
BS1199.H6G77   1998
234'.8—dc21   97-45877
                                                                 CIP

10 9 8 7 6 5

Contents

FOREWORD

There is a wisdom that comes with maturity that cannot be
found in any other way. This little volume is an apt illustration
of that truth.

William Greathouse, early in his life, was captivated by the
noblest of all thoughts, the nature of God in His holiness and
the possibility of our becoming like Him. He has spent a lifetime lovingly exploring that subject. As a scholar, he has lived
with the biblical texts. He has missed none of any significance.
He has explored the treatment of this subject through the history of the church. There is no modern parochialism here. He has
read the literature on the question and digested the insights of
theologians, biblical and systematic, as they have tackled this
biblical theme. The results are all here in a remarkably brief but
thorough compass. He has inevitably put those who will digest
this little volume in his debt.

Dr. Greathouse brings rich gifts and experience to the subject. A university-educated churchman who has spent his life
between the classroom, the pulpit, and the episcopal office, he is
at home with much that is helpful. His control of the language
makes his study of the biblical vocabulary especially illuminating; his stature as a theologian enables him to handle the biblical concept with depth and skill. His knowledge of text and tradition and his natural gifts enable him to critique but draw
positively from contemporary literature on this theme. His position as a child of Wesley enables him to break out of the restric-
tive paradigms of traditional Reformed or contemporary Evan-
gelicalism and see possibilities that too many modern
theologians never glimpse. The result is a conviction that Christ
died on the Cross to do far more for us than most of us have understood. Best of all, William Greathouse's concern is ultimately
pastoral. He loves the truths discussed here—but not truth for
truth's sake. He is a churchman who longs to see these truths

incarnated in ordinary lives. He will be disappointed if in your reading something does not happen to lead you into a fuller experience of the grace that Christ and His cross were meant to provide.

—Dennis F. Kinlaw
President Emeritus
Asbury College

About the Author

William M. Greathouse is an author and scholar well known in Holiness circles. After 23 years as a Nazarene pastor, he served from 1963 to 1968 as president of Trevecca Nazarene College (now University) in Nashville, from 1968 to 1976 as president of Nazarene Theological Seminary in Kansas City, and from 1976 to 1989 as a general superintendent of the Church of the Nazarene. He has taught religion classes at both the institutions he served as president. In 1994 he was named Expositor of the Year by the Christian Holiness Association and in 1997 received the Life Achievement Award from the Wesleyan Theological Society. Among books he has authored are *Love Made Perfect* and *The Fullness of the Spirit*. He coauthored with H. Ray Dunning *An Introduction to Wesleyan Theology* and with Paul Bassett volume 2 of *Exploring Christian Holiness* and has written numerous articles in the *Preacher's Magazine*, the *Herald of Holiness*, and the *Wesleyan Theological Society Journal*. Greathouse lives near Nashville with his wife, Ruth. They have three children and seven grandchildren.

PREFACE

I have written this study of biblical holiness with the prayer that it may make some small contribution to the Church's recovery of its pre-Constantinian understanding of itself as the people of God called to be holy as He is holy and, as the Body of Christ, commanded to be perfect in love as the Heavenly Father is perfect. The title, *Wholeness in Christ*, underscores John Wesley's understanding of salvation as *divine therapy*. "Know your disease," he counseled his early Methodists; "know your cure." God's redeeming work that came to final expression in the death and resurrection of Christ and the accompanying outpouring of the Holy Spirit at Pentecost provides *complete healing* for the disease of sin that afflicts us as members of Adam's fallen race.

The Early Church had experienced Christ's healing grace and took with all seriousness His commandment to love one another—yes, even their enemies and persecutors—with the love that He himself had sealed with His blood and shed abroad in their hearts by the Holy Spirit. Love as understood in the Greco-Roman culture was *eros*, which was sometimes viewed as a noble self-love advocated (but not always practiced) by its ethical teachers but which was more popularly understood as the sensuality and hedonism of its pagan gods. The love that the early Christians had been given was *agapē, God's own love in the Spirit,* which compelled them to die to themselves, at times lay down even their lives, in their response to Christ's self-giving love, as His witnesses (martyrs). Church historian Adolph Harnack somewhere wrote that it was the "charity" and the "chastity" of those early Christians that shook the foundations of the pagan Roman Empire. It is for the revival of such *love* and *purity* in Christ's Body, and for a renewal of the primitive understanding of the Church as *a counter-culture of holy love,* that I pray and dedicate these pages.

I have written these pages frankly and gratefully from within the Wesleyan-Holiness tradition. My acknowledged presuppositions are those of John Wesley (1703-91), who saw his Anglican faith and practice as a "middle way" between Reformation and Catholic understandings of salvation and holiness. The English reformer

9

saw the cause for the rise of Methodism in the *passion for holiness* that marked his life and that of his brother Charles while they were students at Oxford, a passion that came fully into focus when they were grasped by the teaching of justification by faith alone, through the human instrumentality of Moravian missionary Peter Böhler.

In conference with his Methodist preachers Wesley asked:

"Q. What was the rise of Methodism, so called?

"A. In 1729, two young men, reading the Bible, saw they could not be saved without holiness, followed after it, and incited others so to do. In 1737 they saw holiness comes by faith. They saw likewise, that men are justified before they are sanctified; but still holiness was their point. God then thrust them out, utterly against their will, to raise a holy people."[1]

This Wesleyan conviction, that justification is in order to sanctification, is the living heart of the Wesleyan tradition from which these pages are written. This volume makes no claim to being an exhaustive treatment of the subject. *Wholeness in Christ* is "an overture to biblical theology." Hence the subtitle of the book: *Toward a Biblical Theology of Holiness.* I intend this work to provide a credible *scriptural* foundation for an understanding of Christian holiness. With Wesley I subscribe to the "pessimism of nature" as taught by Augustine, Calvin, and Luther, but with the English reformer I am convinced that Rom. 5:12-21 (which with Wesley I view as the recapitulation of salvation history) proclaims an "optimism of grace" that affords Christian believers *true sanctification—* moral and spiritual *wholeness,* "not only in remission of sins, but infusion of holiness . . . a far more noble . . . life than that which we lost by Adam's fall."[2] My deep and unshakable conviction, based on God's redemptive purpose revealed in both the Hebrew and Christian Scriptures and finally in the person and work of His Son Jesus Christ (Heb. 1:1-4), is that there is, indeed, *in the Bible* a divine promise of *wholeness in Christ.* With Wesley I hold the Great Commandment to be a "covered promise" of Christian perfection or entire sanctification.

As important as it is fully to grasp and consider the episto-

---

1. John Wesley, *The Works of John Wesley,* 3rd ed., 14 vols. (1872; reprint, Kansas City: Beacon Hill Press of Kansas City, 1978-79), 8:300.

2. John Wesley, *Explanatory Notes upon the New Testament,* 2 vols. (reprint, Kansas City: Beacon Hill Press of Kansas City, 1981), Rom. 5:20.

lary writings as they plumb the depths of the new covenant promise of the Spirit and inward sanctification (chaps. 6—9), it is even more important that we listen, with both mind and heart, to Jesus himself as He announces the bliss and holiness of life in the kingdom of God, a life that He himself models as "our grand Exemplar" and makes available to us through His Spirit. For this reason I have chosen to conclude this volume with a chapter on the Sermon on the Mount (chap. 10), which spells out in detail what it is to "have the mind of Christ" ("all the mind that was in Him") and "to walk as He himself walked" ("not only in many or most respects, but in all things") (1 Cor. 2:16; see 1 John 2:6).

The Sermon on the Mount is not a perfectionist ethic, enjoining us to keep every jot and tittle of a "new *Law.*" It is not an impossible ideal, given by Jesus to shatter our self-reliance and reduce us to despair. It is not an "interim ethic," calling us to repentance in view of the impending Apocalypse. Nor is it a futurist ethic, relegating the Sermon to the millennial Kingdom, after Christ's return. No! These sayings of Jesus delineate lived faith in the *present* kingdom of heaven. They say to us, "You are forgiven, you are a child of God, you belong to the kingdom. The sun of righteousness has risen over your life, the light of which shines in the darkness. Now you may experience it: out of the thankfulness of a redeemed child of God a new life is growing."[3] Since the Kingdom is present in Christ, every commandment in the Sermon is a "covered promise" of moral and spiritual wholeness—"pure love to God and man" (Wesley) in the power of the Spirit. "The kingdom of God," Paul assures us, "is . . . righteousness and peace and joy in the Holy Spirit" (Rom. 14:17, NKJV). "The time is fulfilled, and the kingdom of God is at hand; repent, and believe in the gospel" (Mark 1:15, RSV).

This little volume is the distilled essence of a lifetime of preaching, teaching, reading, research, and writing. For more than a dozen years I combined pastoral preaching with college teaching. As both college and seminary president I took upon myself the joyous burden of limited classroom teaching. During my years as a general superintendent of my denomination I understood my calling to be that of "pastor and teacher of *all* the churches," usual-

---

3. Joachim Jeremias, *The Sermon on the Mount,* trans. Norman Perrin in *Biblical Series—2,* John Reumann, ed. (Philadelphia: Fortress Press, 1961), 31.

ly carrying with me a biblical journal or some exciting new theological tome! Then since my retirement I have been unable to shake off the urge to teach budding preachers and teachers of the gospel, and to continue writing. These pages are the immediate product of my past seven years of teaching an upper level college course in the theology of holiness.

As I have written this manuscript, I have submitted it to colleagues and scholars for their criticisms and suggestions. My primary indebtedness is to my former student, H. Ray Dunning. Ray has been of invaluable assistance in helping me state more clearly what I was trying to say in these pages and, at my urging, in reorganizing and reworking several chapters. I have also submitted working copies of the study to other scholar-friends with whom I have been in dialogue through the years, among whom were R. E. "Dick" Howard and Richard S. Taylor; both have critiqued chapters and offered helpful suggestions. I am also indebted to Bonnie Perry, managing editor of Beacon Hill Press of Kansas City, for her expert editing of the manuscript, preparing it for book publication. Bonnie has been an inspiration and encouragement as I have sent her my submissions along the way. Paul Martin, book production editor, and Kelly Gallagher, director of Beacon Hill Press, have also been very helpful in shepherding the project toward publication. Finally, to my wife, Ruth, who has patiently endured the several years I have sat at my word processor writing and rewriting these pages, I express my loving appreciation.

As I have worked and written, Paul's reminder to the Corinthians has never been far from my consciousness: "It is because of him that you are in Christ Jesus, who has become for us wisdom from God—that is, our righteousness, holiness and redemption. Therefore, as it is written: 'Let him who boasts boast in the Lord'" (1 Cor. 1:30-31, NIV).

For whatever good this book may accomplish, *sola gratia Deo.*

—William M. Greathouse
Trevecca Nazarene University

Note to the Reader: This revised and corrected reprint takes into account the Eastern Church's social view of the triune God as this understanding is reflected in humankind's creation in God's image for His purposes, with the *imago Dei* further illuminating the idea of scriptural holiness as both corporate and personal.

1

Holiness
in the Old Testament

For many contemporary Christians, the Old Testament seems ancient and remote. It was written thousands of years ago over a vast span of time. It deals with a religion with which we are quite unfamiliar, referring to practices and rules for life that, for the Christian, have long since been invalidated and outmoded by the work of Christ. Hence, we are not too much concerned about our ignorance of it.

However, the truth is, we cannot really understand the New Testament without a knowledge of the Old. As Augustine said many centuries ago, "The New is in the Old concealed; the Old is in the New revealed." The roots of our Christian faith lie deep in the soil of the Old Testament.[1] Informed biblical scholars would concur with the 1975 statement of the National Conference of Catholic Bishops: "Most essential concepts of the Christian creed grew at first in Judaic soil. Uprooted from that soil, these basic concepts cannot be perfectly understood."[2]

The doctrine of Christian holiness, like any other doctrine, is therefore best approached by examining its Old Testament roots. It becomes our first task, then, in seeking an understanding of the

---

1. The student interested in the demonstration of this claim should read Paul and Elizabeth Achtemeier's *Old Testament Roots of Our Faith* (New York and Nashville: Abingdon Press, 1962).

2. Walter Harrelson and Randall M. Falk, *Jews and Christians: A Troubled Family* (Nashville: Abingdon Press, 1991), 13.

Christian doctrine of holiness, to go back to the root of this teaching in the Hebrew Scriptures. As we proceed in our investigation, it should become clear that the New Testament doctrine of sanctification is the flower of Old Testament teaching.

THE BIBLICAL TERMS

While the biblical concept of sanctification cannot be restricted to specific terms, it is important to understand the development of the Hebrew words for "holy," "holiness," "sanctify," and "sanctification," all of which translate one family of Hebrew terms, the *qodesh* family.

The semantic origin of this noun is so lost in the mists of ancient obscurity that there can be no absolute certainty about its earliest meaning. Two major theories have been advanced: the first is based on the similarity of the term with a Babylonian one and suggests that it means "bright, clear"; the other conjectures that it meant "to be separated." While one cannot be dogmatic, the preponderance of scholarly opinion supports the second view. After a careful analysis of the issues, Norman H. Snaith voices this majority view as follows: "With respect to the comparative merits of the two suggestions, the balance, in our view, is definitely in favor of Baudissin's theory (*qodesh* had originally to do with "separation").[3]

As the term comes to expression in the Old Testament, it seems to have passed through three phases of use, neither of the earlier two becoming completely extinct. In all cases it was applied primarily to God and, in a nonderivative sense, only to Him. As Snaith claims, "This is the most intimately divine word of all. It has to do with the very nature of Deity; no word more so, or any other as much."[4]

The first phase may be characterized as a prerational understanding and identifies the boundary line between the natural and the supernatural. It reflects the mystery of the "Wholly Other." It does not necessarily entail any particular characteristic but does generate the feelings of awe and wonder—in fact, of fear.

Rudolph Otto's classic analysis of primordial religious experience, *The Idea of the Holy* (his philosophy of religion), is really an ex-

---

3. Norman H. Snaith, *Distinctive Ideas of the Old Testament* (London: Epworth Press, 1955), 25.
4. Ibid., 21.

ploration of this phase of "the holy." "Holiness," Otto avers, "is a category of interpretation and evaluation peculiar to religion."[5]

For this element he coins the word "numinous" from the Latin *numen* ("supernatural"). The numinous of which he speaks is a "moment," an awareness that defies rational analysis. While it cannot be strictly defined (thus nonrational), we can hint at its meaning by looking closely at the feelings it evokes, feelings to which Otto gives the term *mysterium tremendum.* "The holy" evokes awe—it overwhelms the soul with a sense of majesty; it pulsates with supernatural power. Otto quotes Tersteegen: "A God comprehended is no God."

John G. Gammie finds five major aspects of the numinous. Utilizing Otto's Latin terms, he chose to help capture the ineffability of "the holy." Gammie analyzes it as (1) awefulness, plenitude of power that evokes dread and a sense of divine wrath *(tremendum);* (2) overpoweringness, plenitude of being, absolute unapproachableness *(majestas);* (3) urgency, vitality, will, force, movement, excitement, activity, energy that the mystic experiences as "consuming fire" *(energicum);*[6] (4) being: the "Wholly Other," different, in a category separate to himself, transcendent, supernatural *(mysterium);* and (5) compelling, fascinating, giving rise to spiritual intoxication, rapture, and exaltation *(fascinans).* This latter element may be latently present in longing and in moments of solemnity; it is experienced when one gains mystic insight "and at conversion."[7]

Otto's analysis will constitute a starting point and a frame of reference for the understanding of biblical holiness in this volume.

Gammie sees as an initial example of Otto's approach the magnificent theophany at Sinai in Exod. 19 (all RSV):

> Each one of the elements of the holy is present: (1) *awefulness, dread, wrath:* "And the whole mountain quaked greatly" (v. 18c); "God answered him in the thunder" (v. 19b); "Go down and warn the people . . . lest the LORD break out upon

---

5. Rudolph Otto, *The Idea of the Holy,* trans. J. W. Harvey (London: Oxford University Press, 1957), 5.

6. Otto did not himself employ the Latin *energicum,* but his most avid devotee, Old Testament scholar D. J. Hanel, rightly did.

7. John G. Gammie, *Holiness in Israel,* in *Overtures in Biblical Theology* (Minneapolis: Fortress Press, 1989), 5-6.

them" (vv. 21-22); (2) *majesty and unapproachability:* "Take heed that you do not go up into the mountain or touch the border of it" (v. 12) "lest they break through to the LORD" (v. 21); "The people cannot come up to Mount Sinai" (v. 23); (3) *energy, vitality, and movement:* "The LORD descended upon it in fire; and the smoke of it went up like the smoke of a kiln" (v. 18*ab*); (4) *mystery:* "Lo, I am coming to you in a thick cloud" (v. 9*a*); (5) *fascination:* "Do not let the priests and people break through to come up to the LORD" (v. 24*b*).[8]

The numinous, however, is not the distinctive idea to be found in the Old Testament, although, as we shall see, it is not absent. In fact, it is an essential component of the holiness of God when qualified by other considerations. This fact is reflected in critiques that have been made of Otto, critiques that are legitimate while not denying the validity of what he is examining. For example, Walter C. Kaiser observes, "Otto makes no mention, strangely enough, of Leviticus 19, the key chapter in the Bible on holiness. In his zeal to assert the unique character for religion, he ends up making the ethical content a mere 'extra.' But Leviticus 19 insists that faith and ethics are necessary aspects of the same coin, though they are by no means identical."[9]

In the same vein Gammie writes, "Nowhere does Otto sufficiently probe the notion that the holy calls for purity, cleanness, and that frequently purity is to be attained by means of separation. To be holy is to be separate; to be holy is to be clean and pure. Each of these notions has ethical as well as cultic implications."[10]

Recent studies on the Hebrew cultus have shown that purity, cleanness, is indeed a regular counterpart and requirement of holiness. In Exod. 19, for example, the Lord instructed Moses, "Go to the people and consecrate them today and tomorrow. Have them wash their clothes and prepare for the third day, because on the third day the LORD will come down upon Mount Sinai in the sight of all the people. You shall set limits for the people all around, saying, 'Be careful not to go up the mountain or to touch the edge of it. Any who touch the mountain shall be put to death'" (vv. 10-12).

---

8. Gammie, *Holiness in Israel*, 6-7.
9. Walter C. Kaiser, *The New Interpreter's Bible*, Leander E. Keck, convener of Editorial Board and New Testament editor (Nashville: Abingdon Press, 1994), 1:1132.
10. Gammie, *Holiness in Israel*, 7-8.

These considerations highlight the second and third phases of the use of the *qodesh* terminology. But before we look at these, we need to explore a bit further the statement made earlier that this first aspect is to be found in the Old Testament and ultimately provides an important theological truth.

The validity of Otto's analysis of the numinous consists in its warnings against becoming "cozy" with the "Wholly Other." Anyone who has had a true experience of God's gracious presence may discover, by examining the heart of this awareness, Otto's *mysterium tremendum:* the sense of awe, wonder, and adoration that invades our being when in true worship we sing, "Holy, holy, holy, Lord God Almighty!" (Reginald Heber). In Charles Wesley's words, it is

> *The speechless awe that dares not move*
> *And all the silent heaven of love.*

The second phase to which we have made reference may be termed "the cultic." This use is almost completely a derivative concept; that is, the "holiness" of persons, places, objects, and so on is the result of their being consecrated to the service or ownership of the God who is the primary Bearer of holiness in a non-derivative sense.

"Sanctification" refers to the ritual that effects this result; thus "to sanctify" means "to make holy" in the sense alluded to. But, further, in this context "holiness" may be considered a "contagion" to be communicated on contact. Numerous aspects of this phenomenon may be found in the Old Testament (e.g., Lev. 6:27; 2 Kings 2:13 ff.; Isa. 65:5; Ezek. 44:19). This understanding of *qodesh* becomes a fertile field for idolatry. When a person or place or thing (such as the ark of the covenant) is treated as if he, she, or it has inherent holiness, some aspect of the created world is being elevated to a status that can be attributed only to the Creator; this is idolatry. This implies that "derivative holiness" is an essentially relational concept.

The third and most distinctive phase of the use of the *qodesh* family of terms comes chiefly into view with the work of the eighth-century prophets. Hence, it is sometimes called "the prophetic view." It is here that the ethical aspect becomes dominant. It is essentially a personal concept and becomes the basis for the prophetic call to the ethical requirements of the covenant.

In summary, the "holiness" of God does indeed refer to His "otherness" rather than His "remoteness," but the quality of this "Wholly Other" as manifested in His activity among human beings dictates that those who would "share" His holiness must reflect those same ethical characteristics. Both of these meanings inform the Old Testament teaching about the holiness of God and become the background for the New Testament supposition about holiness in human life.

THE HOLINESS OF GOD

Holiness is not one attribute of God among others or even the chief attribute or even the sum of all the divine attributes, says James Muilenberg, but is "the innermost reality to which all others are related."[11] As Ernst Sellen puts it, "God is *holy.* Herein we touch on that which constitutes the deepest and innermost nature of God in the Old Testament."[12]

THE THREEFOLD MEANING OF HOLINESS

Upon examination, the use of *qodesh* in the Old Testament entails three interrelated ideas: "separation," "glory," and "purity."

Holiness as Separation. We have seen that "separation" is no doubt the primordial meaning of the term. That this is the central significance of it is clear from the 830 occurrences of *qodesh.* Furthermore, God alone is *qodesh.* Persons or things are *qodesh* only as they are related to Him.

Holiness is indeed the very nature of God. When the prophet says in Amos 4:2 that "the Lord GOD has sworn by his holiness," he is saying the same thing he declares in 6:8: "The Lord GOD has sworn by himself." God is *qodesh* in himself. Whatever else the sovereign Lord subsequently makes known of himself is governed by the fact that He is the holy God, the "Wholly Other" who alone is "perfect in pow'r, in love, in purity" (Heber).

The first truth, therefore, to settle in our thinking is that of the absolute and final distinction between God and us creatures. "I am God and no mortal," He announces, "the Holy One [*qadash,*

11. James Muilenberg, *Holiness,* vol. 2 in *The Interpreter's Dictionary of the Bible,* 4 vols., ed. George Arthur Buttrick (Nashville: Abingdon Press, 1962), 616.

12. Gammie, *Holiness in Israel,* 3.

adjective] in your midst" (Hos. 11:9). To fail to acknowledge the distinction between God and ourselves is the root of sin. As we will see later, such a failure occurred in the garden when the serpent promised the first pair that if they would assert their independence from the Lord, they would themselves be "like God," with the right to decide good and evil for themselves. This *hubris* is humanity's "original" sin, the root of all moral evil; it is, as Millard Reed puts it, "the delusion of self-sovereignty." But if to refuse to acknowledge the distinction between Deity and ourselves is the root of all moral evil, to "let God be God" is the root of all holiness.

The first word of holiness is, therefore, "I, I am the LORD, and besides me there is no savior" (Isa. 43:11). God alone is God; the creature alone is creature. This is the axiom of all holiness. As Snaith insists, "God is separate and distinct because He is God. A person or thing may be separate, or may come to be separated, because he or it has come to belong to God . . . [is] now in the category of the Separate."[13] Snaith further insists on the positive, rather than the negative, meaning of the concept of holiness and thus concludes that while holiness certainly involves separation *from* uncleanness and sin, it is primarily separation *to* God.[14] Based on this understanding, H. Ray Dunning has written, "Holiness in human beings (or things) is present only when in relation to God. That is, no finite person or object has any inherent holiness. The holiness of things or persons is derived and dependent. This derived holiness is present only as the person or thing is in right relation to God."[15] To become holy as humans is to be made "partakers of *his* holiness" (Heb. 12:10, KJV, emphasis added; cf. 2 Pet. 1:4).

Holiness as Glory. While separation is the primary meaning of *qodesh*, in many instances it is synonymous with "glory" (Heb. *kabod*), "in the sense of the burning Splendour of the Presence of the Lord."[16] Promising to be with His people in the Tabernacle, God said, "I will meet with the Israelites there, and it shall be sanctified by my glory" (Exod. 29:43). Likewise, upon the dedication of the

13. Snaith, *Distinctive Ideas*, 30.
14. Ibid.
15. H. Ray Dunning, *A Layman's Guide to Sanctification* (Kansas City: Beacon Hill Press of Kansas City, 1991), 23-24.
16. Snaith, *Distinctive Ideas*, 48.

Temple in Jerusalem, which replaced the former tent sanctuary, "the glory of the LORD filled the house of the LORD" (1 Kings 8:11).

In each of these instances, it is clear that the reference is to a visible appearance of the invisible One in order to vouchsafe for the people the fact of His presence. Hence *kabod* refers to a perceptible manifestation of the Reality to which humanity would otherwise have no access. Thus holiness as glory is the corollary of holiness as separation or radical otherness.

The locus classicus of *kabod* in the foregoing sense is found in Exod. 33:18-23, in which the encounter between Moses and God reflects an interplay between these two aspects of holiness.[17] In essence, Moses makes the request to see God "as He is in himself," that is, face-to-face. But this request is denied, since "you cannot see my face, for no one may see me and live" (v. 20, NIV). What God does allow Moses to see is His "glory," anthropomorphically referred to as His "back parts" (v. 23, KJV). But what Moses saw was not God as He is in himself (His holiness as otherness), but His "glory" that is the manifestation of His activity in the world described in terms of "mercy" and "compassion" (v. 19, NIV).

Protestant Reformer John Calvin recognized this fundamental biblical truth about God and developed a doctrine of what is called "accommodation." Because of God's holiness—properly understood—and humanity's finitude, there can be no knowledge of God by human beings unless He "accommodates" himself to our limitation by making himself accessible through the manifestation of His "glory" in some form of incarnation. This is why the New Testament sees the ultimate glory of God to be present in the person of Jesus Christ, *the* Incarnation.

Holiness as Purity. This concept reflects the second significance of *qodesh* as referred to earlier in this chapter. It is a cultic term and is conceived—at least from the priestly perspective—as ritual purity. Its opposite is "uncleanness," and the two are antithetical.

Commenting on holiness as purity, John G. Gammie shows that the ideas of cleanness associated with God's holiness were quite diverse:

---

17. There is a certain ambiguity in this passage, since the term "glory" is used in a double sense. The context enables us to clearly distinguish between the two meanings. The exposition in the text above seeks to make the distinctions clear.

For the entire Old Testament/Hebrew Scriptures, holiness summoned Israel to cleanness. . . . Diversity within unity is to be discerned in the fact that for different groups of religious persons within Israel—prophets, priests, and sages—the kind of cleanness required by holiness varied. For the prophets it was cleanness of social justice (ethical), for the priests a cleanness of proper ritual and maintenance of separation, for the sages [wise men] it was cleanness of inner integrity and individual moral acts.[18]

In the priestly context, holiness requires that everything that is either unclean or common shall be "cleansed" by a ritual act of sanctification prior to being pressed into divine service. Persons who come into the presence of the Holy One must carefully prepare themselves by ritual washings and other means, since to present oneself with any degree of impurity is to invite disaster.

These understandings were always in danger of being perverted into ritualism, and hence we have numerous conflicts between the priestly understanding of "holiness and purity" and the prophetic understanding (see Amos 7:10-17 for a dramatic conflict between priest and prophet). The prophetic view understands "purity" in an ethical sense, and even though cultic language is sometimes used (as in Ezek. 36:24-29), it must be interpreted as having ethical significance.

Isaiah's vision of the divine holiness, recorded in the sixth chapter of his prophecy, embodies the full disclosure of this truth and there moves beyond the cultic to the ethical. The prophet begins, "In the year that King Uzziah died, I saw the Lord seated on a throne, high and exalted, and the train of his robe filled the temple" (v. 1, NIV). Here is the transcendent, incomparable God, the "Wholly Other" who alone is "high and exalted" above all creation and creatures (see 40:12-18, 25).

"Above him were seraphs," Isaiah continues, "each with six wings" (v. 2, NIV). As the seraphs sing, "Holy, holy, holy," they cover their faces so that they may not see God, and their feet so that He might not behold them. Thus they move about the throne, proclaiming to one another the holiness of God: "Holy, holy, holy is the LORD of hosts; the whole earth is full of his glory" (v. 3).[19]

---

18. Gammie, *Holiness in Israel*, 195-96.
19. Th. C. Vriezen, *An Outline of Old Testament Theology* (Newton, Mass.: Charles T. Bradford Co., 1958), 149.

The prophet's response to this vision was a profound existential sense of his own "uncleanness," as well as that of his fellow Judeans. "'Woe to me!' I cried. 'I am ruined! For I am a man of unclean lips . . . and my eyes have seen the King, the LORD Almighty'" (v. 5, NIV). The prophet was struck prostrate with his sinfulness.

What was there about the vision that created this response in one who had been a prophet of the Lord? While the text itself does not explicitly say, the total movement of biblical thought in conjunction with the developing concept of holiness would seem to suggest that it was certainly more than ritual impurity. Perhaps against the background of the death of King Uzziah, who had presumptuously taken upon himself the prerogative of priest, a position for which he was not qualified (and was thus unclean), Isaiah saw himself as having failed to place the Holy One at the center of his own existence and having given more credence to proper political action than to dependence upon the God of Israel.[20] Certainly this latter became the central theme of his preaching in the ensuing years of his ministry.

"Then one of the seraphs flew to me," Isaiah continues his confession, "with a live coal in his hand, which he had taken with tongs from the altar. With it he touched my mouth and said, 'See, this has touched your lips; your guilt is taken away and your sin atoned for'" (vv. 6-7, NIV).

God's holiness is no static quality. "On the contrary," says Snaith, "Jehovah is always active, always dynamically here, in this world. The Hebrew does not say that Jehovah *is*, or that Jehovah *exists*, but that He *does*."[21] Thus, here in Isa. 6 the Holy One becomes the Sanctifier. With Uzziah dethroned and the Lord enthroned, Isaiah was in a position to hear the voice of the Lord saying, "Whom shall I send? And who will go for us?" Instantly he responded, "Here am I. Send me!" (v. 8, NIV). Purged and refined by the fire from God's altar—and now centered in God—Isaiah became the great Old Testament prophet of "the Holy One of Israel."[22]

---

20. King Uzziah was under sentence of death from leprosy for acting as a priest, entering the Temple, and making an offering on the altar of incense (see 2 Chron. 26:16-21).

21. Snaith, *Distinctive Ideas*, 48.

22. "The Holy One of Israel" became Isaiah's favorite appellation of Yahweh, the phrase occurring at least 12 times in chapters 1—39 (1:4; 5:19, 24; 10:20; 12:6; 17:7; 29:19; 30:11, 12, 15; 31:1; 37:23). In addition, we find the phrases "the Holy One of Jacob" (29:23) and "his [Israel's] Holy One" (10:17).

While the cultic and moral aspects of holiness are interwoven throughout the development of the idea in the Old Testament, Peter T. Forsyth is reflecting an important truth in saying, "The very history of the word holiness in the Old Testament displays the gradual transcendence of the idea of separation by that of sanctity. It traverses a path in which the quantitative idea of tabu changes to the qualitative idea of active and absolute purity. The religious grows ethical, that it may become not only more religious but the one religion of the conscience of the world. The one God can only be the holy God."[23]

In Isaiah's Temple experience we have an anticipation of the dispensation of the Holy Spirit. Christianity takes up the prophetic side of the definition of holiness and makes it the standard as the true mark of holiness. What Moses, Isaiah, and a select company of Old Testament worthies found in the presence of God is now promised to every member of the people of God under the new covenant. "And all of us, with unveiled faces, seeing the glory [image] of the Lord as though reflected in a mirror, are being transformed into the same image from one degree of glory to another; for this comes from the Lord, the Spirit" (2 Cor. 3:18).

THE HOLINESS OF GOD EXPRESSED

We now turn to some of the most definitive ways that God expressed His holy nature in the Old Testament. An observation by Bruce C. Birch shows the relation between Yahweh's inherent holiness and the divine activity, which is the expression of that holiness: "Holiness describes the very foundations of the divine being. It is fundamental to divine character and identity, and out of God's holiness a variety of expressions for divine activity grow."[24]

The Steadfast Love of God

The most central of the terms expressive of divine activity within the covenant relationship between God and Israel is *chesed*. God is *qodesh;* He acts in *chesed*. In the context of the theophany on Mount Sinai, God allows His glory to pass by Moses and then

---

23. Peter T. Forsyth, *Positive Preaching and the Modern Mind* (New York: George H. Doran Co., 1907), 310.

24. Bruce C. Birch, *Let Justice Roll Down* (Louisville, Ky.: Westminster/John Knox Press, 1991), 51.

makes this remarkable proclamation: "The LORD, the LORD, a God merciful and gracious, slow to anger, and abounding in steadfast love and faithfulness, keeping steadfast love for the thousandth generation, forgiving iniquity and transgression and sin, yet by no means clearing the guilty, but visiting the iniquity of the parents upon the children and the children's children, to the third and fourth generation" (Exod. 34:6-7).

The Hebrew word *chesed,* here translated "steadfast love," is rendered variously as "mercy," "grace," "loyalty," "goodness," "lovingkindness," and "compassion." The wealth of these terms witnesses to the breadth encompassed in the term.

Chesed is covenant love. On God's part it pledges Him to perform all the promises to His people. For this reason it is sometimes translated "loyalty," but it is not loyalty to a mere contract. Rather, it is the Lord's personal commitment to be faithful to Israel—an attitude manifested in concrete action. Ps. 136, with its oft-recurring phrase "for his steadfast love endures forever," best illustrates the meaning of the divine *chesed.* Katherine Doob Sakenfeld elaborates on this concept: "Divine loyalty within covenant involved both God's commitment to Israel and the ever new free decision of God to continue to honor that commitment by preserving and supporting the covenant community. Divine freedom and divine self-obligation were held together in this single word."[25]

In the Song of the Sea, Moses and the Israelites sang to Him this song: "In your steadfast love you led the people whom you redeemed; you guided them by your strength to your holy abode" (Exod. 15:13).

The Righteousness and Justice of God

God's holiness and steadfast love express themselves most importantly as righteousness (*sedeq,* masc.; *sedeqah,* fem.) and justice *(mishpat).* One of the most significant texts in the Old Testament is found in Isa. 5:16: "But the LORD of hosts is exalted by justice, and the Holy God shows himself holy by righteousness."[26]

---

25. Katherine Doob Sakenfeld, *Faithfulness in Action: Loyalty in Divine Perspective,* in *Overtures in Biblical Theology* (Philadelphia: Fortress Press, 1985), 132.

26. The association of *holiness* and *righteousness* is the great contribution of the eighth-century prophets, where it is *righteousness* that is given special emphasis. Snaith writes, "If we were to choose a passage of Scripture indicative of the new content of *qodesh,* it would be Isaiah [chapter 5] v. 16: 'the holy God *(ha-'el haqqadash)* is sanctified *(niqdash)* in righteousness'" (*Distinctive Ideas,* 51).

Righteousness. One of the most common misunderstandings of the Old Testament is the belief that righteousness is a legalistic concept, devoid of the grace depicted in the New Testament. Although "righteousness" is the most common translation of *sedeq/sedeqah,* is it also rendered as uprightness, vindication, deliverance.

It is now generally conceded that righteousness as a concept is best understood in terms of relationship. Gerhard von Rad has written, "Ancient Israel did not in fact measure a line of conduct or an act by an ideal norm, but by the specific relationship in which the partner had at the time to prove himself true. 'Every relationship brings with it certain claims upon conduct, and the satisfaction of those claims, which issue from the relationship and in which alone the relationship can persist, is described by the term.'"[27]

God's righteousness was not an abstract norm but was revealed in His concrete acts to create and preserve Israel as His chosen people. One of Israel's oldest poems, the Song of Deborah, celebrates "the righteous acts *[sedaqot]* of the LORD" (Judg. 5:11, KJV). In several passages, God's righteousness is equivalent to His "salvation" (Pss. 40:10; 98:2; Isa. 45:21; 61:10; cf. Rom. 1:16-17).

God's righteousness also expressed itself in restoring Israel in time of trouble and need. In this sense God's righteousness appears in a forensic sense, with Him as the righteous Judge (see Pss. 9:4, 8; 96:13; Isa. 5:16; Jer. 11:20).

Justice. The Hebrew word *mishpat* is generally rendered "justice" or "judgment." Although the noun is derived from a root that means "to judge" or "render judgment," it should not be understood in the modern sense of pronouncing a judgment or sentence. Rather, it comprised all the actions involved in the primitive process that took place when two parties presented themselves before a competent authority, each to claim their rights.

Justice is a chief attribute of God's activity in the world: "The LORD of hosts is exalted by justice" (Isa. 5:16). The prophets of Israel were vigorous voices calling for justice, from the burning conviction that God's care extended to every person, particularly the poor and

---

27. Gerhard von Rad, *Old Testament Theology* (New York: Harper and Row, 1962), 371.

the oppressed, and that His law is intended to embody the rights of the faithful community (see Jer. 5:28 for one of many such passages in the prophets). But the call for justice was not a prophetic innovation. Justice was understood by Israel as fundamental to God's activity from earliest history, as evidenced by the Song of Moses: "The Rock, his work is perfect, and all his ways are just. A faithful God, without deceit, just and upright is he" (Deut. 32:4).

The Holiness Command

Dunning points out that the Book of Leviticus contains the most extended discussion of holiness to be found in the Old Testament. In fact, holiness is the key concept of the book, and the motto of Leviticus is the command: "Speak to all the congregation of the people of Israel and say to them: You shall be holy, for I the LORD your God am holy" (Lev. 19:2; cf. 11:44-45; 20:26). The strange thing, he says, is that this motto occurs right in the middle of a lengthy discussion about clean and unclean foods and other matters that seem irrelevant to Christian faith. But precisely this setting, Dunning thinks, is the clue to the meaning of holiness in Christian experience:

> Animals that are unclean are those that have the characteristics from two realms. For example, a catfish swims in the water but does not have scales, which seem appropriate to fish. The best suggestion is that holiness requires that different classes of things not be confused. The same seems to be implied in the command that mixed materials are not to be used. Mixed seeds are not to be sown, mixed cloth is not to be used in a garment. Furthermore, persons who are deformed are forbidden to serve in the tabernacle. All this implies that holiness in human experience requires wholeness, integrity, and normality. Some commentators say that the distinction between clean and unclean animals was to remind Israel that God distinguished them from all other nations on earth to be His own possession, that is, it implies that holiness is separation from the unclean and to the holy God.[28]

In harmony with Dunning's interpretation, Walter C. Kaiser says of holiness in Lev. 19,

---

28. Dunning, *Sanctification*, 24.

The level of ethical performance expected of all persons was that of an imitation of the very character of God: "Be holy because I, the LORD your God, am holy." Holiness is the essential nature of God, as Isa. 6:3 announces: "Holy, holy, holy is the LORD of hosts!" . . .

Holiness stands as the foundational principle of the long list of precepts set forth in this chapter. Holiness is the object of all the moral and ceremonial law. But since God sets the norm and defines just what holiness does and does not include, God's holiness acts both as model and as motivating force in the development and maintenance of a holy character. To make sure that the point is not lost, fifteen times the sixteen subsections end with the reminder that "I am the LORD [your God]."[29]

Birch understands the holiness command to be an injunction to imitate God in His character and actions in His steadfast love and righteous acts toward Israel. "The community of faith," he believes, "is to live its life in imitation of God (imitatio Dei)," noting Martin Buber's passionate claim, "The imitation of God— not of a human image of God, but of the real God, not of a mediator in human form, but of God himself—is the central paradox of Judaism."[30]

At the risk of falling back into the old caricatures of the Old Testament law as legalism, we must put the moral claims of the Law in the framework of God's actions in the world and His redeeming activity in creating Israel as a people for His possession and purposes. As Birch observes,

> Prior to the law is a long narrative through which many elements of the basic character and identity of the Israelite community are established in relation to the understandings of what God has been about in the world. We surely could not imagine focus in the New Testament on the moral resources of Jesus' teachings without attention to what God is doing and modeling for us in the life, death, and resurrection of Jesus.

---

29. Kaiser, New Interpreter's Bible, 1:1131.
30. Birch, Let Justice Roll Down, 125.

One of the clearest and most direct examples of this type of moral norm in the Old Testament material is God's statement, "For I am the LORD who brought you up from the land of Egypt, to be your God; you shall be holy, for I am holy" (Lev. 11:45).[31]

To be holy, Israel must *imitate God,* imitate the kind of love God showed them when they were strangers in Egypt: "Speak to all the congregation of the people in Israel and say to them: You shall be holy, for I . . . am holy. . . . When an alien resides with you in your land, you shall not oppress the alien. The alien who resides with you shall be to you as the citizen among you . . . for you were aliens in the land of Egypt: I am the LORD your God" (Lev. 19:2, 33-34). Examined closely, the *holiness* command becomes the *love* command as Jesus taught (Matt. 5:43-48).

31. Ibid., 126.

2

Perfection
in the Old Testament

s with the teaching of holiness, the doctrine of Christian perfection can be understood only by examining its Old Testament roots.

Because of the misleading connotation of the word "perfect," some theologians propose that the term be abandoned. Our English word derives from the Latin *perfectio*, which implies a state of moral flawlessness and absolute perfection that all Christians agree is reserved for glory. In this sense, of course, "Nobody's perfect."

This chapter follows the suggestion that the author once heard the late H. Richard Niebuhr propose in a university lecture. Niebuhr cautioned that the Christian teacher must not discard biblical terms like "justification," "regeneration," and "sanctification" because they are difficult and no longer meaningful in our biblically illiterate culture. Our task, rather, is to *redeem* these significant words by mining their meaning in the biblical text, and then to *make them live* in the minds of those we address. Such is our endeavor in this study.

More than a dozen words are translated "perfect" in the King James Version of the Old Testament. An examination of these terms sheds light on the scriptural idea of perfection that forms the basis of John Wesley's teaching. All of these terms speak not of a static, absolute perfection but of a dynamic, relative perfection to which God's people have been called since Abraham (see Gen. 17:1).

A faithful reading of the Old Testament reveals that the concept of spiritual perfection—properly understood as blamelessness before God and uprightness of heart and life—lies at the heart of Hebrew piety. This concept is the root of the New Testament teaching. It is also the understanding of perfection that found expression in the writings of the great saints and teachers of both Eastern Orthodoxy and Roman Catholicism. Finally, this truth came to Protestant formulation in the thought and teaching of John Wesley.

We turn therefore to an examination of the Old Testament roots of the distinctive tenet of our Wesleyan faith, the doctrine of Christian perfection.

HOLINESS AND PERFECTION

While the words "holiness" and "perfection" are used by Wesleyans to describe the same experience of grace, an examination of these two terms in the Old Testament reveals that they reflect two different aspects of this grace. George Allen Turner explains: "While the terms associated with 'holiness' stress the contrast between Jehovah and man, which can be bridged by an act of cleansing, those associated with 'perfection' point to man's kinship with God and the possibility of fellowship."[1]

Modern versions translate the several Hebrew words rendered "perfect" in the KJV by such terms as "blameless," "whole," "sincere," "upright," and "upright in heart" in order to avoid the misleading connotations of our English word "perfect." The idea of perfection derived from the Hebrew terms of our Old Testament suggests not a state of perfection reserved for heaven but a state of heart and lifestyle possible *in this present world*. The Old Testament, therefore, provides significant building blocks for the Wesleyan doctrine of *scriptural* perfection.

---

1. George Allen Turner, *The More Excellent Way* (Winona Lake, Ind.: Light and Life Press, 1952), 31. This work is based on Dr. Turner's MS titled "A Comparative Study of the Biblical and Wesleyan Ideas of Perfection, to Determine the Sources of Wesley's Doctrine," accepted by Harvard University for his Ph.D. degree. It is the most extensive exegetical study of Old Testament perfection the author has found.

RELATIVE PERFECTION

The Old Testament ascribes absolute perfection only to God.[2] A typical passage is found in Deuteronomy: "He is the Rock, His work is perfect; for all His ways are justice, a God of truth and without injustice; righteous and upright is He" (32:4, NKJV).

While God alone is absolutely perfect, a relative perfection is ascribed to Old Testament worthies who walked with God in fidelity and fellowship. "Enoch walked with God; and he was not, for God took him" (Gen. 5:24, RSV). "Now before he was taken," we read in the Epistle to the Hebrews, "he was attested as having pleased God" (11:5, RSV). Of Noah also it was said that he "walked with God" (Gen. 6:9). Abraham was commanded, "Walk before me, and be thou perfect" (17:1, KJV). "Since Noah and Abraham at least had serious shortcomings," Turner points out, "the perfection which they embodied was not an absolute and unqualified perfection."[3]

At least seven times in the Old Testament "perfect" is associated with walking, a beautiful and suggestive metaphor for fellowship with God. Persons are perfect "before God" who are sincere and blameless in their hearts, walking in a "straight way," free from crookedness, deviousness, and perversity. Such are perfect in the *relative* sense of living a life *pleasing to God*, even though they fall short of conformity to His perfect law and of faultlessness in the eyes of their fellows. Perfection is a life of dedication and constancy in fellowship with the Almighty.

HEBREW TERMS FOR PERFECTION

Several different Hebrew words and terms are rendered "perfect" in both the KJV and modern versions. It will be helpful in understanding scriptural perfection to look at several of these terms.

PERFECTION AS WHOLENESS

The most common Hebrew term for "perfect" is *tamim*, which means "whole, entire, sound."[4] When referring to animals

2. Only in five instances, where the reference is to God (Deut. 32:4; 2 Sam. 22:31; Job 37:16; Pss. 18:30; 19:7), does "perfect" mean absolute perfection.

3. Turner, *More Excellent Way*, 42.

4. J. Y. Campbell, in *The Interpreter's Dictionary of the Bible*, ed. George Arthur Buttrick (New York and Nashville: Abingdon Press, 1951), 3:730.

offered in sacrifice it means "without blemish" or "without spot," animals not maimed or bruised, but whole, useful, and healthy (cf. Eph. 5:27). The perfect human is one without moral blemish or defect.[5]

Tamim is applied 23 times to the moral character of humans. It is translated in the KJV "perfect" 7 times, "sincere" 3 times, "upright" 12 times, and "undefiled" once. *Tamim* is associated with "walking on the way" 12 times, as in Ps. 101:2, 6—"I will give heed to the way that is blameless. . . . He who walks in the way that is blameless shall minister to me" (RSV).

The Lord appeared to Abraham and said, "I am God Almighty; walk before me, and be blameless" (Gen. 17:1; "blameless" is used also in the NASB, NIV, RSV, and NKJV). Two modern versions retain "perfect." The *New Jerusalem Bible* reads, "Live in my presence, be perfect." Similarly the *Revised English Bible:* "Live in my presence, and be perfect." It was in the gracious, empowering presence of El Shaddai that Abraham could be enabled to be "perfect."

A cognate form of this term is *tom,* which occurs 33 times, with 21 instances referring to human character. It is translated "integrity" 11 times, its central meaning. The adjectival form *tam* occurs 14 times with the meaning of "sincere." This is the term applied to Job, "that man [who] was *blameless* and upright, one who feared God, and turned away from evil" (Job 1:1, RSV, emphasis added).

HOLINESS AS A PERFECT HEART

Another Hebrew term often translated "perfect" is SHLM, which occurs 224 times. In most cases it is the noun *shalom,* which means "peace." The adjective *shalem* is found 27 times, and in 14 instances is translated "perfect" in the KJV. Most scholars agree that the root idea of the noun *shalom* is that of fellowship between God and His people. "Let your heart . . . be perfect with the LORD" (1 Kings 8:61, KJV) is typical, an emphasis common in later Judaism and the New Testament, with the emphasis upon sincerity and singleness of intention. The prayer of Hezekiah reveals an even deeper significance of SHLM, a conviction that one can possess a loyalty and purity of heart that is pleasing to God: "I beseech thee, O LORD, remember now how I have walked before

---

5. The material that follows is based largely on Turner, *More Excellent Way,* 42-51.

thee in truth and with *a perfect heart,* and have done that which is good in thy sight" (2 Kings 20:3, KJV, emphasis added; cf. Isa. 38:3).[6]

PERFECTION AS UPRIGHTNESS OF HEART

Another important term for perfection, found nearly 160 times in the Old Testament, comes from the root Y-SH-R. As an adjective, it usually has the meaning of "upright" and is applied both to God and to persons who are "upright in heart." The verb means "to please, to be right in the sight of" God. Typical of a number of passages in Psalms is the prayer in 7:10: "God is my shield, who saves the upright in heart" (cf. 11:2; 32:11; 36:10; 64:10; 94:15). This concept is clearly parallel to that of a perfect heart. As we will see when we come to Job, who was possessed of the conviction that he was upright before God, purity of intention does not mean faultlessness before either humanity or God. Perfection is uprightness of *heart,* not flawless behavior.

THE PARADOX OF PERFECTION

While the Book of Job addresses the problem of unjust suffering, it is also a treatise on perfection. It opens with the categorical claim that Job was a man who was "blameless ['perfect,' KJV] and upright" (1:1, RSV). Addressing Satan, God asked, "Have you considered my servant Job, that there is none like him on the earth, a blameless and upright man, who fears God and turns away from evil?" (v. 8, RSV).

Although Satan admits Job's uprightness, he is cynical about Job's motive: "Does Job fear God for nothing? Have you not put a fence around him and all that he has, on every side? . . . But stretch out your hand now, and touch all that he has, and he will curse you to your face" (vv. 9-11). The unleashed forces of evil then began to batter Job. While his "friends" taunted him with accusations of wrongdoing (otherwise why would God be punishing him?), Job steadfastly maintained his integrity. Although he felt abandoned by God's presence in the depths of his trials and sufferings (23:1-10), yet he could say, "I have not departed from the commandment of his lips; I have treasured in my bosom the words of his mouth" (v. 12). Satan was wrong. Job's was a *disinter-*

---

6. Ibid., 44.

ested love that could say, "Though he kill me, yet I will trust in him" (13:15, margin). He was indeed scripturally perfect!

Nevertheless, when Job beheld God in His majestic holiness, his lips were silenced. Then he could only say, "Now my eye sees you; therefore I despise myself, and repent in dust and ashes" (42:5-6). The final proof of Job's perfection was the acknowledgment of his folly and shortcomings. So it is today with us. To see and feel the full weight of this paradox is to confess with Charles Wesley,

> *Every moment, Lord, I need*
> *The merit of Thy death.*

3

Toward an Old Testament Theology of Holiness (1)

I t is now our task to attempt to develop an Old Testament theology of holiness. This will involve
(1) an analysis of what the Old Testament means by humankind's creation in the image of God;
(2) an analysis of the Fall and the introduction of sin into history and creation;
(3) a survey of God's redemptive plan, beginning with the call of Abraham as the first step in the creation of Israel; and
(4) a study of God's covenant with Israel instituted at Sinai through Moses.

HUMANKIND IN THE IMAGE OF GOD

The first three chapters of Genesis lay the foundation for the biblical concept of "the creature of God's saving concern."[1]

THE BIBLICAL ACCOUNT

Genesis 1

The Genesis account of creation is to be understood as a *theological* account of origins. Although the first chapter of Genesis suggests several striking parallels to the way modern science

---

1. W. T. Purkiser, *The Biblical Foundations*, vol. 1 of *Exploring Christian Holiness* (Kansas City: Beacon Hill Press of Kansas City, 1983), 34.

views beginnings,[2] it is not to be taken as a "scientific" description of origins. As theology, it declares God to be the "Maker of heaven and earth," who created human beings in His own image and likeness, capable of fellowship with their Creator and called to cooperate with Him in carrying out His purposes on earth.

Few biblical texts are more important for grasping the biblical understanding of humanity as moral beings than Gen. 1:

> Then God said, "Let us make humankind in our image, according to our likeness; and let them have dominion over the fish of the sea, and over the birds of the air, and over the cattle, and over all the wild animals of the earth, and over every creeping thing that creeps upon the earth."
>
> So God created humankind in his own image, in the image of God he created them; male and female he created them.
>
> God blessed them, and God said to them, "Be fruitful and multiply, and fill the earth and subdue it; and have dominion over the fish of the sea and over the birds of the air and over every living thing that moves upon the earth" (vv. 26-28).

In interpreting this passage, we must give special attention to four Hebrew words: bara (create), 'adam (humankind), tselem (image), and demut (likeness).

The term bara signifies an immediate creative act of God. It is used twice in reference to the creation of "the heavens and the earth" (Gen. 1:1; 2:4), once in reference to "every living and moving thing" (1:21, NIV), and three times in reference to human beings. It describes creation de novo, or ex nihilo, in contrast to formation from preexistent matter (cf. 2:7).

'Adam is a generic term meaning "humankind." The transition from the generic term to the personal Adam does not occur until 4:25: "Adam knew his wife again, and she bore a son and named him Seth." In chapter 5 we find the dual significance of the term: "This is the list of the descendants of Adam. When God created humankind, he made them in the likeness of God. Male and female he

2. See H. Orton Wiley, Christian Theology, 3 vols. (Kansas City: Beacon Hill Press, 1940-43), 1:458-61.

created them, and he blessed them and named them 'Humankind' [*'adam*] when they were created" (vv. 1-2, emphasis added). Terrence E. Fretheim comments, "The movement of the meaning of *'adam* back and forth between generic humankind (1:26-27; 5:1-2), the first man, and Adam probably reflects an effort both to tell a story of a past and to provide a mirroring story for every age."[3]

Going back to Irenaeus, Roman Catholic theology has traditionally made a distinction between the *image (tselem)* and the *likeness (demut)* of God in which we humans were created. In this view, *image* defines that which distinguishes humankind from the animal creation (rationality, freedom of will, immortality, and so on), while *likeness* defines the state of holiness in which *'adam* stood before he defected. This interpretation fails to take into account the fact that Gen. 1:26 is an instance of Hebrew parallelism; both terms have to do with parallel representations or models and are simply two ways of saying the same thing.

It is the whole of our being that is like God, a likeness that is passed on through procreation, as Gen. 5:1-3 makes clear (cf. 9:6). *'Adam* is God's special representative by nature and design. Earthly kings would erect images of themselves in distant provinces of their realm to represent them where they could not be personally present. So *'adam* is placed on earth as God's representative and agent. But unlike the image of earthly kings, the image of God is not a fixed image. As Brueggemann points out, "There is only one way in which God is imaged in the world and only one: humanness! God is not imaged in anything fixed but in the freedom of human persons to be faithful and gracious."[4]

Human sexuality is a part of the creation's goodness but is not to be understood as a part of the identity of God. Nothing in the passage suggests the idea that the presence of sexual differentiation in creation is to be read as duality in the nature of God.[5] On this point Wolfhart Pannenberg writes,

---

3. Terrence E. Fretheim, *The New Interpreter's Bible* (Nashville: Abingdon Press, 1994), 1:353. Used by permission. This is the way Paul views Adam (see exposition of Rom. 5:11-21). This "social" understanding of *'adam* also witnesses to the truth that *'adam* reflects the social nature of God, in whose image and likeness we were created (see p. 38).

4. Birch, *Let Justice Roll Down*, 87.

5. Ibid., 88.

While it was a common feature in ancient cultures to conceive of the divine reality as male or female in analogy to human society, the one God of Israel could not be understood to have a divine consort lest monotheism be lost. . . . [The Fatherhood of God in the Old Testament] comes to expression most characteristically in the father-son relationship, when God is said to relate to the king like a father to his son. . . . It expresses not the natural relationship of procreation but rather the social function of providence and care, as it is appropriate in the head of the family.[6]

Following certain Eastern fathers, we may understand humankind's creation in the divine image to be a reflection of the communal nature of the triune God. The Eastern concept of *perichoresis*—that God is a community of Father, Son, and Holy Spirit, whose unity is constituted by mutual indwelling and reciprocal interpenetration—affirms in the Creator both unity in diversity and diversity in unity (see John 14:10-11, 16-18, 20, 23). God is not a monad; He is in himself a fellowship of holy love (17:21-23). The image of God in *'adam* is therefore communal, making possible the divine indwelling of human personality (14:23; 17:26; see chap. 4, fn. 7).

After creating humankind, "God saw everything that he had made, and indeed, it was very good" (Gen. 1:31). This pronouncement contrasts the Hebraic understanding of created existence as essentially good with the Greek valuation of the material world as per se evil.

A reading of the creation account also makes it clear that humankind is not an end in itself but was created for God's purposes. Birch points out, "Creation in the image of God and as male and female is in preparation for the discharge of mission within the created order, and to empower them in this mission God blesses them (Gen. 1:28)."[7]

By creating *'adam* male and female, God empowers them to populate the earth and thereby bring into being human communi-

---

6. Wolfhart Pannenberg, "Feminine Language About God?" *Asbury Theological Journal* 48, No. 2 (fall 1993): 27.
7. Birch, *Let Justice Roll Down*, 89.

ty. But sexuality in the Old Testament is not limited to the procreative act, as we will see when we come to Gen. 2.

The command to exercise dominion over creation was to be carried out by *'adam* as God's representative (image) on earth, in behalf of His sovereignty as Creator. Fretheim points out that a study of the verb *radah* ("have dominion") reveals that "it must be understood in terms of care-giving, even nurturing, not exploitation. As the image of God, human beings should relate to the non-human as God relates to them."[8] The command to "subdue the earth" focuses on the cultivation of the earth and its development as paradise (cf. 2:15). The Judeo-Christian tradition in its image of dominion has been incorrectly charged with major responsibility for the modern ecological crisis. On the contrary, as we will see when we come to the fall of *'adam*, this crisis is the result of *sin*, in which the awareness of our human stewardship over God's created order is forgotten. The command to "have dominion" over and "subdue" the created order is in actuality an *ecological* mandate.

Genesis 2

In the more graphic account of the creation of *'adam* in Gen. 2, a key text occurs: "Then the Lord God formed man from the dust of the ground, and breathed into his nostrils the breath of life, and the man became a living being" (v. 7).

Here God the Creator is pictured as a potter who shapes man according to the divine design. The combination of being formed from dust and in the image of God, made of the same substance of the earth but made to have dominion over it, is a profound statement about human identity, linking to the royal themes we have seen in chapter 1.

Furthermore, *'adam* is seen here as a creature of two worlds. The "breath of life" he received is not simply air but "God's own living breath." The divine act of breathing into *'adam* provides the only distinction here between humans and animals.[9] Physically and biologically, *'adam* is of "the dust of the ground." Personally and psychologically, there is in him "the breath of life," breathed into him by the Lord God, so that he is a "living being" capable of fellowship with his Creator (cf. 3:8-9).

---

8. Fretheim, *New Interpreter's Bible*, 1:346.
9. Ibid., 350.

The creation of a companion for man reveals a second purpose for human sexuality: psychosocial rather than merely biological. Phyllis Bird writes, "Companionship, the sharing of work, mutual attraction and commitment in a bond superseding all other human bonds and attractions—these are the ends for which 'adam was created male and female and these are the signs of the intended partnership . . . a partnership of equals, characterized by mutuality and attraction, support and commitment."[10]

"And the man and his wife were both naked, and were not ashamed" (2:25). This can only mean they were created for a relationship of complete openness and wholeness, with sexuality as a part of God's intention (cf. the Song of Solomon, which celebrates the sexual joys of marriage).

In the midst of the garden God planted a "tree of the knowledge of good and evil" (2:9). The name of the tree is symbolic. "Any meaning assigned to the tree must recognize that it has to do with a 'knowledge' that God has. This makes it unlikely that it has to do either with sexual knowledge/experience which 2:24-25 and 1:27-28 already imply, or knowledge of/experience with sin or wickedness."[11]

The key issue involves discerning what are our best interests as humans placed in God's garden. The tree and the divine command *together* define the limits of creaturehood. To transgress these limits entails the decision to put our own interests first, to become autonomous; in effect it is a *declaration of independence from God.* To refrain from eating is to acknowledge our creaturely limitations and to accept the will of God as making possible true human life. This creational command thus presents a positive use of law, in which certain limits are recognized as being in the best interests of human life and well-being.[12]

The ecological command of 1:28 is repeated in 2:15, where 'adam was commanded to "till . . . and keep" the Garden of Eden. "You may freely eat of every tree of the garden," the Lord God says; "but of the tree of the knowledge of good and evil you shall not eat, for in the day that you eat of it you shall die" (2:16-17; cf.

10. Phyllis Bird, "'Male and Female He Created Them'; Gen. 1:27b in the Context of the Priestly Account of Creation," *Harvard Theological Review* 74 (1981): 138.

11. Fretheim, *New Interpreter's Bible,* 1:350.

12. Ibid., 351.

1:29). This command, says Fretheim, "constitutes a version of the first commandment, a concern not evident in chap. 1."[13]

'*Adam*'s freedom of will is clearly implied. The Creator takes the risk of allowing a choice to be made for obedience or disobedience. What is significant here is humanity's capacity to choose *and* the responsibility to accept the consequences of that choice—obedience to God or disobedience. God has placed boundaries upon the exercise of our freedom. "Without this freedom," Birch reminds us, "our interrelatedness would be no more than the biological connectedness of ecosystems."[14]

THEOLOGICAL INTERPRETATION: *IMAGO DEI*

Clearly, the "image of God" (technically, the *imago Dei*) in Genesis refers to our special human endowment and our special relationship to God. Bernhard W. Anderson has written:

> The image refers to something distinctive in human being that makes possible a sense of awe and wonder, which could lead to prayer and relationship with God. The image refers to those special dimensions of human nature that lift humans above the animal plane: imagination, freedom to be and to become, responsibility and guilt, intellectual inquiry, artistic appreciation. The image refers, above all, to the God-given commission to "image" God on earth, that is, to be the agents who represent and realize God's benevolent and peaceful sway on earth.[15]

The term clearly implies that humans alone, of all God's creatures, stand before Him in an "I-Thou" relationship and in representing Him in dominion over the remainder of creation. Human beings alone are *addressable* by their Creator (1:29), *responsible* and *accountable* before Him (1:28; 2:9), *capable of fellowship* with Him (3:8), and of *"imaging"* their Creator in their very persons as His representatives on earth.

---

13. Ibid.
14. Birch, *Let Justice Roll Down*, 92.
15. Bernhard W. Anderson, *From Creation to New Creation*, in *Overtures in Biblical Theology* (Minneapolis: Fortress Press, 1994), 108.

'ADAM'S DEFECTION; SIN AND DEPRAVITY

In the Epistle to the Romans Paul writes, "Sin came into the world through one man, and death came through sin, and so death spread to all because all have sinned" (5:12).

While Paul's *doctrine* of the Fall reflects a later theological development within Judaism that came to flower in Christian thought, the raw materials for this doctrine are clearly discernible in the early chapters of Genesis we are now to survey.

THE BIBLICAL ACCOUNT

These chapters in Genesis reveal that creation did not remain as God intended but that it has been disturbed and broken by human sin. Disobedience to the divine command broke 'adam's fellowship with God and disrupted the harmony of creation. Now unleashed in the world, sin continues to escalate, corrupting human relationships and even nature itself. These chapters, however, speak not only of sin, which disrupts creation, but also of God's grace, which enables life to continue in spite of sin and gives promise of new creation.

The Temptation and Fall (3:1-24)

In reading the early chapters of Genesis, we must keep in mind the poetic character of biblical language. Wiley and Culbertson call for recognition of the balance between fact and symbolism in chapter 3:

> Without doubt this historical account of the fall contains a large element of symbolism. . . . Such facts as the inclosed garden, the sacramental tree of life, the mystical tree of knowledge, the one positive command representing the whole law, the serpent form of the tempter, the flaming defenses of forfeited Eden—all were emblems possessing deep spiritual significance as well as facts. In defending the historical character of the Mosaic account of the fall, we must not fail to do justice to its rich symbolism.[16]

In Gen. 3 the reader seems to be overhearing the middle of a theological dialogue between the serpent and the woman in the

---

16. H. Orton Wiley and Paul T. Culbertson, *Introduction to Christian Theology* (Kansas City: Beacon Hill Press, 1946), 161.

garden. We hear the serpent raising a question about the amount of freedom God has given the pair: "Did God say, 'You shall not eat from any tree in the garden'?" (v. 1). This question, which is a clever distortion of the divine command in 2:16-17, cannot be answered with a simple "yes" or "no" if the conversation is to continue (a key move on the serpent's part). The "you" is plural in the Hebrew, so that both the man and the woman are implied, even though the man stands "with her" in verse 6 as the silent partner.[17] Eve's initial response was faithful to the divine prohibition.

"But the serpent said to the woman, 'You will not die; for God knows that when you eat of it your eyes will be opened, and you will be like God, knowing good and evil" (v. 5). The key phrase here is "God knows." The tempter's claim was that God had not told them the full truth, that He was keeping something back, depriving them of what was rightfully theirs. Fretheim says,

> The serpent makes it sound as if God's motivation is self-serving; the humans will become like God. Has God, in keeping the full truth from them, divine interests more at heart than interest in humans? The issue of knowledge thus becomes at its deepest level an issue of *trust*. Is the giver of the prohibition one who can be trusted with their best interests? Can the man and the woman trust God even if God hasn't told them everything, indeed not given them every possible "benefit"? . . . *The word of the serpent ends up putting the word of God in question.*[18]

The woman makes no response to the serpent's charge; she focuses only on the potential of the tree, which she saw as "good for food," "a delight to the eyes," and above all, "desirable for gaining wisdom" (v. 6). While the humans may "desire" the trees for their beauty, they shall not "desire" wisdom—that is, the knowledge of good and evil. "The issue involves *the way in which wisdom is gained*," Fretheim observes. "The fear of the Lord is the beginning of wisdom (see Rom. 1:20-21). By using their freedom to acquire wisdom in this way, they have determined that the creational command no longer applies to them."[19]

17. Fretheim, *New Interpreter's Bible*, 1:360.
18. Ibid., 361 (emphasis added).
19. Ibid. (emphasis added).

Distrust thus issued in the denial of their creaturehood. The temptation of us humans is always to overreach our limitations, to try for the prerogatives of God. However, since God has made a specific boundary to be observed, sin is disobedience as well.

Our human temptation is to "be like God, knowing good and evil." "Good and evil encompass all possibilities of benefit and detriment. The temptation is to experience all possibilities, as does God, without regard to limits."[20] "Sin," Millard Reed explains, "is the delusion of self-sovereignty."

The Entrance of Sin and Depravity

The consequences of sin are immediate, as Bruce Birch argues:

> What the man and the woman immediately know (experience) is their own nakedness (3:7). In quick succession they are so ashamed they try to clothe themselves, they are so afraid at the sound of God in the garden that they hide themselves, and they are so unwilling to accept responsibility for their act of disobedience that they try to blame another (7-13). Shame, fear, and guilt enter the human story as signs of brokenness caused by their disobedience. Furthermore, the wholeness and harmoniousness of God's creation is now disrupted and broken (14-19).[21]

Perhaps the most interesting point, in the light of modern ethical issues relating to the roles of men and women, is the recognition that the rule of the man over the woman is *a sign of human fallenness*. Bird writes, "The sign of this disrupted relationship is this, that while the woman's relationship to man is characterized by desire, the man's relationship to the woman is characterized by rule. *The companion of chapter 2 has become a master.*"[22]

Furthermore, the disobedience of the garden is but the first episode in an escalation of sin that tragically unfolds throughout primeval history. In the tragedy of Cain and Abel (4:1-16) sin

---

20. Birch, *Let Justice Roll Down*, 93.
21. Ibid., 99.
22. Bird, "Male and Female He Created Them," 138 (emphasis added).

moves from personal disobedience to murder.[23] In the account of the Flood (chaps. 6—8), wickedness has become so universal that "every inclination of the thoughts of their [human] hearts was only evil continually" (6:5). In the episode of the Tower of Babel (11:1-9), the arrogant desire to "make a name for" themselves launches an attack on the heavens themselves with a tower to give humans access to God. The picture is of a growing gap between God and humanity.

We must not overlook a further point, that the nonhuman creation is a participant in the brokenness and corruption that results from sin. With the apostle Paul we must understand that in the brokenness of sin "the whole creation has been groaning in labor pains until now" (Rom. 8:22). "Throughout the Hebrew biblical tradition," Birch reminds us, "sin is treated as something that disturbs the whole of God's created order and not just the relationship between God and humanity. 'Therefore the land mourns, and all who live in it languish; together with the wild animals and the birds of the air, even the fish of the sea are perishing' (Hos. 4:3)."[24]

THEOLOGICAL ANALYSIS

In summarizing the theological implications of the Fall, W. T. Purkiser provides a threefold view of sin, as intrusion, choice, and condition:[25]

Sin as Intrusion

Sin is not a part of human nature as created or as intended to be. Temptation is seen to come through desires that are themselves *amoral*. "'Each person is tempted when he is lured and enticed by his own desire.' Only when 'desire . . . has conceived' (by impregnation with the consent of the will) does it give 'birth to sin; and sin when it is full-grown brings forth death'" (James 1:14-15, RSV).

Sin as Choice

Sin as an act is a matter of disobedience, of rebellion against God, of an effort to be "like God" (3:5)—and therefore indepen-

---

23. The word "sin" first occurs in 4:7; it is pictured as an invasive power threatening human well-being, an idea suggestive of Paul's concept of sin (Gr. *hē hamartia*) as a tyrannical, irrational force that "entered" the race with Adam's defection (see Rom. 5:12-14).

24. Birch, *Let Justice Roll Down*, 95.

25. Purkiser, *Exploring Christian Holiness*, 1:37-39.

dent of God. "Sin, in the Biblical view," Purkiser quotes James Orr, "consists in the revolt of the creature's will from its rightful allegiance to the sovereign will of God and the setting up of a false independence, the substitution of a life-for-self for life-for-God."

Sin as Condition

"The act of disobedience, of falsely claimed self-sovereignty, brought estrangement and alienation from God." The sin that brought a deprivation of the holiness in which man was created resulted in moral depravation for Adam's race.

It is the New Testament that tells us most specifically of the radical effects of the first sin (specifically, Rom. 5:12-21); yet there is a hint of it in the statement of Gen. 5:3 that Adam "had a son in his own likeness, in his own image" (NIV). The image was still God's image (v. 1), but it was also Adam's image, without the sanctifying relationship with the Creator, deprived and therefore depraved as a branch cut from the vine is corrupt not by the addition of something but by the loss of something (John 15:6).

In the Genesis account we have what theologians speak of as *total depravity*. As members of Adam's fallen race, every imagination of the thoughts of the human heart is "evil" and that "continually" (6:5, KJV).

Even though the picture of fallen humanity is dismal, we must never overlook the balancing truth of *God's grace*, which from the day of the Fall has manifested itself in His immediate and constant endeavor to recover humanity from its sinful predicament. While all humans and creation itself participate in the consequences of sin, so too are they the beneficiaries of God's redemption. As He says in Isaiah, "Behold, I will create new heavens and a new earth. The former things will not be remembered, nor will they come to mind" (65:17, NIV).

The final fulfillment of God's purpose in history is characteristically pictured as a new creation. This theme is most clearly emphasized in the Old Testament in Isa. 40—66, where the author understood himself to be standing just beyond the shadow of divine judgment and on the threshold of God's new age. The Early Church knew itself to be a part of that new creation in Christ, through whom ultimately "the creation itself will be set free from its bondage to decay and will obtain the freedom of the glory of the children of God" (Rom. 8:21).

What God's future redemptive purposes actually entail we mortals can only guess and speak of poetically. Meanwhile we confess ecstatically with the apostle, as he envisioned God's final triumph in redeeming fallen humanity, "O the depth of the riches and wisdom and knowledge of God! How unsearchable are his judgments and how inscrutable are his ways! 'For who has known the mind of the Lord, or who has been his counselor?' 'Or who has given a gift to him that he might be repaid?' For from him and through him and to him are all things. To him be glory for ever. Amen" (Rom. 11:33-36, RSV).

4

Toward an Old Testament Theology of Holiness (2)

In our endeavor to construct an Old Testament theology of holiness, we have considered the meaning of the creation of human beings in God's own image and the meaning of the Fall and the entrance of sin and death into the human family, with the consequent disruption of the round of nature.

We saw further that we must lay equal emphasis upon the balancing truth of the reality of God's grace making redemption possible in the midst of human sinfulness and promising ultimately "a new heaven and a new earth" (Rev. 21:1).

SIN AND GRACE

God's judgment (mingled with grace, as we shall see) was displayed immediately after the sin of the pair in the garden (Gen. 3:9-24). Upon entering the garden, God called to the man, "Where are you?" (v. 9), not because He was ignorant of their whereabouts, but because He wanted the pair to face the consequences of their sin. The man's response, "I was afraid, because I was naked" (v. 10), clarifies the motive of his hiding: guilt and shame. "Partaking of the fruit of the tree," Livingston comments, "had not made him like God, as the serpent had suggested, but had rather compromised his own true essence of being a man before God."[1]

---

1. George Herbert Livingston, "Genesis," in vol. 1 of *Beacon Bible Commentary* (Kansas City: Beacon Hill Press of Kansas City, 1969), 45.

The man was not simply guilty before God; he was ashamed before his wife. "Who told you that you were naked?" God asks in verse 11.

"How could the man have known that he was naked?" Fretheim asks. "Something must have happened so that the nakedness had become a problem to the someone who told him so [namely, the woman]." God then asked the pair whether they had eaten of the forbidden tree. "The response could be viewed as a consequence of their having achieved autonomy; the man could not handle the new 'knowledge.'" But, as Fretheim says, "The man appears fearful, insecure, and ashamed, seeking to justify himself and deflecting blame, both to God for giving him the woman and to the woman for giving him the fruit to eat. . . . This situation attests to a breakdown in interhuman relationships as well as in their relationship with God, whom he does not engage in a straightforward manner."[2]

The woman then blamed the trickery of the serpent, yet she admitted that she, too, had eaten the forbidden fruit. God then proceeded with the sentencing (vv. 14-19). The man then named his wife Eve (v. 20). At this point, Genesis tells us, "the LORD God made garments of skins for the man and for his wife, and clothed them. Then the LORD God said, 'See the man has become like one of us, knowing good and evil'" (vv. 21-22). Driving the man out of the garden, God then blocked its gate with a cherubim and flaming sword (vv. 23-24). Verse 22 strikingly defines original sin—it is self-sovereignty, *the* sin that God will not brook. As we read in Isa. 45:5, "I am the LORD, and there is no other; besides me there is no god."

"The writer presents no naïve theology," Fretheim writes, "but a deeply profound understanding of how God chooses to enter into the life of the world and relate to the creatures. Even more, this God comes to the man and the woman subsequent to their sin; God does not leave them or walk elsewhere."[3] The picture is of God's judgment mingled with grace.

As Creator, we have already noted, God has set the bounds of human creaturehood, saying to the man, "You may freely eat of every tree of the garden; but of the tree of the knowledge of good

---

2. Fretheim, *New Interpreter's Bible*, 1:362.
3. Ibid.

and evil you shall not eat, for in the day that you eat of it you shall die" (Gen. 2:16-17). Despite this warning, the pair disobeyed—and died, as we have just seen: "The wages of sin is death" (Rom. 6:23). God's grace, however, was beautifully displayed immediately after their sin, in the Lord God's entering the garden and calling after the man, "Where are you?" as if he had never sinned!

Then turning to the serpent that had deceived the pair, God said, "I will put enmity between you and the woman, and between your seed and her Seed; He shall bruise your head, and you shall bruise His heel" (Gen. 3:15, NKJV).

In this text the church fathers found the Christus Victor idea of the Atonement: In the very act of bruising Jesus' heel, Satan's head was crushed. Although the serpent's tail still wiggles, his death is certain! In Christ's death and resurrection the decisive victory over sin and death has been won; the final triumph over evil awaits our Lord's return in glory.

In the Lord's making clothes for the pair, other interpreters find the implication that He had offered an animal sacrifice for their sin (cf. 4:4). Whether or not we should read this meaning into the act, the story suggests that God lovingly clothed the pair in the garden.

God, of course, is revealed as the righteous Judge throughout these early chapters of Genesis, exacting the consequences of sin. Yet He also put a mark on Cain to protect him (4:15); He not only saves Noah and his family from the Flood but also guarantees the order of nature and enters into covenant around the promise of the rainbow (8:20—9:17).

Finally, and importantly, in Gen. 12:1-3 the account takes a significant turn to begin the story of Abraham and Sarah and their descendants—Israel. Birch comments, "The testimony of God's creation and the tragedy of broken creation are important in their own right, but they also stand connected to the story of a particular people, beginning with Abraham and Sarah, who understand themselves as called into being to play a part in God's redemptive purposes for a broken creation. . . . God the Creator is also revealed as God the Redeemer, and the story of Israel is to be understood as a part of God's redemptive work."[4]

---

4. Birch, *Let Justice Roll Down*, 96.

Just as creation participates in the consequences of human sin, so, too, creation becomes the final beneficiary of God's redemption. Redemption, which begins with the salvation of the human family, climaxes in a renewed nature rejoicing in the salvation of God's people. "For you shall go out in joy, and be led back in peace," we read in Isa. 55:12-13; "the mountains and the hills before you shall burst into song, and all the trees of the field shall clap their hands. Instead of the thorn shall come up the cypress; instead of the brier shall come up the myrtle."

As we saw in the previous chapter, the final fulfillment of God's purposes in history is often pictured in terms of a new creation, such as we see in the vision of the peaceable kingdom in Isa. 11:6-9. It should not be surprising, therefore, that Paul and the Early Church found in Christ the experience of new creation (2 Cor. 5:17—"The old order has gone, and a new order has already begun," NEB). The climax of God's redemption is seen in the New Testament promise that creation itself will be redeemed when His salvific promise for humankind is consummated (Rom. 8:18-23).

FROM PROMISE TO DELIVERANCE

With the movement from primeval history (Gen. 1—11) to the call of Abraham (12:1-3) we move from the account of humanity in general to begin the story of a particular community—Israel, God's own people.

It is important that we see in these events the beginnings, the roots, of our identity as the Church. We are a continuation of that ancient community called into being by God himself, who was not willing to leave humanity and His creation fallen and broken. To understand more fully the testimony of Genesis and the Exodus story (and their echoes throughout the canon of Scripture) is to gain insight into our character and our mission as God's holy people today.

The birth story of the Israelites is our own birth story as the Church of Jesus Christ. The remembered events that brought ancient Israel into being tell us who we are as God's new Israel—the children of Abraham in whom "all the families of the earth shall be blessed." And in the Exodus event (narrated in chaps. 1—15), in which the Israelites remember their deliverance from Egyptian bondage, we see a foreshadowing of the "exodus" that Jesus accomplished in Jerusalem in His death and resurrection (Luke 9:31), creating the Church as "a chosen race, a royal priesthood, a holy nation, God's own people" (1 Pet. 2:9).

It is as a part of this community of faith and obedience that began with Abraham and became "a priestly kingdom and a holy nation" at the Exodus (Exod. 19:6) that we read the story of Israel in the Old Testament.

THE BEGINNING OF GOD'S PEOPLE: ABRAHAM

In Gen. 12:1-3 God issues both a summons and a promise to Abram: "Go from your country and your kindred and your father's house to the land that I will show you. I will make of you a great nation, and I will bless you, and make your name great, so that you will be a blessing. . . . and in you all the families of earth shall be blessed." God chose Abram, that through him He might raise Israel to be His missionary people, "a light to lighten the Gentiles" (Luke 2:32, KJV) and bring the knowledge of God with all its blessing to the ends of the earth (Isa. 42:5; 43:10-12).

In Abraham we find the true nature of justification, as Paul demonstrates in Rom. 4:1-25. The key passage the apostle quotes is Gen. 15:5-6, where we read that the Lord took Abram out one starry night and talked to him: "'Look toward heaven and count the stars, if you are able to count them.' Then he said to him, 'So shall your descendants be.' And he believed in the LORD; and *the LORD reckoned it to him as righteousness*" (emphasis added; cf. Gal. 3:6-14). The righteousness that the Lord reckoned to Abraham was not ethical, but *relational*.[5] Abraham was *justified by faith,* just as we are who trust in Christ for pardon and acceptance with God.

When Abram was 99, the Lord appeared to him and said to him, "I am the Almighty God; walk before me, and be thou perfect" (Gen. 17:1, KJV). J. G. S. S. Thomson writes concerning this verse, "'Perfect' means ethically blameless, and denotes integrity. And the phrase, 'walk before me' means 'live consciously in my presence.' This suggests progress in ethical conduct consistent with a progressive awareness of God's presence. The aspiration is

---

5. Abraham's ethical behavior reflected the cultural practices of his time. Justification by faith is preethical; yet as Gen. 17:1 clearly implies, implicit within it is the requirement to "walk before me" with integrity (see chap. 8, on Rom. 6:19).

to be well pleasing unto God in whose presence one is constantly walking."[6]

Since Abraham is "the father of us all" (Rom. 4:16), his faith and obedience are instructive to us who through him have been blessed with God's promised salvation.

THE EXODUS AND THE MOSAIC COVENANT

After delivering Israel with a mighty hand from the Egyptians and bringing them across the Red Sea to Mount Sinai, God called to Moses from the mountain and said, "You have seen what I did to the Egyptians, and how I bore you on eagles' wings and brought you to myself. Now therefore, if you obey my voice and keep my covenant, you shall be my treasured possession out of all the peoples. Indeed, the whole earth is mine, but you shall be for me a priestly kingdom and a holy nation" (Exod. 19:4-6).

A significant point to note here is that Israel's holiness was corporate: Israel was God's holy *people.* Individual Israelites were holy as they observed the terms of the covenant. In Exod. 19:4-6 the Hebrew pronoun is *plural.* But not in the Decalogue, which follows; there God employs the *singular,* as the KJV makes clear: "I am the LORD *thy* God. . . . *Thou* shalt have no other gods before me" (Exod. 20:2-3ff., emphases added). That is to say, Israel was truly God's holy people only as they *individually* obeyed His commandments (cf. "The Holiness Command," in chap. 1).

It was in the breakdown of obedience on the part of individual Israelites, we learn, that Israel failed the Lord as His holy people. This defection became obvious at the time of the Exile, when for the first time a prophet would declare, "The soul that sinneth, *it* shall die" (Ezek. 18:4, KJV, emphasis added; see vv. 1-32).[7] Consistent with this new understanding of individual re-

---

6. J. G. S. S. Thomson, *The Old Testament View of Revelation* (Grand Rapids: Wm. B. Eerdmans Publishing Co., 1960), 54.

7. Prior to this, the proverb ran, "The fathers have eaten sour grapes, and the children's teeth are set on edge" (v. 2). H. Wheeler Robinson coined the term "corporate personality" to express this earlier understanding: "Whether in relation to man or God, the individual person was conceived and treated as merged in the larger group of family or clan or nation" (H. Wheeler Robinson, *The Christian Doctrine of Man* [Edinburgh: T. and T. Clark, 1911], 27). While the idea of corporate *sin,* as defined in the proverb, was abandoned, the concept of "corporate personality" has a much wider meaning for bibli-

sponsibility, Jeremiah envisioned a new covenant that the Lord would make with Israel that explicitly promised an experience of personal holiness for every individual of the believing community (Jer. 31:31-34, esp. v. 34; cf. Ezek. 36:25-27). But that is to get ahead of the story.

Our task is now to return to beginnings. We shall give our attention, therefore, to the original covenant the Lord made with Israel at Sinai.

The Mosaic Covenant

Although the experience of God's deliverance from Egyptian bondage formed the faith out of which Israel was born as a community, it required the formative experience of God's covenant making at Sinai to make the community of Israel an ongoing reality.[8]

The traditional view of the Mosaic covenant as a covenant of works and the Decalogue as a list of rules to be kept in order to earn God's favor and blessing must be rejected out of hand. Sufficient to disprove this mistaken idea is the prefatory statement that provides the background of the Ten Commandments: "I am the LORD your God, who brought you out of the land of Egypt [this is redemptive grace] . . . you shall have no other gods before me. You shall not make for yourself an idol . . . for I the LORD your God am a jealous God" (Exod. 20:2-5).

God first redeemed Israel, then commanded their exclusive devotion. In this context, the Decalogue spells out the framework of covenant obedience, first in their relationship to Yahweh, then to one another. The close relationship between obedience in relationship to God and obedience in relationship to neighbor is the basis of Jesus' summary of the two tables of the Law as loving God "with all your heart, and with all your soul, and with all your mind . . . [and] your neighbor as yourself" (Matt. 22:37, 39). Fur-

---

cal theology and therefore must not be set aside (see Gen. 5:1-2; cf. Rom. 5:12-21). Such corporate thinking in fact distinguishes Hebrew from Greek thought. The latter had no idea of social personality—it conceptualized only the *individual*. It is this individualistic way of thinking that renders Greek philosophy incapable of articulating biblical theology. This study of biblical holiness, while recognizing the place of personal freedom, will therefore endeavor to keep in view the corporate nature of personality, with reference to both sin and redemption. As we have seen, such a social understanding of personality also reflects the *imago Dei* (see p. 38).

8. Birch, *Let Justice Roll Down*, 145.

thermore, in thus summarizing the Law, Jesus was drawing directly on the Book of Deuteronomy, where love is explicitly stated to be the essence of the covenant Law.

The Love of God

Although the word does not occur in the Exodus story, it is the *love* of God that is later declared to be the motive of His deliverance of Israel from Egyptian bondage, particularly in Deuteronomy and Hosea.

In his Deuteronomic rehearsal of the Exodus story prior to his death, Moses gave the people of Israel an extremely important reminder: "It was not because you were more in number than any other people that the LORD set his love upon you and chose you, for you were the fewest of all peoples; but it is because the LORD loves you, and is keeping the oath which he swore to your fathers, that the LORD has brought you out with a mighty hand, and redeemed you from the house of bondage, from the hand of Pharaoh king of Egypt" (7:7-8, RSV). God's love was the sole explanation for Israel's redemption. Simply put, God loved them because He loved them!

The prophet Hosea makes the same point in a graphic picture of His fatherly love for Israel: "When Israel was a child, I loved him, and out of Egypt I called my son. . . . Yet it was I who taught Ephraim to walk, I took them up in my arms; but they did not know that I healed them. I led them with cords of human kindness, with bands of love" (11:1, 3-4).

God's deliverance of His people was clearly out of the free initiative of His love, a manifestation of sheer grace. And it is obvious that Israel participated in that love. As Birch writes, "God's deliverance in the Exodus experience establishes relationship with Israel, and that relationship is already characterized from God's side as love."[9]

The Love Command

It is in light of God's love for Israel that we are to understand the Shema: "Hear, O Israel: The LORD our God is one LORD; and

---

9. Ibid., 120. See Snaith, *Distinctive Ideas*, 94-95, in which he distinguishes between *'ahabah* (election love) and *chesed* (covenant love).

you shall love the LORD your God with all your heart, and with all your soul, and with all your might" (Deut. 6:4-5, RSV). Yahweh's love for Israel calls for a responding love on the part of His people, a love that recognizes that Yahweh alone is God and manifests itself in wholehearted devotion and faithful obedience to His revealed will.

As the creed and confession of Israel, the Shema is central to an understanding of the Law, summarizing the Law as it does in terms of loving God. Brevard S. Childs writes, "The ability of Deuteronomy to summarize the Law in terms of loving God with heart, soul and mind is a major check against all forms of legalism. According to Deuteronomy, the whole Mosaic law testifies to the living will of God whose eternal purpose for the life of his people provides the only grounds for life and salvation."[10]

The Law in all its forms is to be understood in terms of Israel as a community of faith. The community formed in relation to the Lord is prior to all else, and the laws are for guidance and instruction in grasping and living out the implications of such a community.[11] "God's prior initiative of grace and freedom is the presupposition on which the Decalogue rests," Birch reminds us. "Obedience to these commands will not establish relationship with God; they but spell out the framework of response in community to a relationship already initiated by God."[12]

The term "Law," therefore, must be carefully defined because of the legalism it calls to mind for most people. The Hebrew word is "Torah," which properly means "instruction" or "guidance." Seen as the expression of God's grace and love, Torah indicated for Israel a way of life, oriented to life in relation to God.

God, as the Giver of Torah, was seen primarily not as the giver of commandments but as the Source of divine teaching and guidance that defined the life of the faithful community. Conversely, the commandments were seen less as stern rules of behavior than as the joyous gift of God's guidance, manifest in the commandments, but in other ways as well.[13]

---

10. Brevard S. Childs, *Old Testament Theology in a Canonical Context* (Philadelphia: Fortress Press, 1985), 56.

11. Birch, *Let Justice Roll Down*, 164.

12. Ibid., 169.

13. Ibid., 172.

John Barton goes to the heart of the matter when he writes,

> "Torah" is a system by which to live the whole of life in the presence of God, rather than a set of detailed regulations to cover every individual situation in which a moral ruling might be called for. . . . Torah . . . is in another aspect the design according to which the world was created, and which makes sense of it; and by adhering to it human beings form part of God's plan, and enjoy . . . fellowship with him. . . . In this sense ethics is not so much a system of obligations as a way of communion with God, which is the cause of joy: hence . . . such passages in praise of the law in Psalm 19. . . . And hence the existence of the text which has so often struck Christian readers as artificial, repetitive and legalistic, but which could well serve as a complete statement in miniature of Old Testament ethics. . . . Psalm 119 [is comprised of] one hundred and seventy-six verses in praise of the Torah.[14]

In this view Torah defines holiness, not as rigid adherence to laws and regulations but as life lived in relationship to God, in praise and in grateful, obedient love. At the very heart of the Law is love—divine love finding a responsive human love. "We love because he first loved us" (1 John 4:19). Even so, such responsive love is at the same time the Law's command: "Do not think that I have come to abolish the law or the prophets," Jesus said; "I have come not to abolish but to fulfill" (Matt. 5:17). The balance of grace and obedience is as pertinent to the Church as to ancient Israel.

In recent years E. P. Sanders has coined the term "covenantal nomism" (nomism deriving from the Greek *nomos*, "law") to express the balance between God's grace revealed in the election of Israel and the obedience He commanded of the chosen people. According to Sanders, the "pattern" or "structure" of covenantal nomism is this:

> (1) God has chosen Israel and (2) given the law. The law implies both (3) God's promise to maintain the election and (4) the requirement to obey. (5) God rewards obedience and punishes transgression. (6) The law provides for means of

---

14. John Barton, "Approaches to Ethics in the Old Testament," in *Beginning Old Testament Study*, ed. John Rogerson (Philadelphia: Westminster Press, 1982), 130.

atonement, and atonement results in (7) maintenance or reestablishment of the covenantal relationship. (8) All those who are maintained in the covenant by obedience, atonement and God's mercy belong to the group which will be saved. An important interpretation of the first and last points is that election and ultimately salvation are considered to be by God's mercy rather than human achievement.[15]

God's covenant under Moses originated in an act of sheer grace, but its origins included the words of acceptance: "'Now therefore, if you obey my voice and keep my covenant, you shall be my treasured possession out of all the peoples.' . . . The people all answered as one: 'Everything that the LORD has spoken we will do'" (Exod. 19:5, 8).

Old Testament history is a detailed and often painful commentary on Israel's failure to live out their pledged obedience as God's covenant people. We turn now to this problem—and to God's further promise to offer His people a new covenant under which He would remove their heart of stone, put His Holy Spirit within them, and write His Law on their hearts and minds.

The Promise of the Spirit

Theologically, it is relatively easy to formulate the balance between divine grace and human obedience; practically, Israel found it virtually impossible to live out their obedience simply in trustful acceptance of God's promise to preserve and save them. Even when received as a covenant of grace, the Law was insufficient in itself to insure the holiness of God's people. Of course the Law's inability to sanctify is as true of Christians today as it was of historic Israel, a truth the apostle Paul drove home in his Epistle to the Romans.

The Powerlessness of the Law to Sanctify

The Old Testament details Israel's repeated failure to live out their covenant obligations to the Lord, despite His persistent love and care for them. Israel's miserable history attests to the fact that the Law could not deliver them from the sin that was lodged in their hearts.

---

15. E. P. Sanders, *Paul and Palestinian Judaism* (Philadelphia: Fortress Press, 1977), 422.

Jeremiah saw the problem most acutely (see 7:21-26; 11:6-8). Crying to his generation, he urged, "Circumcise yourselves to the LORD, remove the foreskin of your hearts" (4:4; cf. Deut. 10:16). Physically circumcised, they were spiritually uncircumcised, as evidenced by their inveterate stubbornness and rebellion against the Lord. The prophet laments, "Can the Ethiopians change their skin or leopards their spots? Then also you can do good who are accustomed to do evil" (13:23). "The heart is deceitful above all things, and desperately corrupt; who can understand it?" (17:9, RSV).

The rock upon which Israel foundered was their "heart of stone" (Ezek. 36:26). Even when understood correctly as a love command, the Law was powerless to dislodge sin and sanctify their hearts.

The Promise of Sanctification

Moses himself, however, foresaw a better day and promised, "The LORD your God will circumcise your heart and the heart of your descendants, so that you will love the LORD your God with all your heart and with all your soul, in order that you may live" (Deut. 30:6). In this verse we see a foregleam of Jeremiah's promise of the new covenant:

> The days are surely coming, says the LORD, when I will make a new covenant with the house of Israel and the house of Judah. It will not be like the covenant that I made with their ancestors when I took them by the hand to bring them out of the land of Egypt—a covenant that they broke, though I was their husband, says the LORD. But this is the covenant that I will make with the house of Israel after those days, says the LORD: I will put my law within them, and I will write it on their hearts; and I will be their God, and they shall be my people. No longer shall they teach one another, or say to one another, "Know the LORD," for they shall all know me, from the least of them to the greatest, says the LORD; for I will forgive their iniquity, and remember their sin no more (31:31-34; cf. Heb. 8:6-12; 10:14-17).

The fundamental weakness of the Law was its powerlessness to provide the requisite motivation to fulfill the love command that lies at its heart. John spelled out the fatal weakness of the Law in one sentence: "The Spirit had not been given" (John 7:39, RSV), that is, as an interior dynamic for the Law's fulfillment.

Ezekiel's version of the new covenant, given to exiled Israel in Babylon, is particularly relevant to this point:

It is not for your sake, O house of Israel, that I am about to act, but for the sake of my holy name, which you have profaned among the nations to which you came. I will sanctify my great name, which has been profaned among the nations, and which you have profaned among them; and the nations shall know that I am the LORD, says the Lord GOD, when through you I display my holiness before their eyes. I will take you from the nations, and gather you from all the countries, and bring you into your own land. I will sprinkle clean water upon you, and you shall be clean from all your uncleannesses, and from all your idols I will cleanse you. A new heart I will give you and a new spirit I will put within you; and I will remove from your body the heart of stone and give you a heart of flesh. I will put my spirit within you, and make you follow my statutes and be careful to observe my ordinances (36:22-27).

During the intertestamental period, the hope voiced by Ezekiel was interpreted as the promise of future sanctification. George Allen Turner writes,

Typical of this entire literature is the paraphrase of Ezek. 36:26 by S. Simeon b. Johai, "And God said, 'in this world, because the evil impulse exists in you, ye have sinned against me; but in the world to come I will eradicate it from you.'" It is remarkable that the rabbis, as well as John Wesley, viewed this passage as a dispensational promise of perfection. To the Christian it had already been fulfilled; to the Jew it remained a hope; to both it involved a fulfillment of the law by love.[16]

---

16. George Allen Turner, *The Vision Which Transforms: Is Christian Perfection Scriptural?* (Kansas City: Beacon Hill Press, 1964), 72.

5

The Age of the Spirit

W hat does this mean?" the amazed and perplexed onlookers asked the apostles at Pentecost upon hearing the untutored Galilean followers of Jesus declaring "the wonders of God" (Acts 2:11, NIV) in their own languages.

"These are not drunk, as you suppose," Peter rejoined, "for it is only nine o'clock in the morning. No," he then explained, "this is what was spoken through the prophet Joel: 'In the last days, it will be, God declares, that I will pour out my Spirit upon all flesh'" (vv. 15-17).

Peter's response to his questioners must be understood in the light cast by several other definitive New Testament passages.

First, in the Sermon on the Mount, Jesus says, "Do not think that I have come to abolish the law or the prophets; I have come not to abolish but to fulfill" (Matt. 5:17). In His person and work as the messianic Son, Jesus claims, God has "filled full" (Gr. *plērō-sai*) both the Law and the Prophets.[1] Everything that was formerly promised in Scripture is now fulfilled in Christ.

Again, the Book of Hebrews opens with the majestic announcement "Long ago God spoke to our ancestors in many and various ways . . . but in these last days he has spoken to us by a Son" (1:1-2). In Jesus, God has spoken His final and definitive word of salvation to humanity (vv. 1-4).

---

1. "God's work, testified to in the Scripture, is not yet complete. The Law and the Prophets point beyond themselves to the definitive act of God in the eschatological, messianic future" (M. Eugene Boring, *New Interpreter's Bible*, 8:186).

Finally, in Romans Paul declares, "Christ is the end *(telos)* of the law so that there may be righteousness for everyone who believes" (10:4). *Telos* here is "a technical term for final cause, goal, or purpose," says Robert Jewett, "a usage reflected in the verbal form *teleō* in Rom. 2:27, 'to fulfill the law.'"[2] Paul means that Christ is the Goal of the Law, that at which it aimed and for which it was intended. "Faith working through love" (Gal. 5:6) is "the just requirement *(dikaiōma)* of the law [which is] fulfilled in us, who walk not according to the flesh but according to the Spirit" (Rom. 8:4; cf. 13:8-10).

To repeat, it is passages such as these that reveal the significance of that which follows Peter's definitive announcement in Acts 2:16-17. (See also Rom. 3:21, 31; Heb. 10:1-10.) Luke intends that Peter's apostolic pronouncement be understood as the frontispiece of his book. The sermon summarizes the New Testament *kerygma*.[3] It centers in "Jesus of Nazareth," who, "according to the definite foreknowledge of God," was "handed over" to the Jews, who "crucified and killed [Him] by the hands of those outside the law" (Acts 2:22-23). "But," Peter declares, "God raised him up . . . and of that all of us are witnesses. Being therefore exalted at the right hand of God, and having received from the Father the promise of the Holy Spirit, he has poured out this that you both see and hear. . . . Therefore let the entire house of Israel know with certainty that God has made him both Lord and Messiah, this Jesus whom you crucified" (vv. 24, 32-33, 36).

"The Holy Spirit in the Church," says C. H. Dodd, is "the sign that the new age of fulfillment has begun."[4] As we will see, the New Testament makes clear that in the coming of the Spirit at Pentecost, the new covenant foretold by Jeremiah (31:31-34) was inaugurated, and the personal sanctification promised in Ezekiel (36:25-27) was now made possible in the long-anticipated gift of the Holy Spirit (Acts 15:8-9; Rom. 6:1-23; 8:1-17; Heb. 8:6-13; 10:14-18). This is in truth the age when Jesus Christ baptizes penitent believers with the Holy Spirit and fire (Matt. 3:11).

---

2. Robert Jewett, "The Law and the Coexistence of Jews and Gentiles in Romans," *Interpretation* 39, No. 4 (October 1985): 354.

3. The Greek term for the apostolic gospel, the "heralding" of Jesus, and the promised Spirit as fulfilling the promised messianic salvation.

4. C. H. Dodd, *The Apostolic Preaching* (New York and London: Harper and Brothers, 1951), 26.

The second chapter of Acts, however, records only the first of four "Pentecosts" in the Book of Acts. Historically, Pentecost is as unrepeatable as Good Friday or Easter; on that day the Holy Spirit came to "abide with [the Church] forever" (John 14:16, KJV). This historic coming of the Holy Spirit explains why the Church celebrates Pentecost Sunday (Whitsunday) each year. In another sense, however, Pentecost ushered in the *age* of the Spirit. The first Pentecost, H. B. Swete contends, did not give the apostles once and for all a full understanding of the universal gift of the Spirit.[5] The three subsequent "Pentecosts" are to be viewed as a *history of the coming of the Spirit:* first, in Samaria (8:14-17); second, at Caesarea (10:44-48; 11:15-17); and finally, at Ephesus (19:1-6). The signs that accompanied these "Pentecosts" are to be viewed as *inaugural,* signifying the extension of the gift of the Spirit to "the ends of the earth" (1:8).

It seems noteworthy that when Paul asked the disciples at Ephesus, "Did you receive the Holy Spirit when you became believers?" they replied, "No, we have not even heard that there is a Holy Spirit" (19:2). The Greek in this verse is identical to that in John 7:39, which reads literally, "as yet there was no Spirit." Of course, this does not mean the Spirit was nonexistent before Pentecost, but rather that the promised *sanctifying* Spirit was not "known" before the glorification of Jesus. Before the Spirit could be given as a permanent endowment to the people of God, a *pattern* was necessary in order to *define* life in the Spirit. The New Testament speaks with one voice in declaring that *Jesus himself* defines the Spirit-filled life. The Spirit who came at Pentecost is the *Spirit of Christ.* The power of the Spirit promised to believers is *the power to be Christlike.*

Late missionary statesman E. Stanley Jones gave this position definitive statement:

> If the power of the Spirit was to be Christlike power, then it was necessary to see that power manifested through the whole gamut of life, from a carpenter's bench to the throne of the universe, from the denial, betrayal, and crucifixion on the one hand to the triumph of the resurrection on

5. Yves Congar, *I Believe in the Holy Spirit*, trans. David Smith (New York: Seabury Press; London: Geoffrey Chapman, 1983), 1:45.

the other. For we had to see this power manifested as supreme modesty and humility, which when he triumphed over his enemies in the resurrection, made him refuse to appear in triumph before them to cow and overwhelm them—he was humble in every circumstance, and yet almighty in this humility. We had to see this power in its total range, for it was universal power.[6]

THE SPIRIT IN THE OLD TESTAMENT

Even though the Holy Spirit was not given until Pentecost, the Old Testament testifies to the Spirit's existence and activity from the dawn of creation to the coming of Christ.

Altogether there are 86 references to the Spirit of God in the Old Testament. For our purposes we can divide the references into three groups: (1) those that refer to God himself as "Spirit," (2) those that have to do with the redemptive action of God in Israel, and (3) those prophetic of Messiah and the age of the Spirit.

GOD "THE HOLY SPIRIT"

In the opening sentences of Genesis we read, "In the beginning . . . the Spirit of God was moving over the face of the waters" (1:1-2, RSV). Several modern versions translate the word *ruach* in this sentence as the "wind" of God (inc. NEB, NJB, NRSV). Something Jesus said to Nicodemus concerning the Spirit comes to mind: "The wind blows where it chooses" (John 3:8), reflecting the fact that the Greek *pneuma*, like the Hebrew *ruach*, also means "wind" or "breath."

After reviewing the many ways *ruach* is used in the Old Testament, Yves Congar sees the term *"ruach of God"* as referring to the Subject by whose powers various effects are produced in the world and in the experience of men and women who receive gifts of leadership or prophecy in Israel: "Sometimes the 'spirit of the Lord' or the 'spirit of God' simply refers to God himself," he writes, "as for example in Is. 40:13; 63:10: 'But they rebelled and grieved his holy spirit.' This brings us to a term that is so important for us here, an expression that is also used in the penitential

---

6. E. Stanley Jones, *The Way to Power and Poise* (New York: Abingdon-Cokesbury Press, 1949), 42.

psalm, 51:11, the 'holy spirit.'"[7] Congar then adds, "The spirit is holy because it comes from God and its reality belongs to the sphere of God's existence. There is no need to find any other reason for the holiness of the spirit. God is holy because he is God, but in the case of this spirit (or Spirit), the Old Testament does not emphasize the value of sanctification very much, at least not in the sense of an inner principle of perfection in life; such holiness is rather the result of observing the Torah."[8]

In Gen. 2:7, *ruach* is seen as the Breath of God. After forming man's body of dust, "the LORD God . . . *breathed* into his nostrils the breath of life; and the man became a living being" (emphasis added). The Breath-Spirit is qualified in various ways: as the spirit of intelligence (Exod. 31:3) or as the spirit of wisdom (35:30-31; Deut. 34:9). God as the Spirit is omnipresent, and from Him no one can escape (Ps. 139:7-18; cf. Acts 17:22-28). God is personal Spirit, permeating, yet distinct from, His creation. He is present, not only as the sustaining Power of the world, but also as a disturbing moral influence within the conscience of humans.

THE ACTION OF THE SPIRIT OF GOD

In a number of passages *ruach* suggests the powerful action of God. The term suggests a desert wind suddenly whipped into tornadic fury. The word thus came to mean *supernatural power laying hold upon a man or woman,* reinforcing natural powers and enabling such a one to perform divinely appointed tasks.

In the Book of Judges we read how "the spirit of the LORD came upon" Othniel, Gideon, Jephthah, and Samson, empowering them to champion the cause of Israel against its enemies (3:10; 6:34; 11:29; 13:25). In 1 Samuel we find an interesting account of Saul of Kish. Samuel announces to Saul, "Then the Spirit of the LORD will come upon you, and you will prophesy . . . and be turned into another man" (10:6, NKJV). "So it was," the record says, "when he had turned his back to go from Samuel, that God gave him another heart. . . . Then the Spirit of God came upon him, and he prophesied among them" (vv. 9-10, NKJV). Later we read how Samuel anointed David to be king, "and the Spirit of the LORD came upon David from that day forward" (16:13, NKJV).

---

7. Congar, *I Believe in the Holy Spirit,* 1:4.
8. Ibid.

In the above accounts, James S. Stewart observes, "the power of the Spirit . . . was abnormal in its nature, intermittent in its action, and non-ethical in its manifestation."[9] The gift of the *sanctifying* Spirit, as "the inner principle of perfection in life," awaited the next chapter in the history of salvation.

PROPHECIES ABOUT MESSIAH
AND THE AGE OF THE SPIRIT

By far the most important Old Testament passages dealing with the Spirit are those predictive of the Messiah and Pentecost.

During the intertestamental period a *dual* hope arose in Israel: (1) the hope of Messiah and (2) the hope of an unprecedented gift of the Spirit to Israel through Messiah.

The *first* strand of Israel's hope was the expectation of the Messiah, the Branch from the roots of David, upon whom the Spirit of the Lord should *rest*. George S. Hendry observes, "In contrast to the heroes, kings, and prophets of the past, upon whom the Spirit came only as an occasional and temporary visitant, the promised shoot of the stem of Jesse is one upon whom the Spirit of the Lord will *remain*."[10]

"And the Spirit of the LORD shall rest upon him, the spirit of wisdom and understanding, the spirit of counsel and might, the spirit of knowledge and the fear of the LORD" (Isa. 11:2, RSV).

Again the Lord says, "Behold, my servant, whom I uphold, my chosen, in whom my soul delights; I have put my Spirit upon him, he will bring forth justice to the nations. . . . He will not fail or be discouraged till he has established justice in the earth; and the coastlands wait for his law" (42:1, 4, RSV).

The *second* strand of Israel's hope was the expectation of a universal outpouring of the Spirit upon the people of God.

"For I will pour water on the thirsty land, and streams on the dry ground; I will pour my Spirit upon your descendants, and my blessings on your offspring" (44:3, RSV).

"And it shall come to pass afterward that I will pour out My Spirit on all flesh" (Joel 2:28, NKJV).

---

9. James S. Stewart, *A Man in Christ* (New York: Harper and Brothers, Publishers, n.d.), 308.

10. George S. Hendry, *The Holy Spirit in Christian Theology* (Philadelphia: Westminster Press, 1956), 17.

Congar speaks of "the two incomparable chapters of Ezekiel 36 and 37," which affirm in powerful language God's purpose to sanctify Israel and renew them as a people of the Spirit, explaining, "The disaster of the invasion and the test of the exile, interpreted by the greatest prophets, led to a vision of the Spirit-breath of God as purifying men's hearts, penetrating into them and making them a holy people of God. This was to be a new beginning, a new exodus, a new covenant and a people renewed."[11]

Because of the sins of the nation, it was believed, the Spirit had returned to heaven after Malachi. The Spirit would return to Israel, however, in the times of Messiah. Then, the rabbis taught, "the evil impulse would be taken out of Israel's heart . . . and the Spirit, as a power for moral renewal, would rest upon her."[12]

John the Baptist's witness to Jesus is an expression of Israel's intertestamental hope: "I saw the Spirit descend as a dove from heaven, *and it remained on him.* I myself did not know him; but he who sent me to baptize with water said to me, 'He on whom you see the Spirit descend *and remain,* this is he who *baptizes* with the Holy Spirit.' And I have seen and have borne witness that this is the Son of God" (John 1:32-34, RSV, emphases added). Jesus the Son of God (Messiah), as the *Bearer* of the Spirit, is also the *Baptizer* with the Holy Spirit (cf. Matt. 3:11-12). In Jesus, as we shall see, the dual hope of Israel finds fulfillment.

THE BAPTISM, CONCEPTION, AND LIFE OF JESUS[13]

Congar sees the baptism of Jesus (Mark 1:1 ff.) as "the beginning of the eschatological period characterized by the gift of the Spirit to a people of God with a universal vocation."[14] At His baptism Jesus was marked out and dedicated as the One through whom the Spirit enters the history of humanity "as a messianic gift, and . . . as the *arrha* or earnest-money, as an eschatological gift."[15]

---

11. Congar, *I Believe,* 1:9.
12. David Hill, *Greek Words and Hebrew Meanings* (Cambridge, Mass.: Cambridge University Press, 1967), 232-33; cited in H. Ray Dunning, *A Layman's Guide to Sanctification,* 25.
13. The material in this section is drawn largely from Congar, *I Believe,* vol. 1.
14. Ibid., 15.
15. Ibid., 15-16.

Although there is no doubt that in both Matthew and Luke Jesus' conception and birth were through the Spirit, both Gospel writers connect the *communication* of the gift through Him to His baptism. Before His baptism Jesus was not seen as someone acting in the power of the Spirit, nor did His fellow townspeople in Nazareth see anything exceptional in Him. From His mother's womb Jesus was indeed the Son of God filled with the Spirit, but it was the Spirit received in an act of God at His baptism that consecrated and empowered Him for His ministry. Congar explains,

> A first sending of the Spirit—Thomas Aquinas speaks of the "mission" of the Holy Spirit—made the little Jesus who was brought to life in Mary's womb "holy" and the "Son of God" (Messiah). A new communication or mission was initiated in the event of his baptism, when he was declared the Messiah, the one on whom the Spirit rests, who will act through the Spirit and who, once he has become the glorified Lord, will give the Spirit. If he was consecrated at the time of his baptism to carry out his prophetic ministry, then he was able to pour out the Spirit when he was "exalted to the right hand of God" (Acts 2:33).[16]

The Father's word to Jesus at His baptism, "You are my Son, the Beloved; with you I am well pleased" (Luke 3:22), is not a call but a declaration that echoed in Jesus' mind and confirmed to Him the kind of Messiah He was to be. The first part of the declaration ("You are my Son") is from Ps. 2:7, recognized as a royal, messianic psalm. The latter part ("with you I am well pleased") is from Isa. 42:1, the first verse of the Song of the Servant, whose death was "for the sins of the many" (52:13—53:12). Congar points out, "The characteristics of the Servant, called to mind by the reference to Is 42:1, are made explicit in the description of Jesus as the 'Lamb of God, who takes away the sin of the world' (Jn 1:29), the declaration made by Jesus in the synagogue in Nazareth (Lk 4:17-21) and Matthew's commentary on Jesus' healings (11:16ff.)."[17]

Jesus came to be baptized with the intention of offering himself to God's plan for His ministry, thereby accepting the role of

---

16. Ibid., 16.
17. Ibid., 17.

the Servant who would give His life "for the sins of the many" (see Heb. 10:5-10). Jesus, in fact, saw His coming death as His true "baptism" (Mark 10:38; Luke 12:50). He offered himself to God as a spotless victim through the "eternal spirit" (i.e., the Holy Spirit [Heb. 9:13-14]). His sacrifice was the consequence of His baptism, and His glory the consequence of His sacrifice. Furthermore, it was an event into which *we as believers* are incorporated when we are baptized (Rom. 6:3-4).

The descent of the Spirit upon Jesus at His baptism was a prophetic anointing for a mission to proclaim and carry out in the power of the Spirit. Furthermore, Pentecost was for the Church what Jesus' baptism was for Him—namely, to *continue* the ministry that Jesus began at His baptism (Acts 1:1). Irenaeus stated this truth beautifully when he wrote, "That is why this Spirit descended on the Son of God who became the Son of man—it was in this way, with him, that he became accustomed to dwell in the human race, to rest on men. . . . It is this same Spirit that the Lord gave to the Church when he sent the Paraclete from heaven."[18]

PENTECOST—THE AGE OF THE SPIRIT INAUGURATED

As we have seen, Peter's sermon at Pentecost is definitive. As the primitive *kerygma*, it is the skeleton of the apostolic declaration concerning Jesus.

Of unparalleled significance is Peter's declaration on that occasion: *"This is that which was spoken through the prophet Joel"* (Acts 2:16, KJV, emphasis added). At His baptism Jesus was anointed by the Spirit and empowered to be the messianic Servant of the Lord, upon whom the Spirit had come to rest (the *first* strand of Israel's hope fulfilled). At Pentecost Jesus was "declared to be Son of God with power" (Rom. 1:4), who baptizes with the Holy Spirit (the *second* strand of Israel's hope fulfilled). If the day of the Spirit was dawning at Jesus' baptism, at Pentecost "the Son of righteousness" had risen "with healing in his wings."[19]

Mark well Peter's declaration:

---

18. Ibid., 127.
19. William M. Greathouse, *The Fullness of the Spirit* (Kansas City: Nazarene Publishing House, 1958), 52.

This is what was spoken by the prophet Joel: "And in *the last days* it shall be, God declares, that I will pour out my Spirit upon all flesh, and your sons and your daughters shall prophesy, and your young men shall see visions, and your old men shall dream dreams; yea, and on my menservants and my maidservants in those days I will pour out my Spirit; and they shall prophesy. And I will show wonders in the heaven above and signs on the earth beneath . . . before the day of the Lord comes, the great and manifest day. And it shall be that whoever calls on the name of the Lord shall be saved" (*Acts 2:16-21, RSV, emphasis added*).

The days of the Messiah—foreseen by the prophets—were finally here in all their glory! The "last days" of which Peter spoke began at Pentecost and will be consummated by Christ's second advent. *Between these two events stretches the age-long day of the Spirit.*

C. H. Dodd writes: "The more we try to penetrate in imagination to the state of mind of the first Christians in the earliest days, the more we are driven to think of the resurrection, exaltation, and second advent as being, in their belief, inseparable parts of a single divine event . . . *The proof that it was here was found in the actual presence of the Spirit, that is, of the supernatural in the experience of men.*"[20]

SANCTIFICATION IN THE ACTS OF THE APOSTLES

We now address the question of sanctification in the Book of Acts. Congar says flatly, "An experience of the Holy Spirit is narrated in the Acts of the Apostles, but it is not combined with any form of teaching."[21] This statement, however, must be qualified.

According to Acts, the primary role of the Holy Spirit is that of empowering the Church to bear witness to Christ. "You will receive power when the Holy Spirit has come upon you; and you will be my witnesses in Jerusalem, in all Judea and Samaria, and to the ends of the earth" (1:8). Accordingly it may be said, "Luke has one master purpose in mind as he writes Acts: to sketch the Spirit-empowered witness of the Church as it begins in Jerusalem,

---

20. C. H. Dodd, *Apostolic Preaching*, 33.
21. Congar, *I Believe*, 1:129.

spreads into surrounding regions, and extends to the wide world. His particular concern is with the preaching of the gospel and the planting of the Church in radiating centers throughout a large part of the Roman empire."[22]

Even so, as Congar himself concedes, "One is bound to ask whether the gift of the Spirit which figures in the Acts of the Apostles, where it is said to be the same as given at Pentecost (11:17), is that of the Spirit as the principle of interior sanctification, or the Spirit of dynamic testimony."[23]

In this connection, as H. Ray Dunning observes, Jesus' high-priestly prayer in John 17 must not be overlooked:

> In particular we are here enabled to see the relation between Jesus' high-priestly prayer and the experience(s) of the Spirit in Acts. In John 17, the theme of mission is likewise inescapably present. . . . The burden of Jesus' prayer for His disciples was that "the world may believe that thou hast sent me" (v. 21 [KJV]). In the course of His prayer He dedicated (sanctified) himself to the completion of His mission and prays that God will dedicate (sanctify) His disciples to the continuance of that mission. The carrying out of this mission involves far more than persuasive speech; it entails a unity . . . that can occur only through a metamorphosis of their nature. Thus the Pentecostal outpouring as well as subsequent ones have as their aim the moral renewal (sanctification) of the disciples so they may carry out this mission. The descriptions of the corporate life of the Early Church validate that Pentecost was clearly effective in accomplishing this result.[24]

Furthermore, according to Acts 1:4-5, Jesus charged the apostles "not to depart from Jerusalem, but to wait for the promise of the Father, which, he said, 'you heard from me, for John baptized with water, but before many days you shall be baptized with the Holy Spirit'" (RSV). "What is the 'promise of the Father'?" Dunning asks. In answering this question, he refers to W. F. Lofthouse.

---

22. William M. Greathouse, *Acts*, vol. 5 in *Search the Scriptures* (Kansas City: Beacon Hill Press, 1954), 6.

23. Congar, *I Believe*, 1:46.

24. H. Ray Dunning, *Grace, Faith, and Holiness: A Wesleyan Systematic Theology* (Kansas City: Beacon Hill Press of Kansas City, 1988), 422.

Lofthouse has argued that since this is asserted to have been given by Jesus, it can only refer to the Johannine passages dealing with the promise of the Paraclete. Hence the promise of the Father is of the Holy Spirit, who is the Spirit of Christ. The content of Jesus has gone into it, with the result that those who received the Spirit in His fullness understood that not only were they being given a special kind of power to carry on Jesus' mission in the world, but they also were being transformed into a new existence that involved a through-and-through sanctification of their natures.

In addition to this, however, one could argue that included in the "promise of the Father" was the prophecy of John the Baptist. They were hearing this from Jesus, too. . . . John's prediction of the "baptism with the Holy Spirit" involved both endowment and moral renewal or sanctification.[25]

Jesus' baptism, John had said, would be with "the Holy Spirit *and fire*" (Matt. 3:11, emphasis added). The Baptist knew himself to be the forerunner of Malachi's promised "messenger of the covenant," of whom the prophet had said, "He will sit as a refiner and purifier of silver" (Mal. 3:3). Commenting on John's prediction, George Buttrick explained, "The ancient refiner watched the silver in the crucible, and kept the flame burning until all the base metal had come to the top and been skimmed off, until all agitation had ceased, and until he could see his face in the silver as in a mirror. This is a parable of the refining fire of baptism in Christ."[26] Our response to the promise of this refining baptism should be that of Charles Wesley:

> *O that in me the sacred fire*
> *Might now begin to glow,*
> *Burn up the dross of base desire,*
> *And make the mountains flow!*

Laurence W. Wood offers an interpretation of Acts 1:8 that sees the empowerment of the Spirit being *in itself* sanctifying grace. "The 'power from on high' which Jesus promised to his disciples,"

    25. Ibid., 423.
    26. George Arthur Buttrick, *The Interpreter's Bible,* ed. George A. Buttrick (New York and Nashville: Abingdon-Cokesbury Press, 1953), 7:266.

he says, "was divine energy *(dynamis)* which empowered them to live truly and completely as disciples and to become effective witnesses of God's reality in a hostile world." He continues,

> This "power" of the Holy Spirit is purifying power (Acts 15:8-9) which cleansed the disciples from their fears . . . and allowed them to be released from the threatening fear of their enemies. This "power from on high" was a power to love God truly and fully (Rom. 5:5). No longer did they "follow afar off," but boldly and with deep devotion and commitment they became witnesses of their Lord. The power of the Holy Spirit given at Pentecost is the power to be true disciples (Jn. 14—17).[27]

But what about the 3,000 at Pentecost who, upon hearing Peter's sermon, received "the gift of the Holy Spirit" upon repenting, believing, and being baptized? Were they *entirely* sanctified? "The great company added to the church that day," Wesley believed,[28] received the Spirit just as believers receive Him today, in justification, which is the *beginning* of sanctification.[29] The 3,000 therefore become a pattern for us rather than the 120 who had a previous experience of Jesus.

The third chapter of Galatians provides a scriptural basis for Wesley's contention. "Did you receive the Spirit by works of the law, or by hearing with faith?" (v. 2, RSV), Paul asked the Galatians, who were being "troubled" by Jewish legalists (1:7). They knew the answer to Paul's question by experience. They had "begun with the Spirit" (3:3) when they had trusted in the crucified Jesus. "Christ redeemed us from the curse of the law, having become a curse for us," the apostle reminds them, "that in Christ Jesus . . . we might receive the promise of the Spirit through faith"

---

27. Laurence W. Wood, "Third Wave of the Spirit and the Pentecostalization of American Christianity: A Wesleyan Critique," *Wesleyan Theological Journal* 37, No. 1 (spring 1996): 125.

28. Against John Fletcher, who after the debate conceded Wesley's point.

29. In a letter to Joseph Benson on Dec. 28, 1770, Wesley cautioned (against some persons at Trevecca in Wales who, following John Fletcher, were speaking frequently of "the baptism with the Holy Spirit"), "If they like to call this 'receiving the Holy Ghost,' they may; only the phrase in that sense is not scriptural and not quite proper; for they all 'received the Holy Ghost' when they were justified" (John Wesley, *The Letters of John Wesley, M.A.*, ed. John Tilford [London: Epworth Press, 1931], 5:215).

(vv. 13-14, RSV). "Because you are sons," he says in the next chapter, "God has sent the Spirit of his Son into our hearts, crying 'Abba! Father!'" (4:6, RSV). The Christian life *begins and ends* with the promised Spirit (3:3).

Conclusion

The importance of the Book of Acts is its announcement that with the coming of the Holy Spirit at Pentecost the long-expected age of the Spirit has dawned in salvation history. What was once only promise is now glorious fulfillment. The crucified Jesus, now exalted to the Father's right hand, gives the Holy Spirit to those who repent and believe. While the Book of Acts provides us with living examples of what it means to be baptized or filled with the Holy Spirit, it is the Epistles that spell out the theological and ethical implications of this distinctive New Testament grace. The chapters that follow will engage this further task.

6

The Christian Experience of the Holy Spirit

The normative understanding of what has been called "the Christian experience of the Holy Spirit" comes to its clearest expression in the Epistles.[1] Although references to the Spirit's work in human life in the Gospels and Acts have lingering aspects of the Old Testament view of the Spirit of the Lord, the Epistles centrally emphasize the truth that the ultimate mark of the Spirit's presence is not "signs and wonders and various miracles" (Heb. 2:4; cf. 1 Cor. 13:1-3), but the transformation of our human existence into the likeness of God. This transforming experience of the Spirit in human life is what we mean by "sanctification." Thus the work of the Spirit in human life defines the meaning of sanctification.

John Wesley recognizes this distinctive work of the Holy Spirit in these words: "The title 'holy,' applied to the Spirit of God, does not only denote that he is holy in his own nature, but that he makes us so; that he is the great fountain of holiness to his church; the Spirit from whence flows all the grace and virtue, by which the stains of guilt are cleansed, and we are renewed in all holy dispositions, and again bear the image of our Creator."[2]

---

1. H. Wheeler Robinson, *The Christian Experience of the Holy Spirit* (London: Nisbet and Co., 1911).

2. John Wesley, Sermon, "On Grieving the Holy Spirit," in *The Works of John Wesley*, 3rd ed., 14 vols. (1872; reprint, Kansas City: Beacon Hill Press of Kansas City, 1979), 7:486.

Strictly speaking, "the Christian experience of the Holy Spirit" is not simply an "experience." It is indeed an experience, but it is more; it is most profoundly a relationship with God, grounded on faith in Christ, and bringing the indwelling Spirit (Rom. 8:1-4, 9). That Spirit, says Paul, is the Spirit of Christ: "Anyone who does not have the Spirit of Christ does not belong to him" (v. 9). (Compare Acts 2:33, where this truth is implicit; but it is made explicit in Acts 16:7.) Positively, this means that every Christian has received the Spirit; negatively, that the person "whose life bears no evidences of the Spirit's sanctifying work is no Christian."[3] This connection is beautifully made by Friedrich Schleiermacher's famous phrase "The fruits of the Spirit are none other than the virtues of Christ."[4]

In our endeavor to demonstrate the foregoing thesis, we will engage in theological exegesis. The term "exegesis" literally means to "lead out" or "read out." It includes all the procedures necessary to identify the true meaning of a given passage of Scripture. Exegesis is often set in contrast to eisegesis, which means to "read in." "The exegete," Dunning explains, "is the one who attempts to bring the passage to expression in its original significance. Donald Miller has this in mind when he defines *exegesis* as 'right listening.'"[5] *Theological exegesis* is that aspect of the interpretative work that attempts to identify the theology that informs the text. It presupposes a structure of theology that is brought to expression with a greater or lesser degree of completeness by a particular passage. The assumption in this procedure is that there is such an identifiable theological structure.

The final aim of the study is to bridge the chasm between the ancient world of the Epistles and our contemporary society and church so that we may understand what the New Testament means by sanctification.[6]

---

3. C. E. B. Cranfield, *The Epistle to the Romans*, 2 vols., in *The International Critical Commentary*, eds. J. A. Emerton and C. E. B. Cranfield (Edinburgh: T. and T. Clark, 1975), 1:388.

4. *The Christian Faith*, trans. H. E. Mackintosh and J. S. Stewart (Edinburgh: T. and T. Clark, 1960), 576.

5. "Introduction," *Biblical Resources for Holiness Preaching: From Text to Sermon*, ed. H. Ray Dunning and Neil B. Wiseman (Kansas City: Beacon Hill Press of Kansas City, 1990), 1:19.

6. Technically this task is generally referred to as *hermeneutics*, a term that in its verb form means "to bring to understanding."

The work of theological exegesis implies that our first task should be to provide a brief summary of the structure of New Testament theology, especially as it comes to expression in the Epistles. We will focus primarily upon the letters of Paul, since he provides the fullest resource for the study, but the other letters will not be ignored.

THE STRUCTURE OF
NEW TESTAMENT THEOLOGY

At the heart of Paul's gospel is the message of the Cross—"Jesus Christ, and him crucified" (1 Cor. 2:2)—a scandal to the Jews and folly to the Gentiles, "but to those who are the called, both Jews and Greeks, Christ the power of God and the wisdom of God. For God's foolishness is wiser than human wisdom, and God's weakness is stronger than human strength" (1:24-25).

By "Christ the power of God" Paul means Christ as God's Power to liberate from the thralldom and entanglements of sin (Rom. 1:16-17) and progressively transform into the image of God everyone who believes the gospel, through the life-giving Spirit bestowed by the risen Lord (2 Cor. 3:17-18; 1 Cor. 15:45).

For "Christ . . . the wisdom of God," see 1 Cor. 2:6-16. By faith in the crucified and resurrected Lord, we receive the Spirit; through the Spirit, those who are "mature" (*teleiois*, v. 6) and "spiritual" (*pneumatikoi*, v. 15) "have the mind of Christ" (v. 16) to understand "God's wisdom," which, had

> the rulers of this age understood . . . they would not have crucified the Lord of glory. But, as it is written, "What no eye has seen, nor ear heard, nor the human heart conceived, what God has prepared for those who love him"—these things God has revealed to us through the Spirit; for the Spirit searches everything, even the depths of God. . . . Now we have received not the spirit of the world, but the Spirit that is from God, so that we may understand the gifts bestowed on us by God (*vv. 8-10, 12*).

These divinely bestowed gifts are summarized in the last two verses of the previous chapter: "It is because of him that you are in Christ Jesus, who has become for us wisdom from God—

that is, our righteousness, holiness and redemption. Therefore, as it is written: 'Let him who boasts boast in the Lord'" (1:30-31, NIV).[7]

God's wisdom in Christ Jesus may be categorized in three ways: as *dikaiosunē* (justification or righteousness), *hagiasmos* (sanctification or holiness), and *apolutrōsis* (redemption).

Rom. 1:18—8:39 illuminates these three terms that define our salvation:

1. Christ Jesus is our Justification or Righteousness. Through faith in Him we are restored to right relationship with God (1:18—4:25).

2. Christ Jesus is our Sanctification or Holiness. By faith we die and rise with Christ and receive the Spirit, who makes us truly holy in this present age (5:1—8:16).

3. Christ Jesus is our Redemption (8:17-39). If, in fact, we suffer with Christ, we will also be glorified with Him (v. 17). "We ourselves, who have the first fruits of the Spirit, groan inwardly as we wait for adoption as sons, the redemption of our bodies. For in this hope we were saved" (vv. 23-24, RSV).

Our salvation in Christ Jesus begins with justification, issues in sanctification, and is consummated in glorification.

The salvific work of Christ, as Paul explains it, is placed in the larger context of all New Testament theology, namely an eschatological dualism of the two ages: the Present Age and the Age to Come. This dualism had become a dominant form of expression for rabbinic theology during the intertestamental period. According to this theology, the present age was under the dominion of demonic powers, with Satan as "the prince of the power of the air" (Eph. 2:2, KJV). For many in Israel, the failure of the hopes of the age of salvation had led to a skepticism, namely that God was still in control of history but had withdrawn from activity in the world. The Age to Come was the Kingdom age, when the anticipated age of salvation would be ushered in through the destruction of the present social order. With apocalyptic signs in the heavens, the Present Age would be brought decisively to an end with the entrance of God.

Under this idiom, it was the central claim throughout the New Testament that the Age to Come had broken into history in the person and ministry of Jesus Christ, even though the Present

---

7. The Greek reads literally, "And of him you are in Christ Jesus, who became wisdom to us from God, both *(te)* righteousness and sanctification and redemption" (1:30).

Age has not yet come to an end, and the upheavals in nature and society were not obvious. Thus there was an overlapping of the two ages, referred to in the New Testament as "the last days." In this "time between the times," those who are in Christ experience the blessings of the future now (see Heb. 6:5). Since one of the major aspects of this promised age involved the giving of the Spirit to all God's people (see chap. 5), it is extremely important to understand the nature of this new relationship to God in the Spirit.

AUTHENTIC AND UNAUTHENTIC SPIRITUAL EXPERIENCE

There is evidence in Paul's Epistles of a struggle in the Early Church to overcome understandings of religious life that were carried over from either pagan or Judaistic backgrounds. These struggles were most clearly seen in 1 Corinthians and Galatians. For the focus of this chapter, these letters are especially important because of their definitive treatment of life in the Spirit (1) as primarily a life of agape love rather than the exercise of charismata, the grace gifts of the Spirit, particularly glossolalia or tongues-speaking (in 1 Corinthians); and (2) as the freedom in the Spirit to serve others in love and to fulfill the law spontaneously, as opposed to loveless legalism (in Galatians).

James S. Stewart has given an important evaluation of Paul's contribution to the maturing understanding of the normative Christian experience of the Holy Spirit.

In the primitive Christian community there was a tendency at the first—perhaps quite natural under the circumstances—to revert to the cruder conceptions of the Spirit, and to trace His workings mainly in such phenomena as speaking with tongues. It was Paul who saved the nascent faith from that dangerous retrogression. Not in any accidental and extraneous phenomena, he insisted, not in any spasmodic emotions or intermittent ecstasies were the real tokens of God's Spirit to be found; but in the quiet, steady, normal life of faith, in power that worked on moral levels, in the soul's secret inward assurance of its sonship of God, in love and joy and peace and patience and a character like that of Jesus.[8]

---

8. James S. Stewart, *A Man in Christ: The Vital Elements of St. Paul's Religion* (New York: Harper and Brothers, n.d.), 308-9.

In the eschatological gift of the Spirit, the Church enjoys a dual heritage of Old Testament promise: (1) endowment by the Spirit, especially the gift of prophecy (Acts 2:17-18) and (2) sanctification by the Spirit: freedom from sin, and moral renewal in the image of God (Rom. 8:1-4; 2 Cor. 3:17-18). "Both these motifs are present in Paul," Dunning writes, "but it is the latter that becomes predominant."[9]

For Paul, the Church is a charismatic community, as 1 Cor. 12—14 demonstrates. "To each is given the manifestation of the Spirit for the common good" (12:7). In verses 8-12 Paul then lists various charismata of the Spirit, "who allots to each one individually just as the Spirit chooses" (v. 11). Barrett says, "The test by which spiritual gifts may be valued is given in 12:3: the work of the Spirit is to declare that Jesus is Lord. The more plainly a gift testifies to the lordship of Jesus the greater its value. Glossolalia bears witness to the fact that I who speak am dominated by a lord, but it does not make clear who that lord is; it might be a demon (1 Cor. 10:20 [12:2]). . . . Who could suppose that the words 'A curse on Jesus!' could be uttered by the Holy Spirit?"[10]

Such is the danger of unbridled emotionalism. When I am filled with the Spirit, my mind is illuminated ("Jesus is Lord"), not overwhelmed with uncontrollable emotion. At best, mindless spirituality is subnormal Christianity. "What should I do then?" Paul asks. "I will pray with the spirit, but I will pray with the mind also. I will sing praise with the spirit, but I will sing praise with the mind also" (14:15). This is the "spiritual worship" (literally, "rational worship") that is acceptable to God (Rom. 12:1) and understandable to others (1 Cor. 14:16-19).

Positively, the measure of any gift is the degree to which it builds up the Body of Christ. To repeat, "To each is given the manifestation of the Spirit *for the common good*" (12:7, emphasis added)—to build up the entire Body in love (vv. 12-27). On this basis, prophecy is the highest, glossolalia the lowest of the gifts.

---

9. Dunning, *Grace, Faith, and Holiness,* 425.

10. C. K. Barrett, *Paul, an Introduction to His Thought* (Louisville, Ky.: Westminster/John Knox Press, 1994), 113. For a discussion of glossolalia in Corinth, see Donald S. Metz, "The First Epistle of Paul to the Corinthians," in vol. 8 of *Beacon Bible Commentary* (Kansas City: Beacon Hill Press of Kansas City, 1968), 423-55; C. K. Barrett, *A Commentary on the First Epistle to the Corinthians,* in *Harper's New Testament Commentaries,* ed. Henry Chadwick (New York: Harper and Row, 1968), 277-334.

After restating the gifts, Paul concludes, "But strive for the greater gifts. And I will show you a still more excellent way" (12:31)—the way of agape love. "If I speak in the tongues of mortals and of angels, but do not have love, I am a noisy gong or a clanging cymbal." Paul continues, "Love is patient; love is kind; love is not envious or boastful or arrogant or rude. It does not insist on its own way; it is not irritable or resentful; it does not rejoice in wrongdoing, but rejoices in the truth. It bears all things, believes all things, hopes all things, endures all things" (13:1, 4-7).

Christlike love is the acid test of the Spirit-filled life. Following Paul, Wesley writes emphatically,

> Love is the highest gift of God; humble, gentle, patient love. . . . It were well that you should be sensible of this,— "the heaven of heavens is love." There is nothing higher in religion; there is, in effect, nothing else; if you look for anything but more love, you are looking wide of the mark, you are getting out of the royal way. And when you are asking others, "Have you received this or that blessing?" if you mean anything but more love, you mean wrong; you are leading them out of the way, and putting them upon a false scent. Settle it then in your heart, that from the moment God has saved you from all sin, you are to aim at nothing more, but more of that love described in the thirteenth of the Corinthians. You can go no higher than this, till you are carried into Abraham's bosom.[11]

In his excellent commentary on 1 Corinthians, Pentecostalist Gordon D. Fee acknowledges,

> It is hard to escape the implication that what is involved here are two opposing views as to what it means to be "spiritual." For the Corinthians it meant "tongues, wisdom, knowledge" (and pride), but without a commensurate concern for Christian behavior. For Paul it meant first of all to be full of the Spirit, the Holy Spirit, which therefore meant to behave as those "sanctified in Christ Jesus, called to be his

---

11. John Wesley, "A Plain Account of Christian Perfection," in *Works*, 11:430.

holy people" (1:2), of which the ultimate expression always is to "walk in love."[12]

In Paul's letter to the Galatians we encounter a different problem, one that commonly threatens a scriptural view of holiness: the problem of legalism. The apostle had brought his gospel of "the grace of Christ" (1:6) to the Galatians, who had initially "welcomed [him] as an angel of God, as Christ Jesus" (4:14). However, someone or some party—probably Jewish Christians from James in Jerusalem (see 2:11-12)—infiltrated the Galatian church preaching "a different gospel" ("not that there is another gospel," 1:7), confusing the Galatians (5:10) by trying to impose the Mosaic system on his converts and compelling them to be circumcised if they expected to be saved (6:12-13).

An imposition of the external legal demands upon believers may take any one of many forms. The danger of such legalism—adding something else to faith in Christ as the condition of being saved—is indeed a denial of the gospel, since it turns believers away from Christ to their own works or "righteousness" (see 2 Cor. 11:2-3). Whatever form this legalism takes, it nullifies "the grace of God" and actually means that "Christ died for nothing" (Gal. 2:21). Consequently, Christians who "want to be justified by the law have cut [themselves] off from Christ" and "have fallen away from grace" (5:4).

As stated earlier, legalism especially dogs holiness teaching. Many sincere Christians in the Wesleyan-Holiness Movement have understandably been turned away from scriptural holiness by legalism masquerading as holiness. The apostle will give major attention to this problem in Romans, in which, as we shall see, he shows that this was in fact the error of Judaism itself in his time, viewing the Mosaic law in this legalistic fashion. But in Galatians the problem was Jewish legalism displacing the gospel and destroying the freedom Christ provides through the gift of the Spirit: freedom to "fulfill the law of Christ" (6:2) in loving service to others (5:13) and in a life of spontaneous moral obedience to God (5:16-25; cf. "the just requirement of the law," Rom. 8:4).

---

12. Gordon D. Fee, *The First Epistle to the Corinthians*, in *The New International Commentary on the New Testament*, ed. F. F. Bruce (Grand Rapids: Wm. B. Eerdmans Publishing Co., 1987), 630.

"For freedom Christ has set us free," Paul writes. "Stand firm, therefore, and do not submit again to a yoke of slavery" (5:1). The legalist does not believe that life in the Spirit is sufficient to guard against the flesh and hence is tempted to resort to the Law as a means of avoiding libertinism.[13] However, in turning to the Law for moral strength, the legalist inevitably lapses into the bondage of fear (see Rom. 8:15-16). Life in the Spirit is sufficient of itself if we obey Paul's gospel imperatives in this Epistle.

First, the gospel imperative is the command to *love*—to die to self-love and give oneself in loving service to others. "For you were called to freedom, brothers and sisters; only do not use your freedom as an opportunity for self-indulgence, but through love become slaves to one another. For the whole law is summed up in a single commandment, 'You shall love your neighbor as yourself'" (5:13-14). "A Christian is a perfectly free lord of all, subject to none," Luther wrote in his definitive *Freedom of a Christian* (1520); "a Christian is a perfectly dutiful servant of all, subject to all."[14] And John Wesley observed that "faith working by love" (5:6) is "the length and breadth and depth and height of Christian perfection."[15]

Second, the gospel imperative is the command to *"walk by the Spirit"* in a life of disciplined obedience. "Live by the Spirit, I say, and do not [or, "you will not," NASB] gratify the desires of the flesh. For what the flesh desires is opposed to the Spirit, and what the Spirit desires is opposed to the flesh . . . to prevent you from doing what you want" (5:16-17).

"Flesh" and "Spirit" stand for two diametrically opposed forms of human existence: living by the flesh, for a self-centered life; living by the Spirit, for a God-centered life. "Desires" (in 5:17) are not necessarily lustful (although they may be); they may be religious desires, aspirations to experience a God-centered existence. Barrett explains,

> Flesh stands over against love; it also stands over against Spirit. "Walk by the Spirit and you will not fulfill the desire of the flesh." To walk—to live—by the Spirit is to lead

13. Dunning, *Grace, Faith, and Holiness,* 427.
14. Martin Luther, *Basic Theological Writings,* ed. Thomas F. Lull (Minneapolis: Fortress Press, 1989), 630.
15. *The Poetical Works of John Wesley,* ed. George Osborn (London: 1868), 1:xxii (Preface to Hymns and Sacred Poems, 1739 Hymnbook).

not only a non-self-centered existence but what is in fact the only practical alternative to this, God-centered existence. Flesh means that I desire things (not for God or my neighbour but) for myself. Hence the stark opposition of verse 17. Flesh and spirit are contraries not because they are higher and lower parts of human nature but because they denote respectively life as directed by and for self and life directed by and for God.[16]

Wesley understands the concluding clause of verse 17 ("to prevent you from doing what you want") to mean "That, being strengthened by the Spirit, you may not fulfil the desire of the flesh, as otherwise you would do."[17] On the other hand, to walk by the flesh is to be unable to fulfill the desires of the Spirit. Spirit-filled, Spirit-led Christians have "crucified the flesh with its passions and desires" (v. 24) by fully appropriating their crucifixion with Christ (2:20; Paul will spell this out in Rom. 6).

By "the works of the flesh" in verse 19, Paul means more than what is sensual, suggesting that the essence of "fleshly works" is self-centeredness.[18] Wesley notes, "Some of the works here mentioned are wrought principally, if not entirely, in the mind; and yet they are called 'works of the flesh.' Hence it is clear, the apostle does not by 'the flesh' mean the body, or sensual appetites and inclinations only, but the corruption of human nature, as it spreads through all the powers of the soul, as well as the members of the body."[19]

To indulge the flesh not only nullifies life in the Spirit—it spells spiritual death: "those who do such things will not inherit the kingdom of God" (v. 21).

"By contrast, the fruit of the Spirit is love, joy, peace, patience, kindness, generosity, faithfulness, gentleness, and self-control. There is no law against such things" (vv. 22-23). Paul means that love does nothing the Law forbids, and more than the Law

---

16. Barrett, *Paul*, 71.
17. John Wesley, *Explanatory Notes upon the New Testament* (London: Epworth Press, 1953), 696 (ed.).
18. Barrett, *Paul*, 71.
19. Wesley, *Notes*, 697.

requires. "The 'fruit of the Spirit' is mentioned in the singular," says Wesley, "as being consistent and connected together."[20]

We will gain further insight on this subject in our discussion of Paul's doctrine of sanctification in Romans, to which we turn in our next chapter.

20. Ibid.

7

Paul's Theology of Sanctification in Romans

I n Paul's major work, the Epistle to the Romans, his soteriology comes to full, systematic expression. For many years he had been engaged in controversy with Judaizing Christians who had troubled his churches, trying to impose the Law upon his converts. He had written the Galatians and the Corinthians in the heat of this controversy. Now in Romans he sets forth the conclusions to which the Spirit had guided him with reference to Christ and the Law, writing to a church that was experiencing serious problems over this very issue.

The fourth-century writer Ambriosater gives what some believe to be the most probable account of Christian beginnings in Rome: "It is established that there were Jews living in Rome in the times of the apostles, and that those Jews who had believed passed on to the Romans that they ought to profess Christ and keep the law. . . . One ought not to condemn the Romans, but to praise their faith; because without seeing any signs or miracles and without seeing any apostles, they nevertheless accepted faith in Christ, although according to a Jewish rite."[1]

This account seems to accord with what we find in Suetonius's *Life of Claudius*, which records that Claudius "expelled the Jews from Rome because they kept rioting at the instigation of

---

1. John Knox, *The Epistle to the Romans,* of *The Interpreter's Bible,* ed. George Arthur Buttrick (New York: Abingdon-Cokesbury Press, 1951), 9:362.

Chrestus."[2] Suetonius, not understanding the name *Christos*, seems to have confused it with the commonly used Greek name *Chrestus*, which at that time would have been pronounced as *Christos*. So Suetonius's text is understood by many modern historians today.[3] Suetonius's statement about *Chrestus* is probably a reference to trouble that arose in the synagogues of Rome when Christianity was introduced. In any event, Christian Jews as well as unbelievers would have been banished by Claudius's edict in A.D. 49. A reference to that edict is given in Acts 18:2 as the reason for the presence in Corinth of Aquila and Priscilla.

We may take it, therefore, that by the year A.D. 49 Christianity had been introduced into Rome. We still must account for the fact, however, that by the time Paul wrote Romans, the Church was predominantly Gentile (see 1:5-6, 13; 11:13-24; 15:15-16). In the Jewish synagogues of Rome where Christ had been introduced, there would have been, in addition to believing Jews, many "God-fearers," Gentiles who had been attracted by the monotheism and ethical teachings of Judaism. This mixture of Jews and God-fearers (and perhaps some Gentile proselytes) would have prevailed among the above-mentioned synagogues of Rome until Claudius's banishment of "Jews" in A.D. 49. It is likely that these Jewish Christians, on their return to Rome, would have found a Christian situation different from what they had left; they would now be a minority in the church that they had shaped at an earlier date.[4]

These returning Jewish Christians, as well as the Gentile Christians, would find themselves under a prohibition against all private and public associations, to stave off any kind of political or quasi-political agitation.[5] This fact probably explains why Paul does not address the "church" (singular) at Rome, for all the Roman Christians met in house churches, some Jewish (who held a strict interpretation of the Torah), others Gentile (who saw themselves set free from the Torah, among whom would have been "Paulinists" like "Prisca and Aquila," 16:3).[6]

---

2. *Claudia Vita*, 25:4, cited by Knox, *Epistle to the Romans*, 9:362.
3. Joseph A. Fitzmyer, *Romans*, in *The Anchor Bible*, ed. W. F. Albright and David N. Freedman (New York: Doubleday, 1993), 33:31.
4. Ibid.
5. Peter Stuhlmacher, *Paul's Letter to the Romans* (Louisville, Ky.: Westminster/John Knox Press, 1994), 7.
6. See *The Romans Debate*, ed. Karl B. Donfried, rev. and expanded ed. (Peabody, Mass.: Hendrickson Publishers, 1991).

The central issue of Romans, we may therefore understand, is the relationship of the Christian gospel to the Mosaic Torah. In its historical setting, this Epistle may be taken as Paul's addressing of the particular problem created by the events sketched above, an acute division that was threatening Roman Christianity circa A.D. 57, when Romans was written. In getting at the "reason" for Romans, these issues are important. From a wider perspective, however, the canonical Epistle to the Romans may be understood as an ecumenical theology designed (1) to show and insure the *true meaning* of the Torah in light of God's final word in Christ, and (2) to liberate the message of Christ from its Jewish trappings in order "to win obedience from the Gentiles" (15:18; see also v. 19; cf. 1:1-6; 16:26).[7] Romans does not simply address the Jewish problem—it addresses the *human* problem.

PAUL'S GOSPEL IN ROMANS

The place to begin in exploring Paul's gospel is his salutation to the Romans, in which he identifies himself as "a servant of Jesus Christ . . . set apart for the gospel" (1:1). Before Paul met Christ, he was a Pharisee (Phil. 3:5)—set apart for Torah. But on the Damascus road the risen Jesus appeared to him "as to one untimely born" (1 Cor. 15:8) and effected a radical reorientation of his life and faith. In that encounter Paul was "called to be an apostle, set apart for the gospel of God"—made a "Pharisee" for the gospel.[8] "Paul, who had set himself apart for the Law," says Nygren, "is set apart by God for the Gospel."[9] *What Torah had formerly been for Paul, Christ had now become* (Gal. 2:19-21).

Christ's displacing of Torah, however, is but one side of Paul's gospel; at the same time his gospel upholds (Rom. 3:31) and fulfills Torah (10:4). We must now look at this other side of the gospel paradox.

---

7. Karl Barth quotes Luther in this regard: "The words of the prophets, long fastened under lock and key, are now set free. . . . Now we can see and understand what was written, for we have an 'entrance into the Old Testament'" (*The Epistle to the Romans*, trans. Edwin C. Hoskyns from 6th ed. [London: Oxford University Press, 1933], 28).

8. The word translated "set apart" (*aphōrismenos*) has the same root as Pharisee (*pharisaios*).

9. Anders Nygren, *Commentary on Romans*, trans. Carl B. Rasmussen (Philadelphia: Fortress Press, 1949), 46. "Are we to name him a Pharisee?" Barth asks. "Yes, a Pharisee—separated, isolated, and distinct. But he is a Pharisee of a higher order" (*Epistle to the Romans*, 37).

First, Paul announces that the gospel *upholds* Torah. The gospel was not an intrusion into God's plan, since God had promised it "beforehand through his prophets in the holy scriptures" (1:2). "The scripture, foreseeing that God would justify the Gentiles by faith," he tells the Galatians, "declared the gospel beforehand to Abraham, saying, 'All the Gentiles shall be blessed in you'" (3:8).

Furthermore, the gospel is also "attested by the law (Torah)" (Rom. 3:21). In speaking of Torah as "the law of faith" in verse 27, Paul will insist that his gospel, far from overthrowing Torah, points to its true nature as a covenant of *grace* (v. 31).[10] The case of Abraham proves the grace nature of Torah, as he will demonstrate in chapter 4. The case study of Abraham means that God has *never* justified anyone "by deeds prescribed by the law" (3:20); rather, He has *always* justified "the ungodly" by "faith . . . reckoned . . . as righteousness" (4:5; see vv. 1-8).

For an understanding of Paul's theology of sanctification, a second point is highly significant. His gospel not only upholds Torah but also *fulfills* it—by providing a salvation impossible under Torah: freedom from "the law of sin and of death" (8:2). By sending His Son to become one of us and to die for us, God has done "what the law, weakened by the flesh, could not do" (v. 3). In Christ God has dealt sin a deathblow, in order that "the just requirement" of Torah—love of God and neighbor, as Jesus said (Matt. 22:34-40; Mark 12:28-34)—might now be "fulfilled in us, who walk not according to the flesh but according to the Spirit" (Rom. 8:4; see 5:5 and 13:8-10). *In Christ God has made possible true sanctification.*

THE GOSPEL OF GOD'S POWER

Leander E. Keck provides an intriguing analysis of Rom. 1—8 that shows the centrality of Paul's doctrine of sanctification:

> Paul states the gospel in such a way that its scope reaches from Eden to the eschaton, from the "fall" to the redemption of the world. . . . The gospel is God's saving power for every human being, albeit for the Jew first. There is one gospel and only one, for all. . . . But if the gospel is God's sav-

---

10. See chapter 4, "The Mosaic Covenant."

ing power for *all* who believe, the one gospel must bring one solution to the one condition in which all find themselves. However important are the election of Israel, the promise to Abraham, the gift of the law, the Davidic ancestry of God's Son, in no way do these exempt "the Jews" from solidarity with the Gentiles in the human condition. It is the *human* problem that the gospel addresses.[11]

In developing the foregoing theme, Paul inevitably "goes back to Adam" and "unpacks the Adamic situation three times," with an argument that moves "in a spiral fashion, each time going deeper into the human condition, and each time finding the gospel the appropriate antidote."[12]

The first exposition (Rom. 1:18—4:25) is an indictment of both Gentile and Jew as guilty before God and under the power of sin (3:9); this indictment reaches its climax in verses 19-20. The indictment is then followed by the good news of God's righteousness now manifest in Christ Jesus, which provides *justification by faith* (vv. 21-26). On the basis of "the faithfulness of Christ" (*pisteōs Christou*, v. 22) as God's atoning sacrifice, *a rectified relationship with God is now open to all* (v. 30).

The second exposition is 5:12-21 (which provides the basis for 6:1—7:6). Our Adamic condition calls for more than a rectified relationship to God; we need liberation from the sin that rules our Adamic condition. For Paul there are two, and only two, alternate realms: that of Adam (the rule of sin and death) and that of Christ (the rule of grace and eternal life through justification). As Paul develops this theme in 6:1—7:6, he will argue that freedom from sin and death is possible only through *participation* in Christ's death and resurrection, which promise "newness of life" (6:4; cf. 7:6, "new life of the Spirit").

The third exposition is 7:7—8:17. In 7:7-25 we are taken deeper into the human situation. As fallen in Adam, Jew and Gentile alike discover "an illegal resident who [has] usurped control of the house, thereby compelling the enslaved self to do opposite of what it intends." This alien resident is "sin that dwells within me"

---

11. Leander E. Keck, "What Makes Romans Tick," *Pauline Theology III, Romans,* ed. David M. Hay and E. Elizabeth Johnson (Minneapolis: Fortress Press, 1989), 24.
12. Ibid., 25.

(7:17, 20), against which Torah is powerless. But what Torah could not do, God has done through Christ—He has won a divine victory over sin that sets free "from the law of sin and of death" all those who "walk not according to the flesh but according to the Spirit" (8:2, 4) whom they have received through Christ (vv. 1-17).

"What makes Rom. 1—8 tick," says Keck, is "the inner logic" of having to show how the gospel deals with the human condition on three ever-deeper levels, each understood as a dimension of our Adamic condition:

> the self's skewed relationship to God in which the norm (law) is the accuser, the self in sin's domain where death rules before Moses arrived only to exacerbate the situation by specifying transgression, the self victimized by sin as a resident power stronger than the law (thereby showing that the problem is not the law itself). Unless Christ is the effective antidote to the Adamic situation, there is no good news for anyone, not even for the Jew because Moses cannot save from the contradiction of Adam. Conversely, if the Adamic situation is redeemed in Christ, then there is one gospel for all people.[13]

PAUL'S THEOLOGY OF SANCTIFICATION EXPLORED, ROM. 5—8

With this background and introduction to the theme, we are now ready to move directly into Paul's theology of sanctification (chaps. 5—8). While the apostle's development of this truth does not technically begin until 5:12 (with his treatment of Adam and Christ), 5:1-11 constitutes a transition from justification to sanctification.

In 1:18—4:25 Paul sets forth his doctrine of justification by grace through faith. Whereas humanity left to itself without the gospel came under the wrath of God, through the gospel and the grace of God therein, all may now find the redemption that is in Christ Jesus—pardon for sin and acceptance by God—on the basis of Jesus' shed blood. The case of Abraham shows the basic harmony between Paul's gospel and Torah. The discussion comes to a conclusion with Paul's declaration that God's "words" to the pa-

---

13. Ibid., 26.

triarch (that "his faith 'was reckoned to him as righteousness'") "were written not for his sake alone but for ours also. It will be reckoned to us who believe in him who raised Jesus our Lord from the dead, who was handed over to death for our trespasses and was raised for our justification" (4:22-25).

Now, to begin the next major section of his argument, Paul proclaims the *result* of justifying faith (5:1-5). All of us who are justified by faith enjoy "peace with God through our Lord Jesus Christ" (v. 1), namely, reconciliation along with God's promised salvation; above all, we now "rejoice in our hope of sharing the glory of God" (v. 2, RSV). While our *eschatological* hope is the overarching theme of verses 1-5 (as also in vv. 6-11), this hope includes within it the Old Testament promise of heart holiness, since "God's love has been poured into our hearts through the Holy Spirit that has been given to us" (v. 5). "The *Shema* is at last fulfilled," N. T. Wright proclaims. "In Christ and by the Spirit the creator/covenant [God] has created a people that, in return for redemption, will love him from the heart" (cf. 8:28; 1 Cor. 8:3).[14] In the same vein Peter Stuhlmacher comments, "In being filled with the Spirit, the promise of Ezek. 36:26ff. is realized for those who believe, so that they become capable of returning the love of God bestowed upon them (v. 8), that is, to love God as their creator in accordance with his will. In this active love, supported by the Spirit, Christians complete the state of grace into which they were transferred through Christ."[15]

Chapter 5, in characteristic Pauline fashion, unfolds from its initial statement about the *result* of justification (vv. 1-2), through the broader development of the Christian experience of the Holy Spirit (vv. 3-5), into a full statement of the position reached now in the Epistle as a whole.[16]

Rom. 5:6-11 draws out, in particular, the correlation between present justification, based on the *death* of Jesus, and final justification, in which believers will be "saved . . . from the wrath of God" by the *life* of God's Son. The source of the Christian's confidence is

---

14. N. T. Wright, "Romans and the Theology of Paul," in *Pauline Theology III, Romans*, 45. This "people of God" is "the Israel of God" (Gal. 6:16), the "true" composed of believing Jews and Gentiles whom Paul will define in chapters 9—11.

15. Stuhlmacher, *Paul's Letter to the Romans*, 80.

16. Wright, "Romans and the Theology of Paul," 45.

God's *love* objectively revealed in the death of Christ. God proved His love toward us, Paul says, in that while we were "weak," "ungodly," and "sinners," Christ died for us. "For if while we were *enemies*, we were reconciled to God through the *death* of his Son, much more surely, *having been reconciled*, will we be saved by his *life*" (v. 10, emphases added). "Saved by his life" denotes salvation in the full and final sense, which, with justification, assumes the restoration of holiness. The mediation by His life completes that begun by His death and assures "the sanctification without which no one will see the Lord" (Heb. 12:14, NASB). Justification is thus distinct from sanctification and is indeed the gateway to it; it rests on "the death of his Son." Sanctification flows from the life of Christ (Heb. 7:25) by the work of the Holy Spirit (Acts 2:33; 2 Thess. 2:13).[17]

Rom. 5 is therefore the hinge between the apostle's doctrines of justification and sanctification, with the latter being understood negatively as freedom from sin and the Law (Torah) (chaps. 6—7) and positively as renewal in the forfeited image (or "glory") of God (3:23) by the eschatological gift of the Spirit (8:17-24, 28-30; cf. 2 Cor. 3:16-18). Initiated at justification and consummated in glory, sanctification in the eschaton ("this present time" of sufferings, 8:18) demands entire consecration to God (6:13, 19), a yielding to Him that opens the way for the indwelling (infilling) of the Holy Spirit (8:9-17), who hallows our beings and becomes "the first-fruits" of our final redemption (vv. 18-27).

CHRIST AND ADAM (5:12-21)

While Paul refers first to Adam and then to Christ in spelling out the Fall and our restoration, the section should properly be titled "Christ and Adam." Adam is but "a type *[typos]* of the one who *was* to come" (v. 14, emphasis added). The reality is in Christ, through whom Paul's existence had been re-created (2 Cor. 5:17). Adam is the shadow; Christ is the substance. The emphasis throughout this section is placed upon the "much more" grace that comes through Christ. The fall of Adam is but the backdrop of our redemption in Christ. The good news is

---

17. Fredric Godet, *St. Paul's Epistle to the Romans,* trans. A. Cusin (New York: Funk and Wagnalls, 1883), 197.

A second Adam to the fight,
And to the rescue came.[18]

This, says Paul, is life's deepest certainty. "The old order has gone; a new order has already begun" (2 Cor. 5:17, REB). The new age has come upon us, and all who are in Christ have been taken out of the realm of sin and death characterizing Adam's race.[19]

For Paul, Christ and Adam are thus more than historical individuals; they are the heads of two contrasting yet overlapping orders of existence. This is the key to our present passage.

As we have already noted in our study of Old Testament holiness, Wheeler Robinson coined the term "corporate personality" to express the biblical concept of solidarity.[20] In contrast to Enlightenment thought, in which humanity is viewed as an aggregate of discrete individuals, Hebrew thought in terms of the group—the family, clan, nation, or race. Their thought, about Israel for example, could oscillate freely between the individual and the group. Israel would be either their father or the nation. On this view Paul can think of Adam as either the first man (Gen. 4:25) or as "humankind" (5:1-2).[21] Adam as a "corporate personality" is both the progenitor of the race *and* "our old man" (Adam—and ourselves in Adam). Christ, on the other hand, is both the Redeemer and "the new man" (Christ—and ourselves in Him). Adam and those in him are the old, fallen humanity; Christ and those in Him are the new, redeemed humanity—His Body, the Church.

Other interpreters prefer to think in terms of representation. When the head of a nation, for example, declares war, he or she does so as its representative. Thus, in his disobedience Adam involved us in his sin. In Adam's fall "all sinned" (v. 12, NIV, Wesley).[22] By the same token, in Christ all are redeemed. "We are convinced that one has died for all; therefore all have died,"

18. J. S. Whale, *Christian Doctrine* (London: Fontana Books, 1960), 50.
19. See William M. Greathouse, "The Epistle to the Romans," in *Beacon Bible Commentary,* 8:119-20.
20. See chapter 4, footnote 7.
21. See chapter 3 of this volume.
22. The NRSV returns to the KJV "all have sinned." The collective aorist can be rendered either way (see 2. following). Actually, both renderings are needed to incorporate Paul's teaching in these chapters. Sin entered with Adam's disobedience, but it does not issue fully into death until we reenact Adam's sin by our own transgression (see 7:8-9).

Paul writes in a complementary passage. "And he died for all, so that those who live might live no longer for themselves, but for him who died and was raised for them" (2 Cor. 5:14-15). These texts mean that in Adam we *potentially* died *in* sin; in Christ we *provisionally* died *to* sin. Each, Adam and Christ, acted as our representative, affecting our destiny. Thinking this way, some modern interpreters speak of Adam and Christ as "fields of force." From each radiates forces that touch us profoundly, either for life or death. When Adam disobeyed, "sin entered into the world, and death by sin" (v. 12, KJV); sin as an *enslaving power* took possession of the *race*.[23] But when Christ obeyed the Father, grace as a *liberating power* became available, so that "where sin abounded, grace did much more abound" (v. 20, KJV).

Whether we think realistically or representatively (or combine the two, as Wesley did), Paul teaches that the crucifixion of Jesus was the crucifixion of "our old man" (cf. 6:6, KJV) and His resurrection the creation of "the new man . . . after God . . . in righteousness and true holiness" (Eph. 4:24, KJV). "Christ on the cross concludes the old Adam," Chilton and Neusner write, "and in his resurrection commences the new."[24] In the purpose and plan of God, the crucifixion and death of Jesus was the "conclusion" of the old Adam (Adam—and ourselves in Adam) and the resurrection of Jesus the "commencement" of the new man (Christ—and ourselves in Him).

With this background in mind we can say:

1. Adam and Christ are the heads of two aeons (ages), two contrasting, overlapping realms or orders of human existence. The old—initiated by Adam's disobedience—is an order in which sin reigns in death (see chap. 7). The new—initiated by Christ's obedience—is an order where grace reigns "through justification" to life eternal (5:20; see chaps. 6 and 8).

---

23. "Sin" here translates a new term appearing in Romans: *hē hamartia*, "the sin," and probably should be capitalized to express its force. Up to this point in Romans, Paul has been dealing mainly with sin as *guilt*; now he introduces the idea of sin as *revolt*. This is indicated by the new phrase *hē hamartia*, which occurs 28 times between 5:12 and 8:10. In each instance, it refers to sin as "a living, hostile, deadly power." See Greathouse, *Beacon Bible Commentary*, 8:114-15.

24. Bruce Chilton and Jacob Neusner, *Judaism in the New Testament* (London and New York: Routledge, 1995), 93.

2. By nature we are in Adam, through whom we have inherited indwelling sin. Sin is a racial fact before it is an individual act. Guilt as culpability, however, does not attach to the inborn propensity to self-sovereignty, which is the essence of original sin; spiritual death does take effect, however, when this propensity provokes to personal transgression (see 7:9; cf. 4:15).

3. By grace we are in Christ, through whom we have received "the free gift" that "leads to justification and life for all" (vv. 17-18). This "free gift" of God's grace is twofold: (1) universal unconditional justification for infants and the "invincibly ignorant" (Wesley), along with (2) prevenient grace counteracting original sin and making personal salvation possible. Every human being born on earth is covered by the Atonement—until "inbred sin" (Wesley's term) provokes to personal transgression. Furthermore, along with the propensity to self-sovereignty, which is our inheritance in Adam, we receive free grace from Christ in sufficient measure to respond to the gospel and be saved.

4. When as sinners we appropriate God's grace by a personal act of saving faith in Christ, we are re-created and transferred to the order of Christ in which grace reigns in righteousness. "If, because of one man's trespass, death reigned through that one man, much more will those who receive the abundance of grace and the free gift of righteousness *reign in life* through the one man Jesus Christ" (5:17, RSV, emphasis added). This abounding grace is ours, Wesley notes, "not only in the remission of that sin that Adam brought on us . . . but infusion of holiness."[25]

5. The grand announcement of this passage is therefore verses 20-21. Paul's pessimism of nature is more than matched by his optimism of grace: "But law came in, with the result that the trespass multiplied; but where sin increased, grace abounded all the more, so that, just as sin exercised dominion in death, so grace might also exercise dominion through justification leading to eter-

---

25. *Notes* on 5:20. Wesley takes into account "the performative aspect of God's declaration" in Paul's use of the verb *katastathēsontai* here: through Christ Jesus "many will be *made* righteous" (v. 19, emphasis added). God *makes* believers what He accounts them to be—righteous and holy (see Joseph A. Fitzmyer, *Spiritual Exercises Based on Paul's Epistle to the Romans* [New York and Mahwah, N.J.: Paulist Press, 1995], 89-90). To be put in a rectified relation with the holy God, through Christ, is the "premoral" condition for moral consequences; thus forensic righteousness issues in ethical righteousness (as we will see when we come to Rom. 6:15-23)

nal life through Jesus Christ our Lord" (vv. 20-21). C. H. Dodd concludes, "Salvation is more than a device for freeing an individual from his guilt; it must cut at the root of that corporate wrongness which underlies individual transgression. That is, according to Paul, what has been effected by the work of Christ. In Him men are lifted into a new order in which goodness is as powerful and dominant as was sin in the order represented by Adam; or, rather, is far more powerful and dominant."[26]

SANCTIFICATION THROUGH DEATH
TO SIN AND SELF (6:1-23)

Paul continues his treatment of Christian freedom by moving from racial redemption to personal salvation—from Christ's historic freeing of the race from sin and death to the justified believer's freedom from sin and self.[27] The link between the two levels of redemption, as will become clear, is Paul's phrase *dia dikaiosunēs*, judiciously translated by the NRSV "through justification" (5:21). For Paul, justification initiates sanctifying grace in a believer's life (the argument of chap. 6).

But a question already raised earlier in Romans resurfaces: If my sinning elicits from God the manifestation of His righteousness, then why should I not go on sinning? "Let us do evil so that good may come" (as Paul's Judaistic critics slanderously charged; see 3:5-8). In chapter 3 Paul gives a Jewish answer to these critics: "Their condemnation is just" (v. 8, RSV). Now this question assumes a gospel form. Picking up on what he has just said in 5:18-21, Paul addresses his critics by asking, "What shall we say then?" (6:1, RSV), saying in effect: If justification is by grace through faith without the works of the Law, and if the Law instead of insuring a life of virtue serves only to increase sin with the result that trespass multiplied, and if where sin increased grace abounded all the more (5:18-21), "Are we to continue in sin that grace may abound?" (6:1, RSV). "By no means!" Paul shouts. "How can we who died to sin still live in it?" (ibid.). Paul reduces his opponents' argument to absurdity. How can we, as Christians who have *died* to sin, as Christians *persist in living* in it? Such is the force of Paul's

---

26. C. H. Dodd, *The Epistle to the Romans,* in *The Moffatt New Testament Commentary* (New York: Harper and Brothers, 1932), 82.

27. Fitzmyer, *Romans,* in *Anchor Bible,* 33:429-33.

Greek sentence. If we have been truly redeemed in Christ, how can we even *think* of sinning?[28]

In developing his thesis, Paul will rephrase Gal. 2:19-20 (to which he will return also in Rom. 7): "As a believer I have been crucified with Christ and with Him raised to newness of life ['new life of the Spirit,' 7:6]. By faith I have *appropriated* Christ's death for myself, His death *for* my sin becoming my death *to* sin." Paul then recasts this indicative, contrasting it with the imperative, saying in effect, "You have been crucified with Christ and with Him raised to newness of life. Therefore, put off sin! Die to self! Become as Christians what you have been enabled to be!—'dead to sin and alive to God in Christ Jesus'" (vv. 10-11).[29] As justified believers, we have participated in the death and resurrection of Christ, as Paul now will show.

In verses 3-5 Paul cites additional evidence in support of his argument. Up to now in Romans his argument has hinged on the place of faith in justification; now he relates faith to baptism.

"How can we who died to sin go on living in it? Do you not know [or "Have you forgotten," REB] that all of us who have been baptized into Christ Jesus were baptized into his death? Therefore we have been buried with him by baptism into death, so that, just as Christ was raised from the dead by the glory of the Father, so we too might walk in newness of life. For if we have been united with him in a death like his, we will certainly be united with him in a resurrection like his" (vv. 2-5).

Paul takes for granted that the Romans had been baptized—there simply were no unbaptized Christians in the primitive Church. Baptism was no mere supplement to faith; it was the way faith symbolically expressed itself. In baptism the believer confessed "Jesus is Lord" (10:9), thereby submitting to the Lordship of the risen Christ.[30] Even more profoundly, when we understand the *symbol*—not as something detached from what it symbolizes

---

28. Fitzmyer, *Spiritual Exercises*, 93.

29. Ibid.

30. In biblical thought symbol and reality are inseparable: in baptism the believer enters into the reality that the rite symbolizes. Taking baptism as a mere "supplement" to saving faith, while correcting the Catholic error of baptismal regeneration, "puts asunder . . . what God has joined together" in Scripture and results in an unduly individualistic view of salvation that violates the corporate nature of life in Christ (1 Cor. 12:12-27). This is what Wesley meant by his assertion that "the gospel of Christ knows no religion but social, no holiness but social holiness" (*Poetical Works*, 1:xxii).

but as the means of entering into the reality it portrays—baptism is *participation in* Christ's death and resurrection so that we are no longer the persons we once were (v. 5).

To the Corinthians in danger of lapsing into antinomianism Paul gave the reminder, "But you were washed, you were sanctified, you were justified in the name of the Lord Jesus Christ and in the Spirit of our God" (1 Cor. 6:11). In baptism we publicly die as sinners in Adam and are resurrected as saints in Christ. Baptism marks us off thenceforth as those who have been "washed," "sanctified," and "justified" in Christ by the Spirit.

Here in Rom. 6 the apostle gives precise formulation to the integral connection between justification, regeneration, and sanctification within the framework of his baptismal thought. The following quotation is from the NASB, which reflects more correctly the participles of Paul's Greek:

> For if we have become united with Him in the likeness of His death, certainly we shall be also in the likeness of His resurrection, *knowing this,* that our old self was crucified with Him, in order that our body of sin might be done away with, so that we would no longer be slaves to sin; for he who has died is freed from sin. Now if we have died with Christ, we believe that we shall also live with Him, *knowing that* Christ, having been raised from the dead, is never to die again; death no longer is master over Him. For the death that He died, He died to sin once for all; but the life that He lives, He lives to God. Even so consider yourselves to be dead to sin, but alive to God in Christ Jesus *(vv. 5-11, emphases added).*

Certain consequences follow our participation in Christ:

• We have died with Christ, and we are now alive to God in Him (v. 11). Paul's statement may be taken as a "summarizing imperative" that looks both backward and forward—backward to our conversion and forward to our total sanctification (see v. 19).

• In baptism our conversion is sacramentally enacted: we have thereby "grown into union with him"[31]—into His death and resurrection. Fitzmyer gives cogent expression as to what this means in Christian experience:

---

31. Literally, "we have become grown-together with him."

We live by a kind of symbiosis with him, by a close bond that unites us with the risen Christ, with the Christ of glory . . . who has become the Lord of our new lives. . . . As a result of faith and baptism we as Christians have to realize that we now live our lives "in Christ." Christ is "the power of God" (1 Cor. 1:24), and he must be recognized as the dynamic force that activates our existence. . . . If we so live "in Christ," then there can be no question of continuing in sin.[32]

• Further, "our old [unregenerate] self has been crucified with Him," *in order that* "our body of sin" (i.e., our body [or self] as the slave of sin) might be released from sin's rule.[33] The compulsion to sinning is thereby broken: "for whoever has died is freed [Gk. *dedikaiōtai* (justified)] from sin" (v. 7).[34] When sin's *guilt* is canceled in justification, its *power* is thereby effectively broken.

> *He breaks the pow'r of cancelled sin;*
> *He sets the pris'ner free.*
> —Charles Wesley

• As justified believers, we are indeed "dead to sin but alive to God in Christ Jesus" (v. 11). This is not a psychological trick—it is moral and spiritual fact: His death has become my death to sin; His life is now my life to holiness. Cranfield points out that *logidzesthe* ("consider") here in verse 11

> denotes not a pretending ("as if"), nor a mere ideal, but a deliberate and sober judgment on the basis of the gospel, in that it accepts as its norm what God has done in Christ, the gospel-events which are only recognizable as such by faith. . . . So here the imperative followed by *heautous einai* ["yourselves to be"] means something like "Recognize that the truth of the gospel means that you are . . ." This seeing oneself as one is revealed to oneself by the gospel and understanding and taking

---

32. Fitzmyer, *Spiritual Exercises*, 95.

33. "The consequence [of our union with Christ] is that 'our old self has been crucified with him' (6:6), the 'old man,' or the self that we once were, the self that belongs to the old aeon, the self dominated by sin, has died with him" (Fitzmyer, *Spiritual Exercises*, 96).

34. "Jesus' death of atonement," Stuhlmacher comments, "sets one free and from the compulsion to have to sin" (*Paul's Letter to the Romans*, 92).

seriously what one sees is a first step—and a decisively important one—on the way to obedience.[35]

Paul now sets forth his gospel imperative in strongest terms.
Verse 11, indeed, points both backward to what was and forward
to what should be. In verses 2-11 he has declared what it means to
have died with Christ in faith and baptism; now in verses 12-23 he
sets forth the consequences of new life in Christ, urging in effect:
"You have died and risen with Christ: *now become the Christians you
can become!* You *have* died with Christ to sin; now *become* dead to sin!
You *are* alive to God in Christ Jesus; now *live to God alone* and give
free scope to His grace! 'For sin will have no dominion over you,
since you are not under law but under grace.'" "In thus obeying,"
says Fitzmyer, "Christians verify in their lives the gift of divine
grace and thus become what they have been enabled to become."[36]
Let Paul now speak for himself: "Therefore do not let sin exercise
dominion in your mortal bodies, to make you obey their passions.
No longer present your members to sin as instruments of wickedness, but present yourselves to God as those who have been
brought from death to life, and present your members to God as instruments of righteousness. For sin will have no dominion over
you, since you are not under law but under grace" (vv. 12-14).

Obviously, Paul does not mean that Christians have become
incapable of sinning. By the grace of God and the power of the
Spirit they are able *not* to sin; this does not mean they are *unable* to
sin. Justified believers are still human beings in "the Adamic condition," a state of physical depravity that will not be healed until
their bodies are redeemed at the Parousia (8:23). Consequently, we
must cope with what Wesleyan scholar William Burt Pope calls
"natural concupiscence": the combustible elements of sin remain
latent in our unredeemed bodies—not sin, but susceptibility to
sin. Paul elsewhere acknowledges this problem for himself: "I discipline my body and make it my slave, so that, after I have
preached to others, I myself will not be disqualified" (1 Cor. 9:27,

---

35. Cranfield, *Romans*, 1:315.
36. Fitzmyer, *Romans*, in *Anchor Bible*, 33:445. Such empowerment is Howard's
understanding of Paul's imperative here: "Use the resources that are yours in Christ!
You are alive in the Holy Spirit; now let Him be the *means* of your living. Live and walk
by the Spirit!" (Richard E. Howard, *Newness of Life* [Kansas City: Beacon Hill Press of
Kansas City, 1975], 165).

NASB). The *epithumiais* (literally "desires," v. 12) of the body are the occasion of temptation and provide the possibility for sin in the Christian life (see James 1:14-16).[37] If we obey these bodily desires, we open the way for sin once more to "exercise dominion" over us. Hence Paul urges, "No longer present your members to sin as instruments of wickedness, but present yourselves to God as those who have been brought from death to life, and present your members to God as instruments of righteousness" (v. 13; cf. 12:1-2). This is Evangelical synergism, a collaboration with God (Phil. 2:12-13) that, if we continue in grace (Rom. 8:17), will issue in the transformation of our mortal bodies (Phil. 3:20-21).

There is more here. Paul is calling for a moral showdown: "Who is in charge here, God or self?" His aorist imperative means that a personal *crisis* is called for: "*Present* yourselves . . . and your members to God"—*once and for all!* In the final analysis, each of us is part, either of God's problem or God's solution, depending on whether the issue of sovereignty has been resolved. Settling this issue is of urgent importance for every believer. It is a call for moral decision—to let God be God!

Even after the matter of sovereignty is settled, however, victory over sin is not automatic. It never is. Because this is true, John Wesley was reluctant to speak of the "state" of holiness; it is always a "condition."[38]

This conditional understanding of sanctification is the significance of what Paul now says:

> What then? Should we sin because we are not under law but under grace? By no means! Do you not know that if you present yourselves to anyone as obedient slaves, you are slaves of the one whom you obey, either of sin, which leads

---

37. Technically, "passions" (also RSV) is incorrect; the Greek word for "passions" is *pathēmata*, which does not occur until 7:5; certainly it does not mean "evil desires" (NIV), which suggests gnosticism. The KJV rendering "lusts" is not far from correct: irrational desires that clamor only for gratification and must therefore be controlled by reason (through the Spirit, 8:12-13).

38. "Does not talking of a justified or sanctified state, tend to mislead men; almost naturally leading them to trust what was done in one moment? whereas we are every moment pleasing or displeasing to God, according to our works; according to the whole of our present inward and outward behaviour" (1770 Declaration of Methodist Conference Minutes). A year later Wesley qualified his position: "Not the merit of works, but by works as a condition" (1771 Minutes).

to death, or of obedience, which leads to righteousness? But thanks be to God that you, having once been slaves of sin, have become obedient from the heart to the form of teaching to which you were entrusted, and . . . having been set free from sin, have become slaves of righteousness. I am speaking in human terms because of your natural limitations. For just as you once presented your members as slaves to impurity . . . so now present your members as slaves to righteousness for sanctification (*vv. 15-19*).

Paul now raises a question that should disarm his Jewish critic who thought the apostle's gospel of grace opened the door to libertinism: "Should we commit *one act* of sin, because we are not under law but under grace?" Some such translation is needed to carry out the force of Paul's aorist. Paul answers his own question in 13:14, "Put on the Lord Jesus Christ, and make no provision for the flesh, to gratify its desires." *Grace makes no provision for a single sin of conscious, willful disobedience!* Paul is not speaking of some mere peccadillo; he means what the Law calls "sinning with a high hand."[39] The Old Testament penalty was physical death; the gospel penalty is *spiritual* death (6:23)! So much for grace encouraging sin.

Rephrasing 6:2-11 in 6:17-19, but now in the specific terms of the Law (as the norm of Christian ethical behavior), Paul concludes with a clarion call to "righteousness, resulting in sanctification" (v. 19, NASB). It is striking that in this Epistle, in which righteousness is presented as a forensic term defining a right relationship with God, Paul, C. K. Barrett understands, means by the word (in vv. 16, 18, 19, 20) "the moral goal, object, or master, to which Christians are expected to be obedient." Taking into account the "paradoxical" nature of the term "righteousness," Barrett goes on to say,

> God has bestowed righteousness on those who believe. This is purely his gift; it is juridical, eschatological righteous-

---

39. For what Wesley called "sins of surprise," forgiveness is promised in 1 John 2:1-6; but even here the final emphasis is "Whoever says, 'I abide in him,' ought to walk just as he walked" (v. 6). Sin in the Christian's life is like a train wreck—it is not on the schedule!

ness, the right relation with God that one may hope to have at the last judgment. It is essentially a relationship word, but there would be an internal contradiction if the relationship word was not accompanied by ethical righteousness. This is because the God with whom the justified believer now stands in a rectified relation is a moral God. He himself is holy, just, good, loving; it is impossible to remain in a right relation with him while denying the values of holiness, justice, goodness, and love. There is a paradox in God's acceptance of the ungodly, but there would be stark contradiction if the ungodly, once accepted, continued in his ungodliness (which provokes God's wrath, 1:18).[40]

It is not straining the language, therefore, to argue that such abandonment to righteousness results in what Wesley spoke of as "entire" sanctification—heart purity and entire conformity of the believer to the character of God. The sin that remains in the justified believer, to be resolved by sanctifying grace, is the sin of *self-sovereignty: deciding how much of myself God can have.* As long as I am reserving *any* part of my being for myself, I—not God—am sovereign.

The Romans therefore, already slaves of God by redemption, are called upon to become God's slaves by virtue of their own free choice. We are reminded of the Hebrew slave who, entitled to his freedom in the Year of Jubilee, refuses to go out, saying, "I love my master, my wife, and my children; I will not go out a free person." Such a slave would then have his ear pierced with an awl; he would thereby become a *love-slave* for life (Exod. 21:2-6).[41]

The closing paragraph of this chapter contrasts a false and true freedom: "But now that you have been set free from sin and have become slaves of God," Paul concludes, "the return [*karpon,* "fruit"] you get is sanctification and its end, eternal life. For the wages of sin is death, but the free gift of God is eternal life in Christ Jesus our Lord" (vv. 22-23, RSV). There is a "freedom" that is slavery; there is a "slavery" that is perfect freedom.

40. Barrett, *Paul,* 136.
41. See Howard, *Newness of Life,* 171.

SANCTIFICATION THROUGH DEATH TO THE LAW (7:1-25)

In 7:1-6 Paul continues his treatment of the role of the Law in sanctification, an argument that he began at 6:15. In the previous passage (6:15-23) his imagery was that of slavery; now (7:3-4) it is marriage. The connection between death to sin (chap. 6) and death to the Law (chap. 7) is suggested by Paul's confession in Galatians: "For through the law I died to the law, so that I might live to God. I have been crucified with Christ; and it is no longer I who live, but it is Christ who lives in me. And the life I now live in the flesh I live by faith in the Son of God, who loved me and gave himself for me. I do not nullify the grace of God; for if justification comes through the law, then Christ died for nothing" (2:19-21). Paul's death to sin was at the same time death to the Law. It is from this perspective that we are to understand Rom. 7.

Torah, God's good gift to Israel, was at the same time His *command* for Israel's obedience as their part of covenant relationship to Him (Lev. 18:5; cf. Exod. 19:4-6; 20:1-20; Lev. 19; Deut. 5:1-21; and so on).[42] Torah, we must see, was both gift and command. As gift, it was "holy" (7:12); as command, it activated sin (v. 9).

The background of Rom. 7 is found in 5:12-21, in which Paul gives his view of salvation history. It is an account in three stages: from Adam to Moses, from Moses to Christ, and finally from Christ to the end. From Adam to Moses people sinned, but they did not violate precepts, as Adam did (vv. 12-14). In the second period, when "law came in," people's evil deeds became violations (v. 20). At that point the Law became "the power of sin" (1 Cor. 15:56) in human life. In the third period Christ has liberated humanity from sin and death (v. 21).[43]

It was God's plan of salvation from the beginning to send His Son to deal with sin (8:3); we conclude therefore that the Law's intended function was to prepare the way for the grace that God would, in the fullness of time, provide through Christ. In the divine drama of salvation, sin has taken possession of Torah and perverted it; it is now "the law of sin and of death," which God also foresaw.[44] It is from this "perverted" form of the Law that Christ came to deliver us, Paul will now tell us.

---

42. This view of Torah is what E. P. Sanders calls "covenantal nomism" (see pp. 75, 236).

43. Fitzmyer, *Romans*, in *Anchor Bible*, 33:467.

44. *Hē hamartia* should probably be capitalized throughout 5:12—8:10.

Freedom from the Law (7:1-6)

Paul begins by addressing his "brothers and sisters . . . who know the law" (v. 1): particularly the Jewish Christians in Rome who believe that holiness is attained by observing the commandments of Torah. Yet a wider audience may be included, since Paul omits the definite article from *nomos*, saying literally, "since you know *law.*" Whatever Paul's intention here, as his argument unfolds it will become apparent that Gentiles as well as Israelites are in his purview. In any case, Rom. 7 is not a digression but an advancement of his thesis—namely, of the powerlessness of the Law to sanctify.

"The law," Paul declares, "is binding on a person only during that person's lifetime" (v. 1). He then elaborates his point with an illustration: "Thus a married woman is bound by the law to her husband as long as he lives; but if her husband dies, she is discharged from the law concerning her husband. Accordingly, she will be called an adulteress if she lives with another man while her husband is alive. But if her husband dies, she is free from that law, and if she marries another man, she is not an adulteress" (vv. 2-3).

Paul recognizes a married woman's obligation to her husband "as long as he lives," so that marrying another would be adultery. But the moment he dies, she is free to marry another. The law is still in effect, but because the woman's situation is changed, the law of adultery no longer applies to her. The point is evident: the Christian, like the widow, stands in an entirely new relationship to the Law and is no longer under its jurisdiction.[45] Paul's application then follows: "In the same way, my friends, you have died to the law through the body of Christ, so that you may belong to another, to him who has been raised from the dead in order that we may bear fruit for God" (v. 4).

Through faith in the crucified body of Christ we Christians have died to the Law's condemnation and jurisdiction (cf. 6:6). We are now free to marry another; but not just *any* other—we are free for One only, "him who has been raised from the dead" (v. 4; that is, the risen, glorified Christ), "in order that we may bear fruit for God" ("the fruit of the Spirit [which] is love . . . against such there is no law" [Gal. 5:22-23, RSV]).

---

45. Victor Paul Furnish, *Theology and Ethics in Paul* (Nashville and New York: Abingdon Press, 1968), 177.

Consider how sharply Paul contrasts the preceding description of life in Christ with *pre*-Christian existence under Torah. Anticipating what he will say in 7:7-25, he writes, "While we were living in the flesh [or *"by* the flesh"[46]], our sinful passions, aroused by the law, were at work in our members to bear fruit for death" (v. 5).[47] If the fruit of the Christian's union with the risen Christ is "the fruit of the Spirit," the "fruit for death" here means "the deeds of the flesh [Law]" (Gal. 5:19, NASB), as Paul elaborates in Gal. 5:19-21.

Cranfield quotes Calvin's comment on verse 5: "The work of the law, in the absence of the Spirit . . . is to inflame our hearts still more, so that they burst forth into such lustful desires." The Greek *pathēmata* ("passions"), occurring here for the first time in Romans, describes the *carnal mind* (as opposed to the *epithumiais,* "bodily desires," in 6:12). "Challenged by the law which claims man for God and his neighbour," Cranfield comments, "man's self-centeredness—the sinful ego—recognizes that it is being called into question and attacked, and so seeks all the more furiously to defend itself."[48]

Then anticipating what he will argue in 8:1-17, Paul concludes this section by explaining what it means ethically to be freed from the Law: "But now we are discharged from the law, dead to that which held us captive, so that we are slaves not under the old written code but in the new life of the Spirit" (7:6).[49]

The Function of the Law (7:7-13)

What Paul has just said about the close connection between sin and the Law seems to indict Torah itself as sin. Aware of this difficulty, he asks, "What then should we say? That the law is sin? By no means! Yet, if it had not been for the law, I would not have known sin" (v. 7). Paul has already said that "through the law comes the knowledge of sin" (3:20; the knowledge of the specific transgressions of the Law that bring divine judgment). Here "the knowledge of the law" is an *experience of sin itself*—as a hostile power opposed to God (7:8).

---

46. That is, life under the Law is life in the flesh *(sarx)*.

47. This sentence is a summary of 7:7-23, defining this as a condition that should be *history* for Christian believers.

48. Cranfield, *Romans*, 1:337-38.

49. See comments on 6:19-23 above.

Paul epitomizes Torah, quoting the climax of the Decalogue in Exod. 20:17, "You shall not covet"—a specific commandment that activates latent sin, provoking it to rebellion and disobedience. "Coveting is related to sin," Fitzmyer points out, "as the commandment is to the law."[50] The "commandment" may sound like God's injunction to Adam in Gen. 2:17 (cf. Rom. 7:11), but it refers to a specific prohibition of the Mosaic Law just cited, a commandment that provides an "opportunity" (*aphormē*, literally, "jump start") for actual sin.[51] Listen to Paul: "I was once alive apart from the law, but when the commandment came, sin revived and I died, and the very commandment that promised life proved to be death to me. For sin, seizing an opportunity in the commandment, deceived me and through it killed me" (vv. 9-11).

Who is this "I"? Historically, it is Israel confronted by the Mosaic Law as divine commandment (5:20). But the *pasan epithumian* ("all kinds of desire," 7:8)—"the passion of asserting oneself against God and neighbor" is universal.[52] As such it can come to expression *religiously* in one's striving for righteousness before God under the Law. However, it may also come to expression as a *moral* dilemma, the ethical cleavage between will and act or wish and reality. By extension then, the "I" here is the *Adamic* "I," not simply of Israel confronted by the specific commandment of Torah, but also the *ego* of Gentile moralists who "though not having the law . . . show that what the law requires is written on their hearts" (see 2:14-15). Understood as a moral dilemma, these verses portray "the paradox of moralism." Whether the plight be religious or moral, it is the condition of the Adamic "I" in which God's Law compounds the problem of sin.

Yet, even having said this, Paul goes on to absolve the Law from the charge of guilt. "So the law is holy, and the commandment is holy and just and good. Did what is good, then, bring death to me? By no means! It was sin, working death in me through what is good, in order that sin might be shown to be sin, and through the commandment might become sinful beyond measure" (vv. 12-13).

50. Fitzmyer, *Romans*, in *Anchor Bible*, 33:446.

51. Ibid., 467.

52. Ernst Käsemann, *Commentary on Romans*, trans. Geoffrey W. Bromiley (Grand Rapids: Wm. B. Eerdmans Publishing Co., 1980), 194.

As the expression of God's holiness, "the law is holy, and the commandment is holy and just and good." Torah was intended to give *life* to those who would obey (Lev. 18:5). "Did what is good, then, bring death to me?" "By no means!" Paul answers. *Rather, sin, that it might be unmasked as sin, produced death in me, that its true colors might be shown for what they are.*[53] Said Irenaeus: "The law was God's poultice to bring the boil of sin to a head."

The Futility of the Law (7:14-25)

Paul's use of the present tense in this new section has led many interpreters (beginning with the later Augustine)[54] to the false conclusion that he is now describing present Christian experience. This position is fallacious in that it views verses 14-25 as an isolated unit. If we accept what Paul has already said in chapter 6 (that as Christians we have died to sin) and what he is about to show in chapter 8 (that the law of the Spirit of life in Christ Jesus has set us free from the law of sin and death), then this chapter cannot be construed as depicting *Christian* experience. He has already made the point in this very chapter that as Christians we have died to the Law (vv. 1-6). *How can one who has died to the Law be said to be dominated by the Law, and therefore by sin* (vv. 14, 23, 25)?

The use of the present tense in this section is understandable if we keep clearly in mind Paul's main point. Although a case can be made for seeing verses 14-25 as his continuing defense of the Law, it is hard to deny that the apostle's real intent in this passage is to show *the controlling power* of the "sin that dwells within me." The transition to the present tense can easily be made from this perspective. After the opening sentence the Law falls into the background, and everything focuses on our plights as the victims of indwelling sin: *The sin that came to life in its encounter with the Law now lives in us and rules our existence apart from Christ.*

Let Paul now speak for himself: "We know that the law is spiritual; but I am carnal, sold under sin" (Fitzmyer: "Adam's sin and personal sin derived from it") (v. 14, RSV).[55] Torah has its origin in the Spirit of God and derives its character from that Spirit; "but

---

53. Ibid.
54. After his debate with Pelagius and the publication of his *Retractions*.
55. Fitzmyer, *Romans*, in *Anchor Bible*, 33:474.

I am unspiritual" (NIV). Apart from the Spirit living in me and revealing Christ in me and through me, I *am* "flesh." By flesh here Paul means my total self alienated from the life of God and therefore in servitude to sin:[56]

> I do not understand my own actions. For I do not do what I want, but I do the very thing I hate. Now if I do what I do not want, I agree that the law is good. But in fact it is no longer I that do it, but sin that dwells within me. For I know that nothing good dwells within me, that is, in my flesh. I can will what is right, but I cannot do it. For I do not do the good I want, but the evil I do not want is what I do. Now if I do what I do not want, it is no longer I that do it, but sin that dwells within me *(7:15-20).*

Once again we ask, "Who is this 'I'?" If we take the verb *ginō-skein* (v. 15) in its biblical sense meaning "to choose" (see Amos 3:2), then Paul, employing the historic present, is speaking as Saul the Pharisee, persecutor of the Church: "I do not determine my own actions"—sin does (see v. 20). "A person thinks he knows what he is doing and what he can expect," Käsemann explains. "But he lives under an illusion, since the will of God becomes the basis of one's own pious self-assertion and thus leads to one's own destruction."[57]

"Indeed, an hour is coming," Jesus warned His disciples, "when those who kill you will think that by doing so they are offering worship to God" (John 16:2). According to Paul Achtemeier, this was exactly the case with Paul's persecution of the Church:

> Paul's good intentions—to do the will of God as he understood it from the law—led him to oppose Christ, and so to do the opposite of what he wanted. Zealous for the law, Paul the Pharisee sought to do God's will, yet in that zeal opposed God and did the very evil he sought to eradicate through his persecuting activity. Seeking God's will in the law (and hence blameless; Phil. 3:6), Paul the Pharisee had been led to oppose Christ, and hence to do the opposite of

---

56. "The flesh here signifies the whole man as he is by nature" (Wesley, *Notes*, 545).
57. Käsemann, *Commentary on Romans*, 203.

God's will. So had sin taken control of the law, and so it led him astray.[58]

"The crucifixion of Christ is the logical sequence of self-righteousness," Emil Brunner said. *Anyone* who centers on God's law rather than Christ may unwittingly "crucify to themselves the Son of God afresh" (Heb. 6:6, KJV)—even in Christ's Church! Thus, while describing Paul's Jewish predicament under the Law, this passage can be extended to a principle operative in Adamic humanity (v. 22). Fitzmyer says, "Paul uses [the present tense, vv. 14-25] to show the uselessness of *any* attempt to fulfill demands of legal righteousness apart from God's grace."[59]

We should now be in a position to understand the more common translation of verse 15: "I do not understand my own actions. For I do not do what I want, but I do the very thing I hate."

"I am a bafflement to myself," Paul is saying. "The mystery stems from a conflict in the inmost depths of a human being," Fitzmyer comments, "the cleavage between reason-dominated desire and actual performance."[60] Ovid's plaintive confession is often cited in this connection:

> *My reason this, my passion that, persuades;*
> *I see the right, and approve it too,*
> *I hate the wrong, and yet the wrong pursue.*
> —*Metamorphoses* 7.19-20

Epictetus's words are even closer to Paul's: "What he wants he does not do, and what he does not want he does" (*Discourses* 2.25.4). Every ethically sensitive human being understands the apostle's conclusion: "Now if I do what I do not want, it is no longer I that do it, but sin that dwells within me" (v. 20).

The closing section of this chapter not only depicts the powerlessness of the Law to deliver from the power of sin but also reveals the ultimate function of the Law (i.e., to bring us to Christ, who alone can sanctify):

---

58. Paul J. Achtemeier, "Some Things Hard to Understand," *Interpretation* 38 (July 1984): 267. See Paul J. Achtemeier, "The Law in Paul's Conversion," in *Romans*, in *Interpretation: A Bible Commentary for Teaching and Preaching*, ed. James Luther Mays (Atlanta: John Knox Press, 1985), 126-30.

59. Fitzmyer, *Romans*, in *Anchor Bible*, 33:473.

60. Ibid., 474.

So I find it to be a law that when I want to do what is good, evil lies close at hand. For I delight in the law of God in my inmost self, but I see in my members another law at war with the law of my mind, making me captive to the law of sin that dwells in my members. Wretched man that I am! Who will rescue me from this body of death? Thanks be to God through Jesus Christ our Lord!

So then, with my mind I am a slave to the law of God, but with my flesh I am a slave to the law of sin *(7:21-25).*

Paul now rounds off his discussion of the role of the Law. Human beings are carnal (v. 14), creatures of the flesh (*sarx*, v. 18), weak and prone to succumb to the attacks of sin that dwells within them (v. 20). Yet not all that is within them is sinful; there is also the mind (*nous*, v. 23), which recognizes the Law of God and its claims (v. 22). But the mind of itself is unable to resist the seductive power of sin. "So I find it to be a law that when I want to do what is good, evil lies close at hand" (v. 21). Playing on the different senses of *nomos*, Fitzmyer thinks, Paul here uses it as a "law of experience."[61] "I delight in the law of God in my inmost self, but I see in my members another law at war with the law of my mind, making me captive to *the law of sin* [emphasis added] that dwells in my members" (*nomos* as the "principle" of indwelling sin— Fitzmyer).[62] As attractive as this thesis may be, it is probably better to translate verse 21, "This then is what I find the Law to be" in experience.[63] James Dunn points out that "all Paul's references to the law so far in the letter (3:27 not excluded) have been to the Jewish law."[64] The sense, however, is virtually the same either way we translate: under the Law the "sin principle" is activated—"the law of sin that dwells in my members" (v. 23).

In verses 22-23 we see what Jacob Arminius called "the war of laws": the Law of God and the law of sin, diametrically opposed to and at war with one another. Corresponding and subor-

61. Ibid., 475. Stuhlmacher agrees, seeing Paul's usage as "a rhetorical variation on the concept of Law" (*Paul's Letter to the Romans,* 111).

62. Fitzmyer, *Romans,* in *Anchor Bible,* 33:476.

63. Literally, "I find then the Law, for he who wishes to do the good, that for me the evil lies ready to hand."

64. James D. G. Dunn, *Romans 1—8,* vol. 38A in *Word Biblical Commentary,* eds. David A. Hubbard and Glenn W. Barker (Dallas: Word Books, 1988), 393.

dinate to the Law of God is the law of my mind; and to the law of sin, the law of my members.

The War of Laws

| The Law of God *(verse 22)* | directly contrary | The Law of Sin *(verse 23)* |

consentaneous & subordinate *indirectly*

The Law of the Mind *(verse 23)*   directly contrary   The Law of the Members *(verse 23)*

contrary & subordinate *indirectly*

Carl Bangs, *Arminius: A Study in the Dutch Reformation* (Nashville: Abingdon Press, 1971), 190.

"Wretched man that I am! Who will rescue me from this body of death?" (v. 24).

"Jesus Christ our Lord!" Paul shouts, He who brings "the war of laws" to an end by introducing "the law of the Spirit of life" (8:2)—the life principle of the Spirit introduced by faith in Christ that supplies what the Law could never bring.[65]

65. Fitzmyer, *Romans,* in *Anchor Bible,* 33:482-83. See Carl Bangs, *Arminius: A Study of the Dutch Reformation* (Nashville: Abingdon Press, 1971), 188-92.

Verse 25 is Paul's conclusion: "So then, with my mind I [*autos ego*, "I of myself," RSV] am a slave to the law of God, but with my flesh I am a slave to the law of sin." This is the sum of what he has been saying in the past 11 verses. Verse 25 is not out of place (as Moffatt thought). "It is the expression of exultation that is out of place," says Donald M. Davies, "but only because Paul could not contain himself longer."[66] "I of myself" is the key to the dilemma Paul has described—"I . . . left to myself" (MOFFATT); "I relying on myself" (A. M. Hunter). As long as I am the Adamic "I," I am flesh *(sarx)*; and *to the extent* that I am relying on my "autonomous ego" for deliverance from indwelling sin, I am *to that degree* "in the flesh" (cf. 8:8-9). This is why Godet can say, "Paul speaks of the unregenerate man without concerning himself with the question of how far the unregenerate heart remains in the regenerate believer."[67] My death to the Law must become, therefore, a death to self and self-reliance: a death of the Adamic "I" (see Gal. 2:20).

SANCTIFICATION BY THE SPIRIT (8:1-39)

The grand announcement of this chapter is that "what the law, weakened by the flesh, could not do" (v. 3) God has done in Christ. "There is therefore now no condemnation [neither legal nor personal] for those who are in Christ Jesus" (v. 1), for to be in Christ is to be saved from both the *guilt* and *power* of sin.

The first section of Rom. 8 can be divided into two parts: (1) Sanctification by the Spirit *through* Christ (vv. 1-8) and (2) Sanctification by the Spirit *of* Christ (vv. 9-17).

Sanctification by the Spirit Through Christ (8:1-9)

First, the Spirit fulfills the Law (vv. 1-4).

There is therefore now no condemnation for those who are in Christ Jesus. For the law of the Spirit of life in Christ Jesus has set you free from the law of sin and death. For God has done what the law, weakened by flesh, could not do: by sending his own Son in the likeness of sinful flesh, and to deal with sin, he condemned sin in the flesh, so that the just requirement of the law might be fulfilled in us, who walk not according to the flesh but according to the Spirit *(vv. 1-4).*

66. Donald M. Davies, "Free from the Law," *Interpretation* 7 (April 1953): 162.
67. Godet, *Romans*, 282-83.

"What the law, weakened by the flesh, could not do" (v. 3) God has done for us—in Christ and by the Spirit through Him. "For the law of the Spirit of life in Christ Jesus has set you free from the law of sin and death" (v. 2).[68] From Christ, and Christ alone, flows the Spirit of life and holiness.

"The law of the Spirit is nothing more than the Spirit himself in his ruling function in the sphere of Christ," says Käsemann. "He creates life and separates not only from sin and death but also from their instrument, the perverted law of Moses."[69] But observe—He separates us from that perverted law in order that He may establish and fulfill in us "the just requirement" (v. 4) of God's original Torah.

What was not possible to the Law in its perverted form because of indwelling sin, God has made possible by "sending his own Son in the likeness of flesh, and to deal with sin" (v. 3), that is, to *meet* sin in the place where it dwells and rules, and there to condemn, judge, and remove it.[70] As a denizen of the flesh, the Son of God "'condemned' that 'sin' which was 'in' our 'flesh,'" says Wesley; "gave sentence, that sin should be destroyed, and the

---

68. Strong MS evidence supports *se* ("you") here (as also NASB), instead of *me* (KJV, RSV). This interpretation means that Paul is addressing the Roman Christians as justified believers freed from the sin's dominion.

69. Käsemann, *Commentary on Romans*, 215-16.

70. Karl Barth, *A Shorter Commentary on Romans* (Richmond, Va.: John Knox Press, 1959), 90. "As Origen noted, we human beings have 'the flesh of sin,' but the Son had the 'likeness of sinful flesh.' He came in a form like us in that he became a member of the sin-oriented human race; he experienced the effects of sin and suffered death, the result of sin, as one 'cursed' by the law (Gal. 3:13). Thus in his own person he coped with the power of sin. Paul's use of the phrase *sarx hamartias* denotes not the guilty human condition, but the proneness of humanity made of flesh that is oriented to sin" (Fitzmyer, *Romans*, in *Anchor Bible*, 33:485). "Those who believe that it was fallen human nature which was assumed have even more cause than had the authors of the Heidelberg Catechism to see the whole of Christ's life on earth as having redemptive significance; for, on this view, Christ's life before His actual ministry and death was not just a standing where unfallen Adam had stood without yielding to the temptation to which Adam succumbed, but a matter of starting from where we start, subjected to all the evil pressures which we inherit and using the altogether unpromising and unsuitable material of our corrupt nature to work out a perfect, sinless obedience" (Cranfield, *Romans*, 1:383 n. 2). "To bear fallen flesh is necessary if Jesus is to complete the work to which he was called. What is important soteriologically was that Jesus was enabled to resist temptation not by some immanent conditioning, but by virtue of his obedience to the guidance of the Spirit" (Colin E. Gunton, *Christ and Creation*, Didsbury Lectures, 1990 [Carlisle, England: Paternoster Press; Grand Rapids: Wm. B. Eerdmans Publishing Co., 1992], 54). For *us*, gaining mastery over fallen flesh requires that we be born again. Jesus needed no second birth—His birth of Mary was of the Spirit. From His conception Jesus was a man of the Spirit, *God-centered*, not self-cen-

believer wholly delivered from it."[71] On the very ground where sin had established itself—in human flesh—the Son of God has vanquished sin and potentially sanctified our human existence!

The first Adam disobeyed God and died; the last Adam died rather than disobey God, becoming "obedient to the point of death—even death on a cross. Therefore God also highly exalted him" (Phil. 2:8-9). And "being . . . exalted at the right hand of God, and having received from the Father the promise of the Holy Spirit, he has poured out" (Acts 2:33) the sanctifying Spirit, *reproducing in the yielded believer the holiness Jesus himself won by His perfect obedience to the Father.*[72] Thus the glorified Christ, through the gift of the Pentecostal Spirit, inaugurated the new covenant promised in Jer. 31:31-34.

Through the Spirit from Christ "the just requirement [*dikaiōma*] of the law [is] fulfilled in us, who walk not according to the flesh but according to the Spirit" (v. 4). And what is that requirement? It is to love God (v. 28 and 1 Cor. 8:3) with an undivided heart and one's neighbor unselfishly (Mark 12:28-34)—in response to God's love poured into our hearts by the Holy Spirit (see comments on 5:5).[73] The Shema, indeed, is now fulfilled (Deut. 6:4-5; 30:6; cf. Ezek. 36:26-27), and by the love of neighbor the requirement of the second table of the Decalogue is met (Rom. 13:8-10).

Second, the Spirit deposes the flesh (vv. 5-9).

---

tered like *us* in our fallenness. Jesus' assumption of our fallen flesh was the sine qua non of our redemption. "He could heal only what he assumed" (Gregory of Nazianzus). This understanding was the basis of Irenaeus's position that Jesus sanctified humanity from infancy to maturity (see William M. Greathouse, *From the Apostles to Wesley* [Kansas City: Beacon Hill Press of Kansas City, 1979], 36).

71. Wesley, *Notes*, 546. "He 'pronounced the Doom of Sin.' Sin was henceforth deposed of its autocratic power" (C. Anderson Scott, *Abingdon Bible Commentary* [New York: Abingdon-Cokesbury Press, 1929], 1153). John Chrysostom held that the statement "he condemned sin in the flesh" refers specifically to "the crucified 'flesh' of Christ: the Father passed judgment against sin in that the death that Christ died on the cross 'in the flesh' sentenced to impotence sin that reigned in human flesh, which could touch him only in the flesh that he had in common with all human beings" (Fitzmyer, *Romans*, in *Anchor Bible*, 33:487).

72. Godet, *Romans*, 300-301.

73. "The fulfillment spoken of here . . . is something which God, the author of all, works in us through the Spirit as a consequence of the Christ-event. There is a fulfillment of the moral demand . . . [but this] righteousness is entirely the creation of God operating through the Spirit" (Fitzmyer, *Romans*, in *Anchor Bible*, 33:487).

For those who live according to the flesh set their minds on the things of the flesh, but those who live according to the Spirit set their minds on the things of the Spirit. To set the mind on the flesh is death, but to set the mind on the Spirit is life and peace. For this reason the mind that is set on the flesh is hostile to God; it does not submit to God's law—indeed it cannot, and those who are in the flesh cannot please God. But you are not in the flesh; you are in the Spirit, since the Spirit of God dwells in you. Anyone who does not have the Spirit of Christ does not belong to him *(vv. 5-9)*.

By dethroning sin and establishing the reign of grace in us, the Spirit *deposes* the flesh. "But you are not in the flesh, you are in the Spirit, *if* in fact the Spirit of God dwells in you" (v. 9, RSV, emphasis added). This word is addressed not to the saints in heaven, but to the saints in Rome!

For Paul "flesh" and "Spirit" are two conflicting forces; every person is controlled by one or the other. To "walk . . . according to the flesh" is to be under the control of indwelling sin; to "walk . . . according to the Spirit" is to be and live under the control of the indwelling Spirit (v. 4).

In verse 5 Paul shows the relation of a believer's "walk" to his essential "being" (a point not clear in either RSV or NRSV but demanded by the Greek). The NASB correctly translates, "For those who are *[ontes]* according to the flesh." "This is literally an ontological statement," says Wood, "for the Greek particle *ontes* from which the philosophical term is derived appears here in the text."[74] If we are of the flesh, we have the mind-set of the flesh; if we are of the Spirit, the mind-set of the Spirit. The Greek noun for "mind" *(phronēma)*, the aspiration of which this verse speaks, proceeds from the *einai* or "being" and produces the *peripatein*, the "walking" of verse 4. Godet explains, "The *I, egō*, is distinct from both tendencies; but it yields itself without fail to the use of the one or the other—to the former as the *I* of the natural man; to the latter, as the *I* of the regenerate man." As our state, so our tendency; as our tendency, so our conduct.[75]

74. A. Skevington Wood, *Life by the Spirit* (Grand Rapids: Zondervan Publishing House, 1963), 105.

75. Godet, *Romans*, 302.

The mind-set of the flesh is that of the autonomous self, "the life of the *I* for itself."[76] This is "death" to the essential self—separation from God and personal disintegration and corruption that inevitably follow. The mind-set of the Spirit, on the other hand, is a mind set on things "above, where Christ is, seated at the right hand of God" (Col. 3:1, RSV), a life "hid with Christ in God" (Col. 3:3, RSV). This is a life that draws its sustenance, direction, and satisfaction from God in Christ. "To set the mind on the Spirit is life and peace" (v. 6)—God's *shalom*, "which surpasses all understanding" (Phil. 4:7).

"The mind that is set on the flesh," Paul continues, "is hostile to God; it does not submit to God's law—indeed it cannot, and those who are in the flesh cannot please God" (vv. 7-8). Cranfield comments with penetration, "Fallen man's fierce hostility to God is the response of his egotism (which is the essence of his fallenness) to God's claim to his allegiance. Determined to assert himself, to assert his independence, to be the centre of his own life, to be his own god, he cannot help but hate the real God whose very existence gives the lie to all his self-assertion."[77]

"But you are not in the flesh, you are in the Spirit," Paul triumphantly announces, "if in fact the Spirit of God dwells in you" (v. 9, RSV). Although still in the "body" (*sōma*, which must be disciplined, v. 13), Spirit-indwelt believers are not in the "flesh" (*sarx*)! Rudolph Bultmann's comment merits attention: "For the Christian, the flesh is dead and deposed (Rom. 8:2ff); it is excluded from participation in the Reign of God (1 Cor. 15:50), while the *sōma*—transformed (i.e., released from the dominion of the flesh)—is the vehicle of resurrection life. The *sōma* is man himself, while *sarx* is a power that lays claim to him and determines him."[78]

So, Paul writes, "you are not in the flesh, you are in the Spirit, if in fact [*eiper*] the Spirit of God dwells in you" (RSV).[79] *Eiper* here is

---

76. Ibid., 303.

77. Cranfield, *Romans*, 1:386-87.

78. Rudolph Bultmann, *Theology of the New Testament*, trans. Kendrick Grobel (New York: Charles Scribner's Sons, 1951), 1:201.

79. While the NRSV translates *eiper* "since" here in verse 9, in verse 17 it renders it "if, in fact," with respect to the hope of our glorification with Christ. Fitzmyer catches the tension in verse 9 when he writes, "*Yet you are not in the flesh.* The status of the justified Christian is not that of the unregenerate human being. Here Paul formulates the indicative of Christian existence. On it he will base his imperative: Live like a Christian. So Paul counsels Roman Christians directly, using the 2d pl. pron. *hymeis*. He wants them to realize that even their earthly life is now one ruled by God's Spirit" (Fitzmyer, *Romans*, in *Anchor Bible*, 33:490).

a call for the Romans—and us—to be sure that the Spirit now has the same controlling influence that sin formerly exerted. "The use of *oikein en* ("dwells in") denotes a settled permanent penetrative influence," say Sanday and Headlam, possession by a power superior to self.[80] "If the indwelling of the Spirit is spoken of here as that of sin in 7:17ff," Käsemann thinks, "in both cases radical possession is indicated which also affects our willing according to v. 5."[81]

"Anyone who does not have the Spirit of Christ does not belong to him" (v. 9). "This," say Sanday and Headlam, "amounts to saying that all Christians 'have the Spirit' *in greater or less degree.*"[82] Here is the clear implication that a Christian who "is in fact" *fully* indwelt by the Spirit is to be distinguished from one only "having the Spirit" through faith. "The man who does not have the Spirit (whose life bears no evidence of the Spirit's sanctifying work)," says Cranfield, "is no Christian, however much he may claim to be one."[83]

What Paul means here by being "in fact" indwelt by the Spirit is what he elsewhere refers to by being "filled" with the Spirit (Eph. 5:18; 3:14-21). The degree of indwelling is dependent upon the degree of yieldedness to God (see comments on 6:12-14, 19). "The Spirit-filled life, or Spirit-possessed life," Myron Augsburger points out, "is not one in which we have a certain amount of the Spirit, but rather one in which He possesses all of us. The Spirit-filled life is one in which the Spirit expresses Himself within an individual as a controlling and overflowing force. The condition is one of yieldedness on our part. We are filled with the Spirit as we are emptied of self."[84] It is one thing, therefore, to "have" the Spirit; it is quite another for the Spirit to *have us.* In the Spirit-filled life the Holy Spirit is the exact counterpart of the "sin that dwells in me" as a person of the "flesh" (7:17, 20).

Sanctification by the Spirit of Christ (8:9-11)

The most significant claim that Paul makes in Rom. 8 now becomes clear: The Spirit who comes through Christ is the Spirit

---

80. W. Sanday and H. C. Headlam, *The Epistle to the Romans,* in *The International Critical Commentary* (New York: Charles Scribner's Sons, 1929), 196.

81. Käsemann, *Commentary on Romans,* 223.

82. Sanday and Headlam, *Romans,* 197 (emphasis added).

83. Cranfield, *Romans,* 1:388.

84. Myron S. Augsburger, *Quench Not the Spirit* (Scottdale, Pa.: Herald Press, 1961), 39-40.

of Christ. So of the Spirit of God's indwelling he now can say, "But if *Christ* is in you" (v. 10, emphasis added). The passage before us (vv. 9-11) treats "the Spirit," "the Spirit of God," "the Spirit of Christ," and "Christ" as *experientially* synonymous. C. H. Dodd makes a trenchant observation here:

> *In Christ, in the Spirit, the Spirit within, Christ within* were in effect only different ways of describing one experience, from slightly different points of view. This is not to say that Paul, in a strict theological sense, identified Christ with the Spirit. But his virtual identification of the experience of the Spirit with the experience of the indwelling Christ is of utmost value. It saves Christians from falling into a non-moral, half-magical conception of the supernatural in human experience, and it brought spiritual experience to the test of the historical revelation of God in Christ.[85]

To be truly Christian is to be able to confess with Paul, "With Christ I have been co-crucified, and *ego* lives no more, but Christ lives in me" (Gal. 2:20, literal trans.; i.e., to have the sinful *ego* displaced by the living Christ). Paul admonished his Corinthian critics to *self*-examination in these words: "Examine yourselves to see whether you are living in the faith. Test yourselves. Do you not know that Jesus Christ is in you?—unless, indeed, you fail to meet the test!" (2 Cor. 13:5). Bonhoeffer sees here "the" test of what it means to be Christian: *to have "the precise space once occupied by the old man" to be now "occupied by Jesus Christ."*[86] This understanding informs Mildred Wynkoop's claim (commenting on the "second work of grace") that "'second' is *depth*." To be truly sanctified is not to be a *super* Christian (there is no such thing); it is to be a *true* Christian (cf. Rom. 6:11).

While "the Spirit is your life because you have been justified" (v. 10c, REB), Paul reminds his readers, "Your bodies are dead because of sin" (v. 10b, RSV).[87] The full manifestation of Christ in their mortal bodies awaits the resurrection (v. 11). This is the truth

---

85. Dodd, *Romans*, 124.

86. Dietrich Bonhoeffer, *Ethics*, ed. Eberhard Bethge (New York: Macmillan, 1965), 41 (emphasis added).

87. This rendering by REB literally translates this verse and follows the Vulgate in rendering *dia dikaiosunē* "because you have been justified" (Latin, *propter iustificationem*). "This life is nothing but 'justification' (5:18)" (Fitzmyer, *Romans*, in *Anchor Bible*, 33:491).

that underlies the next paragraph (vv. 12-17). Christians are no longer what they once were, but they are not yet what they will be when Christ returns to consummate their redemption (vv. 18-23).

Standing in the Spirit (8:12-17)

Käsemann introduces this section by relating this new section to the Christological understanding of the Spirit in the previous passage, showing how the gospel imperative again arises out of Paul's indicative:

> The christological relation of the Spirit finds expression in the new section in the fact that Christ as prototype, as in Heb. 2:1ff, creates new sons of God, i.e., bearers of the Spirit. The antithetical parallelism of vv. 12-13 take up those of vv. 5-8 at the hortatory level and form a transition to the new theme. . . . The Christian necessarily stands in conflict with the power of the flesh if he is not to fall under the doom of death which this brings. . . . What is at issue is . . . the maintaining of the new life against temptation.[88]

1. Sarx and Sōma

"So then, brothers and sisters, we are debtors, not to the flesh [sarx], to live according to the flesh—for if you live according to the flesh, you will die [paraphrastic future, meaning necessary and certain spiritual death], but if by the Spirit you put to death the deeds of the body [sōma], you will live" (vv. 12-13).[89]

Like sin and the Law, the flesh constitutes a threat to the Spirit-filled Christian. These powers remain as a part of the old order still to be overcome. The sōma, with its appetites, urges, and mechanisms, offers sarx a point of attack. Our task as Christians is to "cut the nerve of [these] instinctive actions" (Rom. 8:13, PHILLIPS) of the body which, if yielded to, would cause us to disobey God (1 Cor. 9:27)—and die.

The Christian has "no obligations" (v. 12, TLB) to the flesh—that is, to the self as an autonomous entity. There is a proper self-regard, which Christ enhances; but there is also an improper self-love. "If anyone wishes to be a follower of mine," Jesus said, "he

---

88. Käsemann, Commentary on Romans, 225.
89. Fitzmyer: "You are going to die, you are bound to die" (Romans, in Anchor Bible, 33:492).

must leave self behind" (Luke 9:23, NEB). "But if by the Spirit you put to death the deeds of the body, you will live" (v. 13). "By the power of the Spirit" is what Paul means here. As the body strives to reassert its autonomy, we have the gracious assistance of the promised Comforter, who will strengthen us to overcome (John 14:15-17). This idea is the biblical doctrine of "counteraction"—not of sin, but of the body's (self's) strivings (cf. 6:12).

2. Sonship and Holiness

Verses 14-17 make it clear that the discipline of the holy life is the discipline of filial *love.* Christians are the obedient children of their Heavenly Father, not slaves to an impersonal legal system.

The danger of overemphasizing discipline is that of causing believers who have found the joy of divine adoption to "fall back into [slavish] fear" (v. 15). Having begun in the Spirit, we are also perfected by the Spirit (see Gal. 3:1-3). Thank God, "There is therefore now no condemnation for those who are in Christ Jesus"—*even for remaining sin*—provided they "walk not according to the flesh but according to the Spirit" (8:1, 4).[90]

In clarifying the nature of Christian discipline, Paul makes two points. First, we are "led by the Spirit of God . . . children of God" (v. 14).[91] Second, as believers we enjoy the "witness" of the Spirit (v. 16), enabling us to cry out, "Abba! Father!" (v. 15). "The joy of the LORD is [our] strength" (Neh. 8:10) as His children, joy arising from the inward assurance that He loves us and accepts us *as we are* in Christ. Assured by the Spirit that He loves us, we love Him in return—and do His will in joyful gratitude. This is the holy life: the joyous and free obedience (perfect love) of God's "adult" children (Wesley).

> *If our love were but more simple,*
> *We should take Him at His word;*
> *And our lives would be all sunshine*
> *In the sweetness of our Lord.*
> —F. W. Faber

---

90. See John Wesley's sermon, "Satan's Devices," in *Works,* 6:32-43, for a powerful sermon on this truth.

91. Paul uses *huioi* ("sons") here in verse 14, but in verses 16-17 he will use *tekna,* "children," which shows the inclusive nature of *huioi.*

Holiness as Hope in the Spirit (8:18-30)

The last verse of the previous section (v. 17), by its movement of thought from sonship to heirship ("if children, then heirs"), makes the transition to the subject of Christian hope. The immediate link in the preceding section is verse 15, in which Paul speaks of "the Spirit of adoption" (KJV). He realizes that our adoption is incomplete. Skevington Wood explains our adoption:

> It is assured the believer, but it is not yet apparent to the world. It is a concealed sonship . . . obscured by the body of our humiliation. But at the end of the age, when the Lord returns for His own, that sonship will be revealed. All will see that the adoption is a fact. The Spirit is the firstfruits of that disclosure. "Beloved, we are God's children now; it does not yet appear what we shall be, but we know that when he shall appear we shall be like him, for we shall see him as he is" (1 John 3:2).[92]

In view of the concealed nature of our adoption, we understand that our existence as Spirit-filled Christians must include "the sufferings of this present time" (v. 18)—the time between Pentecost and the Parousia. "As to the *spirit*, we are in *the age to come*," Godet explains; "as to the *body*, in *the present age*."[93] Our bodies are no longer the instruments of sin, but they are not yet redeemed (v. 23).

This present age is a time when "the whole creation has been groaning in labor pains" (v. 22), waiting "with eager longing for the revealing of the children of God" at the Parousia (v. 19). "And not only the creation, but we ourselves, who have the first fruits of the Spirit, groan inwardly while we wait for adoption, the redemption of our bodies" (v. 23). Although (if we are really indwelt by the Spirit) the *tyranny* of the flesh is past, the "weakness" (v. 26; "infirmities," KJV) of the flesh remains. Those "infirmities" include, of course, the bodily weakness and pain that eventuate in physical death with the anguish of spirit implied by what we call human suffering. But surely more than this is meant. The "groanings" (v. 26, KJV) of the Spirit are the birth pangs of our bodily redemption, just as the groanings of "the whole creation" are the travail of na-

---

92. A. Skevington Wood, *Life by the Spirit*, 86.
93. Godet, *Romans,* 313 (emphasis added).

ture's redemption (v. 22). As the creation is frustrated, or subject to "futility" (v. 20), so our "weaknesses" frustrate the Spirit within us and cause Him to groan "with sighs too deep for words" (v. 26).

Our weaknesses surely encompass the whole array of human frailties: the racial effects of sin in our bodies and minds, the scars of past sinful living, emotional damage from traumatic childhood experiences, our prejudices, our neuroses, our temperamental idiosyncrasies, our human infirmities and fretfulness, and a thousand faults to which our flesh is heir. We may add to this our "involuntary transgressions" of God's perfect law.[94] A full-orbed doctrine of Christian perfection therefore must put the truth within the framework of "this present time" of human suffering and frailty.

But if we believe the gospel, "this present time" is also pregnant with hope—a joyful expectation of the Parousia and final glory (vv. 23-24). "If Christianity is not altogether thoroughgoing eschatology," Barth says incisively, "there remains in it no relationship whatever to Christ."[95]

The indwelling Spirit is not only the Witness to our adoption but also the "first fruits"—the "foretaste" (Weymouth et al.) and "guarantee" (Eph. 1:14, RSV)—of the glory that shall be ours when Christ appears (2 Cor. 1:21-22; Eph. 1:13-14). "Beloved, now are we the sons of God, and it doth not yet appear what we shall be: but we know that, when he shall appear, we shall be like him; for we shall see him as he is" (1 John 3:2, KJV). "In this hope we were saved" (Rom. 8:24, RSV). Such hope is not wistful longing; it is confident expectation based on the Resurrection (1 Cor. 15:20-23, 51-58) and confirmed by "God's love[, which] has been poured into our hearts through the Holy Spirit that has been given to us" (Rom. 5:5).

Superficially, "the sufferings of this present time" seem to hinder God's purpose for us, but in fact everything that seems to frustrate that purpose serves finally only to further it (v. 28). The "good" that God all the while is working in those who love Him is His purpose finally to conform us "to the image of his Son, in order that he might be the firstborn within a large family" (v. 29). *God's ultimate concern is not our happiness, but our holiness: the restora-*

---

94. See Wesley, "A Plain Account of Christian Perfection," in *Works,* 11:395-96.
95. Barth, *Epistle to the Romans,* 314.

tion of the divine image lost in the Fall. "And all of us"—when we love God with disinterested love—"with unveiled faces, seeing the glory of the Lord as though reflected in a mirror, are being transformed into the same image from one degree of glory to another; for this comes from the Lord, the Spirit" (2 Cor. 3:18; cf. 1 Cor. 15:45).

Security in Christ (8:31-39)

This final majestic paragraph is Paul's inspired peroration, celebrating the glorious truth that we are "superconquerors" through Christ. Chapter 8, which begins with "no condemnation," climaxes in effect with "no separation"!

Wright says of Rom. 8:31-39,

> The divine love, which has been under the argument ever since 5:6-10, reemerges as the real major theme of the entire gospel message. This is covenant love, promised to Abraham and his family, a family now seen to be the worldwide people who benefit from Jesus' death. Since this love is precisely the Creator's love, it remains sovereign, though the powers of earth and heaven may seem to be ranged against it. . . . [The love of God is] the covenant faithfulness of the Creator God, revealed in the death and resurrection of Jesus the Messiah and the gift of the Spirit.[96]

TRANSFORMED LIVING—PERSONAL AND COMMUNAL—THE FRUIT OF SANCTIFICATION (12:1-9)

We now turn for a brief look at the fruit of sanctification: transformed living. A point to underscore heavily is the fact that Christian holiness is at once personal and communal. As we have already noted, John Wesley insisted that "there is no holiness but *social* holiness" (i.e., *love* lived out in all human relationships, within the Christian community *and* in the world). While the limitations of our study will not permit us to explore this truth, which Paul sets forth in 12:1—15:13, the verses to which we now shall give attention adequately introduce Paul's ethic of the holy life: "I appeal to you therefore, brothers and sisters, by the mercies of God, to present your bodies as a living sacrifice, holy and acceptable to God, which is your spiritual worship. Do

---

96. Wright, "Romans and the Theology of Paul," 55.

not be conformed to this world, but be transformed by the re-newing of your minds, so that you may discern what is the will of God—what is good and acceptable and perfect" (12:1-2).

"Therefore" indicates that what is about to be said follows from what has already been said in Romans up to this point: God's merciful dealing with us through Christ, "the sweetness of that grace in which our salvation consists" (Calvin). The verb translated "appeal" is a technical term for Christian exhortation, an earnest appeal. "In view of God's mercy" (v. 1, NIV) Paul ex-horts those who are already believers to "present" themselves as "a living sacrifice" to God.

"Present" reminds us of 6:13, 16, and 19, where it is used in the sense of "putting oneself at the disposal of" another (i.e., God). Here the verb seems to be used in the technical sense of religious ritual with the meaning of "presenting a sacrifice." The Greek speaks of our "bodies" being offered—as the instru-ments by which all human service is rendered to God. "Body" equals "self." So "present your bodies as a living sacrifice" upon God's altar, to be consumed in His service. When we do this, we are no longer our own but have come completely under the pow-er of God. "The Christian, already God's by right of creation and right of redemption," Cranfield writes, "has yet again to become God's by virtue of his own free surrender of himself."[97]

Thus offered to God, we become "a living sacrifice, holy and acceptable to God." We are "a living sacrifice" in the sense that we are now *fully alive to God* (cf. 6:11). We are "holy," not only because we belong absolutely to God, but also because we are being "sanc-tified by the Holy Spirit" (cf. 15:16). "The Christian's concrete liv-ing," Cranfield observes, "is henceforth to be marked by the con-tinuing process of sanctification."[98] And we are now "acceptable to God"—a true and proper sacrifice that He will accept.

This action of *worshiping*—the continuous offering of our whole selves in all our concrete living—is our "logical" (Gr. *logikēn*) action of worshiping. "Worship" is literally "service" (KJV) and im-plies that the worship God desires embraces the whole of our lives from day to day. "Spiritual" is literally "logical" (from *logos*). The worship that is "acceptable to God" is not merely "a worship expe-

97. Cranfield, *Romans*, 2:600.
98. Ibid., 601.

rience," something ecstatic or mystical. For Paul, true worship is "reasonable" (KJV), an intelligent offering of ourselves, issuing in a practical daily life reflecting Jesus Christ (the divine *logos*) in our thoughts, aspirations, words, and deeds. This "rational" worship is truly "spiritual worship" (cf. John 4:24).

"Do not be conformed to this world" ("the pattern of this world," NIV), Paul continues in verse 2. J. B. Phillips's familiar paraphrase catches Paul's thought: "Don't let the world around you squeeze you into its own mould, but let God re-make you." This passive imperative is consistent with the truth that, while the transformation is not our own doing but the work of the Holy Spirit, we all have responsibility in the matter—to *let ourselves be transformed* (Gr. *metamorphousthe*) as we mind the checks and obey the promptings of the Holy Spirit. The Greek verb is used of Jesus' transfiguration in the Gospels (Matt. 17:2; Mark 9:2). It is also Paul's word in 2 Cor. 3:18, in which the Christian's "transfiguration" by the Spirit is spoken of as "from one degree of glory to another."

But how does this transformation take place? *By the renewing of the mind.* "Let God re-make you so that your whole attitude of mind is changed" (PHILLIPS). This takes place as we permit the Spirit to renew our thinking—through the Word. "Sanctify them in the truth; your word is truth" (John 17:17). The Spirit transforms us as we attend God's Word prayerfully and obediently.

By worship consonant with the gospel we are able to "discern what is the will of God—what is good and acceptable and perfect" (v. 2). Cranfield thinks that this admonition was prompted by Paul's knowledge that some in the Roman church were inclined to place a higher value on the more spectacular gifts of the Spirit to the neglect of love. This seems to be indicated by what the apostle next says, reminiscent of what he had recently written to the Corinthians—that the gifts of the Spirit are not for personal aggrandizement, but are *communal:* "To each is given the manifestation of the Spirit for the common good" (1 Cor. 12:7; see vv. 12-27). Thus Paul continues:

> For by the grace given to me I say to everyone among you not to think of yourself more highly than you ought to think, but to think with sober judgment, each according to the measure of faith that God has assigned. For as in one

body we have many members, and not all the members have the same function, so we, who are many, are now one body in Christ, and individually we are members one of another. We have gifts that differ according to the grace given to us: prophecy, in proportion to faith; ministry, in ministering; the teacher, in teaching; the exhorter, in exhortation; the giver, in generosity; the leader, in diligence; the compassionate, in cheerfulness (vv. 3-8).

As suggested above, this is the beginning of an ethical exhortation addressed to a congregation who were recipients of various gifts of the Spirit that so easily tempt to spiritual pride. They must think of themselves, therefore, "with sober judgment" in the light of the gospel, and apply "the measure of faith," which declares love to be the true validation of the Spirit-filled life and service to Christ's Body the yardstick of every gift they have received (cf. 1 Cor. 12:7, 31; 13:1-3).

Those who measure themselves by God's standard must understand that their estimate of themselves is always in relation to their fellow believers. All Christians belong to a single whole, the "one body" of Christ; and when they estimate themselves according to the gospel, they will recognize that they do not exist for themselves, but rather that "we are members one of another" (v. 5).

"We have gifts that differ," Paul continues, "according to the grace given to us" (v. 6). What he now says indicates the sober, unself-conscious way in which Christians who measure themselves by the gospel will give themselves to fulfilling the several tasks apportioned to them by God's grace. For Paul, the true manifestation of the Spirit is not in flashy endowments that call attention to the gifted individual, but in the practical living-out of the gospel of loving service to others (vv. 7-8). This reminder is always in order when the Church understands itself as the Spirit-indwelt Body of Christ.

After the above introduction, Paul admonishes, "Love must be sincere" (v. 9, NIV)—and then goes on to apply the principle of love to all human relationships (12:9—15:13). Sanctification is not getting on one's horse and riding off like the Lone Ranger in one's endeavor to be holy! No, sanctification is living out the love of the Spirit within community. No one put this more forcefully or unforgettably than John Wesley, who, more than any other, restored the truth of Christian holiness to its merited position within a Protestant understanding of the gospel. "'Holy solitaries,'" said Wesley, "is a phrase no more consistent with the gospel than 'holy adulterers.' The gospel of Christ knows no religion but social, no holiness but social holiness. Faith working by love is the length and breadth and depth and height of Christian perfection."[99]

---

99. *Poetical Works*, 1:xxiii.

8

Toward a Doctrine of Sanctification

We come now to the heart of the matter, to what has been called "the central idea of Christianity": the purification of the heart from sin and the renewal of our nature in the image of God.[1] Drawing upon the raw materials of our biblical studies, we will attempt to formulate a *doctrine* of "sanctification."

The New Testament words for this divinely wrought spiritual metamorphosis are *hagiadzein* ("to sanctify") and *hagiasmos* ("sanctification" or "holiness"). These words belong almost exclusively to biblical Greek (see Appendix); in both the LXX (the Greek translation of the Old Testament) and the New Testament, the sanctification denoted by these terms "presupposes the religious process of atonement."[2]

SANCTIFICATION—A WHOLE LIFE PROCESS

In three passages in the Epistles—1 Cor. 1:30; 2 Thess. 2:13; and Heb. 12:14—*hagiasmos* is used to signify the total process of sanctification. Concerning this important word, John Allen Knight wrote, "Unless limited by the context, the term encompasses the total work of God—both state and process—in the life of the 'holy one' from the first moment of conviction (spiritual awakening) to

1. Jesse T. Peck, *The Central Idea of Christianity* (Kansas City: Beacon Hill Press, 1951 reprint).
2. Gerhard Kittel, *Theological Dictionary of the New Testament*, trans. Geoffrey Bromiley (Grand Rapids: Wm. B. Eerdmans Publishing Co., 1964), 1:113.

the final 'conformity' (if we may properly speak of 'final') to the image of Christ. This continuing, or progressive, divine work of sanctification produces holy character, which is evidenced by a distinct life-style."[3]

In the three passages cited above we see how Knight's definition of *hagiasmos* applies.

In 2 Thess. 2:13 Paul reminds the Church, "God chose you from the beginning to be saved, *through sanctification by the Spirit [en hagiasmō pneumatos]* and belief in the truth" (RSV, emphasis added). The NIV renders the same Greek phrase as "through the sanctifying work of the Spirit." The scriptural evidence that we are saved is, therefore, that we are being *sanctified*. As Kittel says, *"Hagiasmos,* or sanctifying effected by the Spirit, is the living form of the Christian state."[4] "Sanctification" is, then, the moral description of "salvation."

In 1 Cor. 1:30 we read, "It is because of him [God] that you are in Christ Jesus, who has become for us wisdom from God— that is, our righteousness, *holiness* and redemption" (NIV, emphasis added). Here *hagiasmos* defines the total work of "holifying" made available to us in Christ Jesus: our complete deliverance from sin and our full restoration to the image of God (including all that is involved in such a process). Christ is the believer's Sanctification as well as his or her Justification.

In Heb. 12:14 the author exhorts his readers, "Pursue peace with everyone, and the *holiness* without which no one will see the Lord" (emphasis added). Here *hagiasmos* defines the work of the sanctifying Spirit, which goes forward in us as we cooperate with God in His endeavor to make us completely holy and Christlike. It is not so much a question of where we are in the process as of whether the process is going forward with our full and joyful participation.

The lowest degree of obedience acceptable to God at any point in our pilgrimage, says Mildred Wynkoop, is the highest of which we are capable at that moment by the grace of God. Therefore, says Knight, "it is inconceivable that one who is genuinely converted, born of the Spirit, could oppose the divine cleansing at any stage, or draw back from the ultimate goal of Christlike-

---

3. John Allen Knight, *The Holiness Pilgrimage* (Kansas City: Beacon Hill Press of Kansas City, 1973), 37.

4. Kittel, *Theological Dictionary,* 1:113.

ness." Such a person, he continues, "may wait for more light—being obedient as he does so. There may be a relatively brief ambivalence or hesitating reluctance to move on to entire sanctification once he sees clearly the implications of his initial commitment, but he cannot *stubbornly resist* and at the same time be worthy of the name 'holy one.'"[5]

THE GENESIS OF HOLINESS

Holiness has its genesis in prevenient grace, as Simon Peter makes clear when he speaks of "the *sanctifying work of the Spirit [hagiasmo pneumatos]*," who enables the awakened sinner to "obey Jesus Christ and be sprinkled with His blood" (1 Pet. 1:2, NASB, emphasis added). Furthermore, throughout our pilgrimage, to its very end, the Spirit of God is the sole explanation of any holiness that we may experience. While "prevenient grace" technically refers to the grace of God that comes before justification, it applies to every stage of salvation.

The mission and ministry of the Spirit is to apply to our hearts the benefits of Christ's death on our behalf. He comes to work *within* us all that Christ died to provide *for* us. Charles W. Lowry says of the Spirit that it is His ministry "to enter into the recesses of the human spirit and to work from within the subjectivity of man. From within our human being the Spirit vitalizes, stabilizes, renews, admonishes, warns, recalls, interprets, enlightens, guides, and gives comfort (or strength). He is God in His special activity of secret invasion and invisible occupation."[6]

Thus, as Wesley says, the Holy Spirit is "the immediate cause of all holiness in us,"[7] from the first moment of our spiritual awakening, to the final moment of glory. Harriet Auber expresses this truth poetically:

> *And every virtue we possess,*
> *And every victory won,*
> *And every thought of holiness*
> *Are HIS alone.*[8]

---

    5. Knight, *Holiness Pilgrimage*, 38-39.

    6. Charles W. Lowry, *The Trinity and Christian Devotion* (San Francisco: Harper and Brothers, 1946), 73.

    7. Wesley, *Letters*, 3:9 (emphasis added).

    8. Harriet Auber, "The Holy Spirit," *Masterpieces of Holy Verse* (New York and London: Harper and Brothers Publishers, 1948), 248.

INITIAL SANCTIFICATION—HOLINESS OF LIFE

While the Spirit plays an active role in bringing us to repentance and faith in Christ, sanctification proper has its beginning in conversion, "by the washing of regeneration and renewal in the Holy Spirit" (Titus 3:5, RSV). Wesley spoke of regeneration as the "gate to sanctification." Later Wesleyans coined the term "initial sanctification." However we choose to speak of this miracle of divine grace, conversion is the beginning of both outward and inward holiness.

First, conversion initiates outward holiness. The life imparted by the Spirit in regeneration is a holy life. "If anyone is in Christ, there is a new creation; everything old has passed away; see, everything has become new!" (2 Cor. 5:17; cf. Rom. 6:2-11). Born of God, we begin to "walk in the same manner as He walked" (1 John 2:6, NASB). The old pattern of disobedience has given place to a new pattern of obedience to God. "No one who is born of God will continue to sin," John writes, "because God's seed remains in him; he cannot go on sinning, because he has been born of God" (1 John 3:9, NIV). The new life is a holy life.

One standard, therefore, is required of all: "As obedient children, do not be conformed to the former lusts which were yours in your ignorance, but like the Holy One who called you, be holy yourselves also in all your behavior" (1 Pet. 1:14-15, NASB).

In 1 Cor. 6:9-11 and Titus 3:4-7 Paul makes it clear that conversion initiates a life of holiness. "Do you not know that wrongdoers will not inherit the kingdom of God?" he inquires of the Corinthians. "Do not be deceived!" he warns them. "Fornicators, idolaters, adulterers, male prostitutes, sodomites, thieves, the greedy, drunkards, revilers, robbers—none of these will inherit the kingdom of God. And this is what some of you used to be. But you were *washed*, you were *sanctified*, you were *justified* in the name of the Lord Jesus Christ and in the Spirit of our God" (6:9-11, emphases added).

The passage in Titus also described conversion in terms of regeneration, sanctification, and justification: "But when the goodness and loving kindness of God our Savior appeared, he saved us, not because of any works of righteousness that we had done, but according to his mercy, through the *water of rebirth* and *renewal by the Holy Spirit*. This Spirit he poured out on us richly through Jesus Christ our Savior, so that, having been *justified* by his grace, we might become heirs according to the hope of eternal life" (3:4-7, emphases added).

In 1 Cor. 1:2, Paul refers to the Corinthians as "called to be saints." "Saints" is a translation of the Greek noun *hagios* (see Appendix), which is found only in the plural.

New Testament saints are holy both objectively and subjectively.

First, "saints" are *objectively* holy. They are, like ancient Israel, "a chosen race, a royal priesthood, a holy nation, God's own people, in order that [they] may proclaim the mighty acts of him who called [them] out of darkness into his marvelous light" (1 Pet. 2:9). Once "not a people," they are now "God's people" (v. 10), redeemed "with the precious blood of Christ" (see 1:19; see also 2:4-8). They are also "God's temple" (1 Cor. 3:16-17), His very "dwelling place" on earth in the Spirit (Eph. 2:22).

The objective holiness of the Church is sometimes referred to as "positional perfection," suggested by Heb. 10:14: "For by a single offering he has perfected for all time those who are sanctified." All saints (sanctified ones) enjoy a perfected relationship to God provided by Christ's self-offering, *provided* they "walk in the light as he himself is in the light" (1 John 1:7; see Heb. 12:19-31, the exhortation that follows v. 14).[9]

Second, saints are *subjectively* holy. "Like obedient children," Peter exhorts the new Israel of God, "do not be conformed to the desires that you formerly had in ignorance.[10] Instead, as he who called you is holy, be holy yourselves in all your conduct; for it is written, 'You shall be holy, for I am holy'" (1 Pet. 1:14-16). Here, as in every New Testament holiness passage, the call is to a holy life. New Testament holiness is godlikeness, with all that this implies in one's spirit and lifestyle. To the Ephesians Paul writes, "Blessed be the God and Father of our Lord Jesus Christ, who has blessed us in Christ with every spiritual blessing in the heavenly places, just as he chose us in Christ before the foundation of the world to be holy and blameless before him in love" (1:3-4).

The two key words here are *hagios* and *amōmos*, "holy" and "blameless." "The word *hagios,*" says Barclay, "always has in it the idea of *difference* and of *separation*. A thing which is *hagios* is *different*

---

9. "Positional perfection" is synonymous with "positional sanctification" or "imputed holiness." It is not, however, unconditional; we are "perfect in Christ" and "holy in Christ" as long as we *continue* in Christ (1 Cor. 9:27; 10:6-13; Heb. 6:4-6).

10. "The exiles of the Dispersion" (1 Pet. 1:1).

from ordinary things." This difference applies to a temple, a priest, a sacrificial animal, the Sabbath day, and so on. "God is supremely *holy* because He is *different.*"[11] "So then," says Barclay, "God chose the Christian to be different from other men." He continues:

> In point of fact, a Christian should be identifiable in the world. It must always be remembered that this difference on which Christ insists is not a difference which takes a man out of the world; it makes him different within the world. It should be possible to identify the Christian in the school, the shop, the factory, the office, the hospital, the ward, anywhere. And the difference is this—that the Christian lives and works and behaves, not as any human laws compel him so to do, but as the law of Christ compels him to do.[12] . . .
>
> The second word blameless is the Greek word *amomos.* It is a sacrificial word. Under the Mosaic law such an animal must be examined and inspected; if it has any blemish it must be rejected as unfit for an offering to God.
>
> This word *amomos* thinks of the whole life . . . as an offering to God. It thinks of taking every part of our life, our work, our pleasure, our sport, our home life, our personal relationships, and making them all such that they can be taken and offered to God. This word does not mean that the Christian must be respectable; it means that he must be perfect.[13]

Nevertheless, as precious as is the work of divine conversion, it is only the *beginning* of holiness. In his sermon on "Sin in Believers," Wesley comments on 1 Cor. 6:9-11 (KJV). "'Ye are washed,' says the Apostle, 'ye are sanctified;' namely, cleansed from . . . all . . . *outward* sin; and yet at the same time, in another sense of the word, they were unsanctified; . . . not *inwardly* cleansed from envy, evil surmising, partiality."[14]

Wesley's reference is to the apostle's strong words to the Corinthian church found in chapter 3. After declaring that "those who are spiritual discern all things" and "have the mind of Christ," he addresses the Corinthians directly:

---

11. Difference here carries the significance of *qodesh.* See chapter 1 of this study.

12. William Barclay, *Letters to the Galatians and Ephesians,* in *The Daily Study Bible* (Philadelphia: Westminster Press, 1958), 4.

13. Ibid., 19.

14. Wesley, *Works,* 5:150 (emphasis added).

Brothers and sisters, I could not speak to you as spiritual people, but rather as people of the flesh [*sarkinois*, "carnal"], as infants in Christ. I fed you with milk, not solid food, for you were not ready for solid food. Even now you are still not ready, for you are still of the flesh. For as long as there is jealousy and quarreling among you, are you not of the flesh, and behaving according to human inclinations? For when one says, "I belong to Paul," and another, "I belong to Apollos," are you not merely human? *(3:1-4)*.

The NIV renders *sarkinois* "worldly," a paraphrase that fits the context. Although the Corinthians were Paul's "brothers and sisters" in Christ, their spiritual infantilism, their jealousy and quarreling, their worldly standard of values, their party spirit were all reflective not of Christ, but of the unregenerate world. They were "yet carnal" (v. 3, KJV), behaving like those who were "merely human."

The problem of remaining inward sin calls for the deeper purging of *entire* sanctification. To this topic we now turn.

ENTIRE SANCTIFICATION—HOLINESS OF HEART

The term "entire sanctification" derives from the words of Paul's prayer for his Thessalonian converts: "May the God of peace himself sanctify you *entirely;* and may your spirit and soul and body be preserved sound and blameless at the coming of our Lord Jesus Christ. The one who calls you is faithful, and he will do this" (1 Thess. 5:23-24, emphasis added).

First Thessalonians is Paul's earliest surviving letter and most probably the oldest piece of Christian literature in existence. Of it George Lyons writes, "If vocabulary demonstrates anything, First Thessalonians must be a crucial document in any account of the Apostle's understanding of holiness. The frequent utilization of explicit holiness terminology in this brief letter is particularly noteworthy. Paul's benedictory prayer in 5:23-24 witnesses to the centrality of holiness in 1 Thess."[15]

---

15. George Lyons, "Modeling the Holiness Ethos: A Study Based on First Thessalonians," *Wesleyan Theological Journal* 30, No. 1 (spring 1995): 188-89. Lyons points out that "1 Thess. has a higher density of explicit holiness terms than any other Pauline letter. With 1,452 words in the Greek text (Nestle-Aland 26), 1 Thess. makes up only 4.6% of the total words in the Pauline corpus (32,440). Yet its explicit holiness words are more than twice the corpus average" (ibid.).

This prayer was offered for believers whose authentic Christianity was undeniable but whose faith stood in need of a further manifestation of God's sanctifying grace.

Everything Paul says about the Thessalonians witnesses to their genuine conversion from paganism to Christ (1:9-10). He clearly affirms their election to salvation (v. 4). "In spite of persecution" they had "received the word with joy inspired by the Holy Spirit," thereby becoming "an example to all the believers in Macedonia" (vv. 6-7).

The account continues in chapter 2, in which we see the warm bond of love that existed between this church and the apostle (vv. 1-12). Paul had been forced to leave Thessalonica because of a riot instigated by Jews offended by his preaching of Jesus as their crucified and risen Messiah (cf. Acts 17:1-10). After the apostle's departure, persecution against his converts occasioned his earnest but futile efforts to return to the beleaguered Thessalonians (vv. 13-20).

Chapter 3 opens with Paul's grave concern for the spiritual welfare of the church. When he "could bear it no longer," he dispatched Timothy "to strengthen and encourage [them] . . . so that no one would be shaken by these persecutions" (vv. 1-3). When Timothy returned with a report that the church was standing true, Paul dispatched this Epistle, expressing great relief: "For now we live, if you continue to stand fast in the Lord" (v. 8).

Nevertheless, despite this good news about the believers, Paul was "night and day praying exceedingly" for them, that he might see them face-to-face and *"perfect* that which [was] lacking in [their] faith" (vv. 9-10, KJV, emphasis added). The Greek verb translated "perfect" *(katartidzein)* in the KJV and NKJV comes from a root word meaning "to render complete" or "to fit together" and was used in the Gospels for the disciples' "mending" their nets (see Matt. 4:21). It is used here to mean to "supply" (RSV, NIV) what was lacking in order for the Thessalonians to fully discharge the functions for which God had designed them (cf. Eph. 4:12—"to equip the saints for the work of ministry").[16]

---

16. The NRSV translation "restore" is etymologically possible but does not fit the Thessalonian context. There is no evidence of spiritual loss on the part of the church, only of the need for completing their faith and experience.

Some scholars think Paul's prayer for a "face to face" visit has theological significance. Elsewhere the apostolic presence is linked with the desire to strengthen a church's faith (cf. Rom. 1:11). Having been abruptly removed from Thessalonica, Paul now longs to return in person to perfect their faith and experience.

Their imperfection was in two interrelated areas: in their *love* and in their *holiness* (3:11—4:12). In addressing these remaining deficiencies, the apostle is noticeably positive. He prays that their love may "increase and abound" (3:12) and that they might reflect "more and more" the sanctification to which they had been called (4:1-3). The specific injunctions that follow in chapter 4 spell out what it means to be holy in a pagan culture rife with immorality and seething with lustful passion. Lyons explains, "Paul's theological assumption is that Christian believers are different from pagans because of the character of their God. Pagans behave as they do because they do 'not know God' (4:5; cf. 2 Thess. 1:8; Gal. 4:9). Paul characterizes his moral teaching to the Thessalonians as an exhortation 'to live a life worthy of God who calls you into his kingdom and glory'" (2:11-12).[17]

He reminds these Christians, "This is the will of God, your *sanctification:* that you abstain from fornication" (4:3, NRSV, emphasis added). His instruction was not "Do as I say," but "Do as I do" (cf. 2:10; 1:5). God did not call the Thessalonians "to impurity but in *holiness*" (4:7, emphasis added). The use of *hagiasmos* here must be taken to mean that the Thessalonians had been called of God "in the realm of holiness." Therefore, anyone who rejects the call to *entire* sanctification "rejects not human authority but God, who also gives his Holy Spirit to you" (v. 8). Holiness is not a human dogma—it is the *Holy* Spirit's work that we reject at the danger of our own loss (see Heb. 12:14). Although self-idolatry is the root of sin, sexual immorality is its first and most obvious *fruit,* then and now (Rom. 1:21-27; Gal. 5:19). The holy life is a life of moral purity, the authentic mark of those who know God.

Paul's prayer in 5:23-24 is clearly "the summit of the Epistle." It repeats Paul's "prayer-wish" in 3:9-13 and pulls together all the vital elements of his instructions in 4:1—5:22, bringing the entire Epistle to a climax. Within this prayer we see a conscious and de-

---

17. Lyons, "Modeling the Holiness Ethos," 191-92.

liberate summary of all that has come before, in a broad and comprehensive benediction.[18]

The benedictory prayer is threefold, revealing the subject, the scope, and the surety of entire sanctification.

The Subject of Sanctification. "The emphasis is on God *himself* as the acting subject," says Daniel Spross.[19] While the Holy Spirit is the active Agent in effecting sanctification (2 Thess. 2:13), the Spirit does not operate without human cooperation, as Paul's exhortations to holy living clearly imply (1 Thess. 4:3-7). God's call to holiness can be rejected (4:8). The Spirit purifies, motivates, and enables holy living, but our personal participation is always presupposed (cf. Rom. 6:12-19).

Paul employs the aorist tense here *(hagiasai),* a usage that lends itself to the view that sanctification comes to completion (as the purification of our hearts and their perfection in love) within a process that, as we have seen, begins at conversion and, as this passage shows, is consummated at the return of Christ. God himself sanctifies us in our consecration, in our total separation from sin (2 Cor. 7:1), and in our self-abandonment to His working within us (Rom. 6:19). Leon Morris points out that "while there is a human element, in that a man must yield himself up to God (see 1 Thes. 4:4), yet the primary thing is the power of God which enables this to be made good."[20]

The Scope of Sanctification. "May the God of peace himself sanctify you *entirely,*" Paul prays. The compound adverb *holoteleis,* found only here in the New Testament, literally means "wholly and perfectly." "Carrying the sense of fullness, completeness, and totality," Spross explains, "the sanctification prayed for is an entire sanctification."[21] The NIV "through and through" follows Luther's German *durch und durch.*

Some scholars find a further implication in the adverb. Leon Morris observes, "The point is that the word is a compound of which the first part has the meaning of 'wholly.' If the second part is to have its proper significance we need something to bring out

18. Daniel Brett Spross, "Sanctification in the Thessalonian Epistles in a Canonical Context" (Ph.D. diss., Southern Baptist Seminary, 1987), 41-42.

19. Ibid., 43.

20. Leon Morris, *The First and Second Epistles to the Thessalonians,* in *The New International Commentary on the New Testament* (Grand Rapids: Wm. B. Eerdmans Publishing Co., 1959), 180.

21. Spross, "Sanctification," 46.

the thought of reaching one's proper end, the end for which one was made."[22] To be sanctified entirely, then, is to be scripturally "perfect" (i.e., to be attuned to our true "end" as persons fashioned in the divine image). What such "perfection" involves awaits our further exploration of this corollary doctrine.

Paul's prayer for the Thessalonians' sanctification includes the further petition for their preservation in holiness (5:23). Most scholars take the terms "spirit and soul and body" in a collective sense, signifying the totality of personality. Even though the apostle is using Greek terms, he is probably thinking like a Hebrew, like Jesus when He commanded that we love God with all our heart and soul and mind (Matt. 22:37) (i.e., with our whole being).[23] Entire sanctification is spiritual health restored and preserved by the power of God.

Thank God, we may be kept "blameless at the coming of our Lord Jesus Christ." Blamelessness is not to be taken, however, as something to be reserved for the moment of Christ's appearing. The word translated "kept" (tērētheiē) has a double connotation, including not only the idea of conservation and preservation, but also the idea of shielding, defending, and protecting. According to Wiles, the term "implies the continuation of that which already exists—so their present sanctification will be maintained at the parousia. The prayer that they may be kept wholly blameless at the parousia therefore implies their present sanctification as well."[24] Ernest Best concurs when he writes, "Holiness, of course, will not come suddenly into existence then unless they are now al-

---

22. Morris, *Thessalonians*, 188. The second half of the adverb, *teleis*, derives from the root *telos*, meaning "end," "goal," "purpose." D. Edmond Hiebert explains *holoteleis*: "wholly effecting the end, reaching the intended goal, hence has the force of no part being left untouched" (*A Call to Readiness: The Thessalonian Epistles* [Chicago: Moody Press, 1971], 251).

23. Cf. Robinson, *Christian Doctrine of Man*, 108-11. Don Wellman, however, finds in the Greek terms a "functional" trichotomy that seems to be implied elsewhere in Paul (e.g., in 1 Cor. 2:9-14, in which the human "spirit" [or *pneuma*] is the receptor of the Holy Spirit, and the *psychē* is the human "soul" we have in common with the lower animals, along with the "body" [*sōma*]). Wellman makes a strong case for this functional distinction between "spirit," "soul," and "body" as illuminating the experience of entire sanctification in 1 Thess. 5:23, while at the same time preserving the Hebrew understanding of the unity of personality (Don Wellman, *Today's Disciple* [Kansas City: Beacon Hill Press of Kansas City, 1996], 25-26, 40-61). See also Myron S. Augsburger, *Quench Not the Spirit*, 3-5.

24. Gordon Pitts Wiles, "The Function of Intercessory Prayer in Paul's Apostolic Ministry with Special Reference to the First Epistle to the Thessalonians" (Ph.D. diss., Yale University, 1965), 132; cited by Spross, "Thessalonians," 50.

ready 'holy' and seeking holiness. If believers are preserved in the Day of Judgment, this will imply preservation until then."[25]

The Surety of Sanctification. "The one who calls you is faithful, and he will do this." Like justifying faith, sanctifying faith gives glory to God, being fully persuaded that what God has promised He is able also to perform (see Rom. 4:21, KJV).

"But what is that faith whereby we are sanctified;—saved from sin, and perfected in love?" Wesley asks. He then gives an answer well worth our pondering:

> It is a divine evidence and conviction, First, that God hath promised it in the Holy Scripture. . . . It is a divine evidence and conviction, Secondly, that what God hath promised he is able to perform. . . . It is, Thirdly, a divine evidence and conviction that he is able and willing to do it now. . . . To this confidence, that God is both able and willing to sanctify us now, there needs to be added one thing more,—a divine evidence and conviction that he doeth it. . . . If you seek it by faith, you may expect it *as you are;* and if as you are, then expect it *now.* . . . Expect it *by faith,* expect it *as you are,* and expect it *now!*[26]

CHRISTIAN PERFECTION

Barclay's definition of the word for "perfect" in the New Testament—the Greek *teleios*—demonstrates that the term is functional (see Appendix). Christians are "perfect" as they are conformed to their *telos,* their divinely intended "end." When this is the case, they are realizing their raison d'être, their "reason for being." To illustrate, my fountain pen is "perfect"—if it *writes.* Filled with ink, it performs the task for which it was designed and made.

"What is the chief end of man?" is the first question in the Westminster Shorter Catechism. "Answer: The chief end of man is to glorify God and enjoy Him forever." "Therefore, whether you eat or drink, or whatever you do, do all to the glory of

25. Ernst Best, *A Commentary on the First and Second Epistles to the Thessalonians* (New York: Harper and Row, 1971), 182; cited by Spross, "Thessalonians," 51.
26. John Wesley, "The Scripture Way of Salvation," in *Works,* 6:52-53.

God." So Paul urges in 1 Cor. 10:31 (NKJV). "In all things what-ever," Wesley comments, "keep the glory of God in view, and steadily pursue in all this one end of your being, the planting or advancing the vital knowledge and love of God, first in your own soul, then in all mankind."[27]

Both Wesley and Adam Clarke had problems with the term "perfect." Wesley considered letting it drop; however, since "perfect" is a scriptural word, it cannot be discarded. Clarke said, "Had I a better name, I would gladly adopt and use it. . . . But there is none in our language, which I deplore as an incon-venience and loss." Instead of discarding the term, Clarke, lin-guist as he was, focused on the central idea of *teleios:* fitness for purpose. So in his *Christian Theology* we read: "As God requires every man to love him with all his heart, soul, mind, and strength, and his neighbour as himself, then he is a perfect man that does so; he answers to the end for which God made him."[28]

After the glory of God, and subordinated to it, is God's eternal purpose in Christ to transform every justified believer into the likeness of Jesus. "We know that in everything God works for good with those who love him, who are called ac-cording to his purpose. For those whom he foreknew he also predestined to be conformed to the image of his Son, in order that he might be the first-born among many brethren" (Rom. 8:28-29, RSV). And the Father's eternal purpose for us is worked out in time as we expose ourselves to His radiant glory reflected in Christ: "And all of us, with unveiled faces, seeing the glory of the Lord as though reflected in a mirror, are being transformed into the same image from one degree of glory to another; for this comes from the Lord, the Spirit" (2 Cor. 3:18).

Two passages, one from Paul and the other from John, fur-ther illustrate the meaning of Christian perfection.

First, Paul's personal testimony:

> But whatever things were gain to me, those things I have counted as loss for the sake of Christ. . . . that I may know Him and the power of His resurrection and the fel-lowship of His sufferings, being conformed to His death;

---

27. Wesley, *Notes,* 617.

28. Adam Clarke, *Christian Theology,* ed. Samuel Dunn (New York: T. Mason and G. Lane, 1840), 246.

in order that I may attain to the resurrection from the dead. Not that I have already obtained it or *have already become perfect* [*ēdē teteleiōmai,* "already have been perfected"], but I press on so that I may lay hold of that for which also I was laid hold of by Christ Jesus. Brethren, I do not regard myself as having laid hold of it yet; *but one thing I do:* forgetting what lies behind and reaching forward to what lies ahead, I press on toward the goal for the prize of the upward call of God in Christ Jesus. *Let us therefore, as many as are perfect [teleioi],* have this same attitude; and if in anything you have a different attitude, God will reveal that also to you; however, let us keep living by that same standard to which we have attained *(Phil. 3:7, 10-16, NASB, emphasis added).*

Paul's testimony and admonition illustrate the tension between the "already" and the "not yet" of Christian experience in "this present time" between Pentecost and the Parousia (cf. Rom. 8:17-23).

The scriptural evidence that Paul was among the "perfect" was his frank and unabashed confession, "Not that I . . . already have been perfected." The ripest saints are "but Christians in the making" (E. Stanley Jones). As Wesley points out, "There is a difference between one that is *perfect* and one that is *perfected.* The one is fitted for the race (verse 15), the other, ready to receive the prize."[29]

Neither Paul nor the most mature believer has yet attained to perfect Christlikeness. This perfection is reserved for the resurrection (Phil. 3:20-21). By the grace of God, however, ordinary believers may enjoy with Paul the singleness of purpose that permits the Spirit to carry us steadily forward "toward the goal for the prize of the heavenly call of God in Christ Jesus" (v. 14). On this topic P. T. Forsyth wrote, sounding quite Wesleyan, "Our perfection, therefore, is not to be flawless, but to be in tune with our redeemed destiny in Christ."[30]

The second key passage is from 1 John, in which the apostle of love writes, "If we love one another, God lives in us, and his

---

29. Wesley, *Notes,* 735.
30. P. T. Forsyth, *Christian Perfection* (London: Hodder and Stoughton, n.d.), 111.

love is perfected in us. . . . God is love, and those who abide in
love abide in God, and God abides in them. Love has been perfected among us in this: that we may have boldness on the day of
judgment, because as he is, so are we in this world. There is no
fear in love, but perfect love casts out fear; for fear has to do with
punishment, and whoever fears has not yet reached perfection in
love" (4:12, 16-18; cf. 2:5).

All the Greek verbs and nouns in this passage pertaining to
perfection derive from *telos*. God's love, incarnate in the Son,
reached its goal (accomplished its purpose) in Christ's atoning
sacrifice for our sins (4:9-10). God lives in us, and "his love is perfected in us" (accomplishes its purpose in us) when we truly "love
one another" (v. 12; 2:5-6). John sums up perfect love when he
adds, "Love has been perfected among us in this: that we may
have boldness on the day of judgment, because as he is, so are we
in this world" (4:17).[31] God's love, first incarnate in Christ, is now
incarnate in us.

"When love comes, fear goes," Barclay writes. "Fear is the
characteristic emotion of someone who expects to be punished."[32]
And Wesley notes, "No slavish fear can exist where love reigns;
because such fear hath torment—and so is inconsistent with the
happiness of love." For him, four classes of persons are revealed
in this passage: "A natural man has neither fear nor love; one that
is awakened, fear without love; a babe in Christ, love and fear; a
father in Christ, love without fear."[33]

God's perfect love producing perfect love in us, casting out
the tormenting fear of judgment and making us Christlike—this is
the essence of Christian perfection.

THE NEW COVENANT FULFILLED

We can do no better to conclude this chapter than with Paul's
demonstration of the surpassing glory of the new covenant, when
he writes in 2 Corinthians: "Now if the ministry of death, chiseled
in letters on stone tablets, came in glory so that the people of Israel
could not gaze at Moses' face because of the glory of his face, a

31. The pronoun *ekeinos* ("that one"), occurring five times in 1 John, refers to Christ.
32. William Barclay, *The Letters from John and Jude,* in *The Daily Study Bible* (Philadelphia: Westminster Press, rev. 1976), 98.
33. Wesley, *Notes,* 915.

glory now set aside, how much more will the ministry of the Spirit come in glory?" (3:7-8).

As mediator of the old covenant, Moses ascended Mount Sinai, where for 40 days he had face-to-face communion with God. Descending from the mountain, he placed a veil on his face to hide the glory that bathed his countenance. Moses here represents a select company of Old Testament worthies who were granted the exceptional privilege of a sanctifying communion with the Lord. Paul vividly contrasts this privileged holiness of the Old Testament with the universal holiness now available to those who worship God through Christ. "And all of us," he assures us who know God under the terms of the new covenant. "*And all of us*, with unveiled faces, seeing the glory of the Lord as though reflected in a mirror, are being transfigured into the same image from one degree of glory to another; for this comes from the Lord, the Spirit" (v. 18, emphasis added).

In Old Testament times a spiritual aristocracy existed; a few were privileged to ascend the mount of spiritual transfiguration—Enoch, Abraham, Elijah, Moses, Isaiah. But in the gospel dispensation we enjoy a spiritual democracy; "all of us" may climb the mount of face-to-face communion and be transfigured into the likeness of "Christ, who is the image of God" (4:4).

Furthermore, in contrast to the *fading* glory that eventually disappeared from Moses' countenance, we may know a *progressively increasing* glory. "We are not like Moses, who veiled his face to prevent the Israelites from seeing its fading glory. . . . But all of us who are Christians have no veils on our faces, but reflect like mirrors the glory of the Lord . . . in ever-increasing splendour into his own image" (3:13, 18, PHILLIPS).[34]

The crowning ministry of the Spirit in the new covenant is directed toward a metamorphosis of the believer into Christlikeness. This transfiguration of the Christian believer is the distinctive feature of New Testament sanctification.

---

34. The Greek expression may be rendered in this way as well as how NRSV translated it; cf. KJV, RSV, NIV. When over a lifetime we expose ourselves to God's glory mirrored in Christ, our very countenances also are transfigured by that glory (cf. 4:3-6).

9

Sanctification and Perfection in Hebrews

O ur task in this chapter is to explore the teaching of sanctification and the related doctrine of perfection in the Epistle to the Hebrews, one of the major books of the New Testament. Admittedly, for the Western mind Hebrews is one of the most difficult of the New Testament; the author does not develop his theme systematically but treats Scripture in rabbinic fashion as a Jewish *maschal*, a parable or mystery that awaits explanation. Old Testament characters and incidents are seen as types of Christ and the gospel, temporary foreshadowings of the fulfillment that has now taken place once and for all in the Christian gospel. It is this historical perspective—seeing the age of anticipation as foreshadowing the age of fulfillment—that provides the clue to the author's interpretation of the Old Testament.[1] The purpose of Hebrews accordingly, says F. F. Bruce, is "to establish the finality of the gospel by contrast with all that went before it (more particularly, by contrast with the Levitical cultus), as the way of perfection, the way which alone leads men to God without any interruption of access.

---

1. Hebrews, therefore, is not to be taken as Platonic idealism (the earthly tabernacle being the "shadow of heavenly things" [8:5, KJV] understood as metaphysical forms in heaven) but as "eschatological idealism" (the earthly tabernacle and all therein being rather "a shadow of good things *to come*" [10:1, KJV, emphasis added; cf. 9:9]).

He establishes the finality of Christianity by establishing the supremacy of Christ, in His person and in His work."[2]

The origins of the Book of Hebrews are "shrouded in mystery."[3] Interestingly, in recent years the theory has been advanced that Hebrews reflects a position advocated by Hellenistic Jews in one of the Roman house churches that stood in a direct line from the sermon of Stephen recorded in Acts 7. William Manson proposed this theory in 1950, finding at least eight subjects treated quite similarly by both Stephen and Hebrews. Although the particulars of Manson's argument are in dispute among scholars, Brevard Childs believes that his theory "cannot be simply dismissed. In my judgment," he says, "his ability to bring the letter of Hebrews out of its position of isolation within the New Testament and to show important lines of theological connection with Acts is more significant than his detailed historical reconstruction which remains quite hypothetical."[4]

Stephen, a Hellenistic Jew from outside Palestine, seems to have been the first in the primitive Church to see clearly, and to declare boldly, the passing of the Mosaic law with its institutions and the finality of Christ and the gospel. Brought before the Sanhedrin (Acts 6:12) by "those from Cilicia and Asia" (v. 9), Stephen was charged with "saying things against this holy place [the Tem-

---

2. F. F. Bruce, *The Epistle to the Hebrews*, in *The New International Commentary on the New Testament*, ed. F. F. Bruce (Grand Rapids: Wm. B. Eerdmans Publishing Co., 1973), lii.

3. Modern scholarship has not advanced beyond Origen, who said, "Who wrote Hebrews, God only knows." The author was a second-generation Christian who was well versed in the Greek of the Septuagint, the master of a fine rhetorical style completely different from that of Paul. Of him it could be said that "he was an eloquent man, well-versed in the scriptures" (Acts 18:24, a reference to Apollos, who Luther believed wrote the book). Hebrews differs from other New Testament letters in that while it does not begin like an Epistle, it ends like one. Its conclusion (13:22-25) sounds Pauline, but even here Timothy is referred to as the author's "brother," not his "son," as Paul would have written (cf. 1 Tim. 1:2 et al.).

4. Brevard S. Childs, *The New Testament as Canon: An Introduction* (Valley Forge, Pa.: Trinity Press International, 1994), 412. Alongside the fact that the earliest Christianity in Rome was an intra-Jewish phenomenon, a recent scholar writes, "there are signs of a radical Hellenistic Christianity, also of early origin . . . preaching a law-free gospel to Gentiles and God-worshippers associated with the synagogues. With the expulsion of Jewish Christian leaders, it may be that more radical forms of Gentile Christianity developed in the house-churches in the period prior to the succession of Nero" (William S. Campbell, "The Rule of Faith," *Pauline Theology III, Romans*, 265-66).

ple] and the law. . . . We have heard him say," they claimed, "that this Jesus of Nazareth will destroy this place and will change the customs that Moses handed on to us" (vv. 13-14).

The charge presented, the high priest asked Stephen, "Are these things so?" (7:1). Rather than giving a direct answer to this question, Stephen defended his position with an elaborate address to the Sanhedrin. His defense was so masterful in its use of the Old Testament, so penetrating in its insights, and Stephen himself so obviously anointed by the Spirit of God (6:8) that at its climax his accusers were forced either to confess their sins or kill their accuser.

Though Stephen did not give a direct answer to the charge raised against him, his sermon did indeed point to a setting aside of Temple worship and the Mosaic system. His argument was threefold: *(a)* God's revelation had never been confined to the Temple (7:2-50); *(b)* Old Testament revelation was progressive and pointed unmistakably to Christ; Moses himself had said, "God will raise up a prophet for you from your own people as he raised me up" (v. 37; Deut. 18:15, 18). *(c)* A survey of sacred history showed that these Jews were following in the steps of their forefathers who rejected the prophets, having betrayed and murdered "the Righteous One" whom the prophets had foretold (vv. 51-53).

Beyond question, Stephen did see the old wineskins of Judaism bursting under the ferment of Christ's Spirit. Saul from Tarsus, a leading city of Cilicia, would certainly have been one of those who "stood up and argued with Stephen" (6:9). According to Acts, the enraged witnesses who stoned Stephen "laid their coats at the feet of a young man named Saul" (7:58) who, Luke adds, "approved of their killing him" (8:1). How Stephen's position may have impacted the young Saul we can only speculate.

This much we do know, that in his letter to the Colossians Paul advocates a position reminiscent of Stephen's argument and sounding like Hebrews. Opposing an incipient gnosticism in Colossae, the apostle declares that God, in the death of Christ, had indeed "nail[ed] . . . to the cross" the Law with its "legal demands." "Therefore," he urges, "do not let anyone condemn you in matters of food and drink or of observing festivals, new moons, or sabbaths. These," he concludes, "are only a shadow of what is to come, but the substance belongs to Christ" (Col. 2:14, 16-17). "Here it is asserted," Rordorf observes, "that together with all the other festivals and food laws the Jewish Sabbath was also fulfilled in Christ, and in such a way that the real meaning of the Old Testament ordinances was for the first time made plain in Christ."[5] It is a bold picture. Now that the "substance" that cast these shadows has come, the Jewish Sabbath along with the Mosaic taboos are no longer binding for Christian believers.

The above passage in Colossians, while not contradictory to Paul's theology, does not represent the position he argues in his magnum opus, the Epistle to the Romans. There, as we have already seen, he demonstrates the *emergence* of Christianity from the Mosaic system. The writer of Hebrews, on the other hand, argues his position from the idea of Col. 2:17 (that the Law only foreshadows Christ and the gospel) to show the *finality* of Christianity as a world faith, in the context of which, according to Chilton and Neusner, "the entire scriptural inheritance of Israel will be reread." In this rereading of Scripture, "in light of its systemic message," these scholars observe, "a self-evident truth will impose itself on the details of the ancient narratives and prophecies and laws, and the whole will emerge renewed. . . . The power is [thereby] generated to impose upon the received Torah an entirely fresh set of meanings, new issues, unanticipated possibilities."[6]

In Romans, Paul sees Christ as *reestablishing* the Mosaic covenant as "the law of faith" that also *fulfills* its "just requirement" of love. The writer of Hebrews, however, declares that Christ has rendered Torah, *as a means of salvation, obsolete:* "He abolishes the first in order to establish the second. And it is by God's will that we have been sanctified through the offering of the body of Jesus Christ once for all" (10:9-10).[7] On these grounds

---

5. Willy Rordorf, *Sunday: The History of the Day of Rest and Worship in the Earliest Centuries of the Christian Church*, trans. A. A. K. Graham (Philadelphia: Westminster Press, 1968), 101.

6. Chilton and Neusner, *Judaism in the New Testament*, 160.

7. Both Paul and the author of Hebrews, however, agreed that God, in providing sanctification through His Son, has accomplished what Torah could not; it is only in their *perspectives* that the two differ. "Moreover," as Childs points out, "a remarkable feature of the letter [to the Hebrews] is that it reflects no interest in the contemporary Judaism of the period" (*New Testament as Canon,* 414). In light of the tragic and embarrassing story of the

Chilton and Neusner title the Epistle to the Hebrews "From Salvation to Sanctification."[8]

"One of the chief contributions to our theme found in Hebrews," Purkiser writes, "is the linking of perfection and sanctification."[9] E. C. Blackman summarizes the teaching of Hebrews at this point:

> The main theme of the Letter to the Hebrews is the work of Christ as priest and sacrifice. It can be stated as the provision of "purification for sins" (1:3), implying the imagery of sacrifice, as in 2:17b; 5:1 and in the whole central argument of chs. 5—10. But the metaphor changes to that of sanctification when Christ is referred to as the sanctifier (2:11; 7:26-27; 13:12). These metaphors are used interchangeably, as we see from 9:11-14—a peak point in the argument—and 9:22-23. The point of contrast here between Christian and Jewish me-

---

church's persecution of Jews through the centuries, those who find in Hebrews the final revelation of the gospel for the world must balance its message with what Paul writes in Rom. 9—11 (esp. 11:28). To draw anti-Semitic conclusions from Hebrews is not only to misunderstand its true message (see Chilton and Neusner) but, even more seriously, to make mockery of the holiness Christ died to provide (10:10; 13:12) and which the book exhorts the people of God to pursue and exemplify if they would see Him (chap. 12).

8. Chilton and Neusner, *Judaism in the New Testament*, 175.

9. W. T. Purkiser, *Exploring Christian Holiness*, 1:196. In Hebrews God is the One who "perfects" the Son (2:10) as "the pioneer and perfecter of our faith" (12:2). The verb "perfect" *(teleiōsai)* is important in the author's vocabulary. In its verbal form it occurs 14 times in Hebrews—as an adverb *(teleiōs)* once, as an adjective *(teleios)* twice, as a noun *(teleiotēs, teleiōsis, or teleiotēs)* three times. "Depending on its context," says Buchanan, "this verb means to perfect, accomplish, fulfill, complete, or become mature. In a relative sense it usually describes a person who was fully cleansed from sin, qualified for full membership in a religious order. . . . Other terms that are closely allied to the word 'perfect' are 'sanctified' and 'worthy.' A person judged worthy of full admission into a sect was considered 'perfect'" (George Wesley Buchanan, *To the Hebrews*, in *The Anchor Bible* [Garden City, N.Y.: Doubleday and Co., 1976], 31). "Although he was a Son, [Jesus] learned obedience through what he suffered" and thereby was "made perfect" and "became the source of salvation for all who obey him" (5:8-9). The essence of this salvation is our "holiness" (12:10) or "sanctification" (v. 14). These latter terms all derive from the verbal form *hagiadzein* ("to sanctify") and occur eight times; other synonymous terms and concepts, however, are too numerous to list.

diatory rites is that whereas the latter effected outward sanctification, Christ offers an inward one ("conscience"; v. 14b) which fits men for God's service, or, more precisely, for the sharing of God's own holiness (*hagiotes;* 12:10), which is the greatest need of man. The vision of God is not possible for the unholy (12:14). "Sanctification" is a synonym for "perfection," a key word in this letter (2:10; 10:14; 11:39—12:2). This sanctification or perfection is due to Christ, who identified himself with man, made man fit for God's presence, and pioneered a way thither as "forerunner" (6:20; 10:19 ff; cf. 3:1a).[10]

With the preceding observations as background, we must now examine more closely the development of the central theme of this letter.

INTRODUCTION: GOD'S FINAL REVELATION IN HIS SON (1:1-4)

We read:

Long ago God spoke to our ancestors in many and various ways by the prophets, but in these last days he has spoken to us by a Son, whom he appointed heir of all things, through whom he also created the worlds. He is the reflection of God's glory and the exact imprint of God's very being, and he sustains all things by his powerful word. When he had made purification for sins, he sat down at the right hand of the Majesty on high, having become as much superior to angels as the name he inherited is more excellent than theirs (*vv. 1-4*).

"He has spoken." This statement is basic to the entire argument of Hebrews, as indeed it is to the Christian faith. God has not remained silent, shrouded in thick darkness, leaving His creatures to grope after Him, "if haply they might feel after him, and find him" (Acts 17:27, KJV); no, He "has spoken to us" His revealing, life-giving, redeeming word, and in His light we see light. He has spoken in two stages: first to our fathers through the prophets, and

---

10. E. C. Blackman, *The Interpreter's Dictionary of the Bible,* ed. George Arthur Buttrick (New York and Nashville: Abingdon Press, 1962), 4:211-12.

finally in His Son. These two stages correspond to the Old and New Testaments respectively, in a progressive revelation. Bruce explains, "The progression is from promise to fulfillment, as is made abundantly clear in the course of this epistle: the men of faith in Old Testament days did not in their lifetime experience the fulfillment of the divine promise in which they had trusted, 'because, with us in mind, God had made a better plan, that only in company with us should they reach their perfection'" (11:40, NEB).[11]

"This Son, in the fulness of time, was manifested in the flesh," Adam Clarke writes, "that he might complete all vision and prophecy, supply all that was wanting to perfect the great scheme of revelation for the instruction of the world, and then die to put away sin by the sacrifice of himself."[12]

Three things that the author here says about the Son are pertinent for the doctrine of holiness:

First, Jesus is "the reflection [or "effulgence"] of God's glory" (v. 3). The Greek word signifies "the radiation of a light flowing from a luminous body."[13] "The God who said, 'Let light shine out of darkness' . . . has shone in our hearts to give the light of the knowledge of the glory of God in the face of Jesus Christ" (2 Cor. 4:6).

Second, Jesus is "the exact imprint of God's very being" (v. 3). Just as a coin bears the image and superscription of the die with which it is stamped, so the Son of God "bears the very stamp of his nature" (RSV). The Greek word *charactēr*, found only here in the New Testament, expresses this truth even more emphatically than *eikōn*, employed elsewhere to denote Christ as the "image" of God (2 Cor. 4:4; Col. 1:15). "What God essentially is, is made manifest in Christ," says Bruce. "To see Christ is to see what the Father is like."[14]

Finally, "When he had made purification for sins, he sat down at the right hand of the Majesty on high" (v. 3). Wiley understands this to mean that Christ has made "the expiation of sins by

11. Bruce, *Hebrews*, 2.
12. Adam Clarke, *A Commentary on the Old and New Testaments* (New York: Methodist Book Concern, n.d.), 6:685.
13. H. Orton Wiley, *The Epistle to the Hebrews*, ed. Morris Weigelt, rev. ed. (Kansas City: Beacon Hill Press of Kansas City, 1984), 38.
14. Bruce, *Hebrews*, 6.

blotting them out. . . . He is Priest and Sacrifice, Altar and Incense, and everything needed to make full atonement." He continues,

> The language in which this fact of expiation is presented is evidently a reference to the purification by sacrifice under the Levitical economy and is a fulfillment of that which was accomplished in symbol on the great Day of Atonement. This purification, therefore, is a provision and potency for the taking away of sin, whether in act or nature. The provision for purging or cleansing away sin was completed once for all by Christ's vicarious sacrifice on earth and before His ascent to heaven.[15]

Now, in His human nature as man—and continuing as man—Jesus has "sat down at the right hand of the Majesty on high," *finishing* His work of atonement. "No priest under the old covenant ministered except in a standing position," Wiley points out, "for his work was never finished."[16] "But when Christ had offered for all time a single sacrifice for sins, 'he sat down at the right hand of God.' . . . For by a single offering he has perfected for all time those who are sanctified" (10:12, 14).

In this prologue, Bruce notes, Christ is seen in His threefold role as Prophet, Priest, and King. "He is the Prophet through whom God has spoken His final word to men; He is the Priest who has accomplished a perfect work of cleansing for His people's sins; He is the King who sits enthroned in the place of chief honor alongside the Majesty on high."[17]

THE SANCTIFIER AND THE SANCTIFIED (2:10-11)

This key passage (2:8-11) must be interpreted in the light of its broader context (1:5—2:9). First, the author declares the *deity* of Jesus as God's Son and cites seven Old Testament passages in support of his claim (1:5-14). His first quotation is Ps. 2:7: "You are my son; today I have begotten you," a verse understood within Judaism as a messianic promise. The seventh and last quotation is from Ps. 110:1: "The LORD says to my lord, 'Sit at

---

15. Wiley, *Hebrews*, 42.
16. Ibid., 43.
17. Bruce, *Hebrews*, 8.

my right hand until I make your enemies your footstool.'" Jesus himself, disputing with the Pharisees just prior to His crucifixion, quoted this psalm as a personal claim of divine Sonship (Matt. 22:44). And in Acts 2:34-35 Simon Peter, concluding his sermon on the Day of Pentecost, quoted Ps. 110:1 as supporting his claim "that God has made this Jesus, whom you crucified, both Lord and Christ" (v. 36, NKJV).

After asserting Jesus' deity, the author then declares His *humanity*. He who is the Son of *God* is likewise the Son of *Man*, a true human being "now crowned with glory and honor because of the suffering of death, so that by the grace of God he might taste death for everyone" (2:9). In His incarnation Jesus "did not come to help angels, but the descendants of Abraham. Therefore," our author tells us, "he had to become like his brothers and sisters in every respect, so that he might be a merciful and faithful high priest in the service of God, to make a sacrifice of atonement for the sins of the people. Because he himself was tested by what he suffered, he is able to help those who are being tested" (vv. 16-18).

It is within this context—the understanding of Jesus as the incarnate Son of God—that we must now examine our key passage: "It is fitting that God, for whom and through whom all things exist, in bringing many children to glory, should make the pioneer of their salvation perfect through sufferings. For the one who sanctifies and those who are sanctified all have one Father. For this reason Jesus is not ashamed to call them brothers and sisters" (vv. 10-11).

The "so great a salvation" the gospel proclaims was not only "declared at first through the Lord" (v. 3) but was procured for us by Him through His passion. Jesus is the "pioneer" of our salvation. The Greek word *archēgos* means "one who has blazed a trail." As the Pioneer of our salvation, Jesus has blazed the trail to God for us to follow. But how was He enabled to do so? The Greek verb signifying "to make perfect" is *teleioun*, which means to carry out the purpose or plan for which a thing is designed. Applied to Jesus here, Barclay says, the writer of Hebrews is saying that through His suffering and death Jesus was made fully able to the task of being the Pioneer of our salvation.[18] "He is the Savior who blazed the

---

18. William Barclay, *The Letter to the Hebrews*, in *The Daily Study Bible* (Philadelphia: Westminster Press, 1957), 19-20.

trail of salvation along which alone God's 'many sons' could be brought to glory," Bruce explains.[19] Human beings, created by God for His glory, were prevented by sin from attaining that glory, until the Son of Man came and by His death opened up a new way by which they might reach the goal for which they were made. As our Representative and Forerunner, Jesus has now entered into the presence of God to secure *our* entrance there. Bruce then asks, "But what is meant by His being made 'perfect' through His sufferings? If the Son of God is the effulgence of His Father's glory and the very impress of His being, how can He be thought of as falling short of perfection?"

The answer is this: the perfect Son of God has become His people's perfect Savior, opening up their way to God; and in order to become that, He must endure suffering and death. The pathway of perfection that His people must tread must first be trodden by the Pathfinder; only so could He be their adequate Representative and High Priest in the presence of God.[20]

"For the one who sanctifies and those who are sanctified all have one Father," our passage says. "For this reason Jesus is not ashamed to call them brothers and sisters" (v. 11). The Sanctifier and the sanctified, having one Father, are in some sense "all of one piece." Our Lord, as at once Son of God and Son of Man, is of the Father. So are we. Therefore it may be said that the Son of God and the sons of men equally have one common origin: both have one Father. But there the equality ends. As the "only begotten" (John 1:14, KJV) and eternal Son, Jesus is of the very essence of the Father. We humans are sons and daughters of God by rebirth of the Spirit (John 3:3-8) and adoption into God's family (Gal. 4:4-7). Jesus' Sonship is original and infinite; ours is derived and finite. However, the being of both is from God.[21]

We humans, however, fell into sin and forfeited the divine image. Fellowship was broken, and depravity spread over the entire race like a dread disease. "It was fitting," therefore, for God's Son to partake of our *natural* condition in order that He might deliver us from our *sinful* condition. "As His unity with us made

---

19. Bruce, *Hebrews*, 43.
20. Ibid.
21. Wiley, *Hebrews*, 83.

possible the Incarnation," says Wiley, "so also our unity with Him makes possible our spiritual restoration."[22]

We have before us the statement that the Sanctifier and the sanctified both have one Father. We must now examine the meaning of the terms relating to their "sanctification." The Greek verb *hagiadzein*, "to sanctify," is used in Hebrews in both an objective and subjective sense. Objectively, it defines the work that God has done for us in expiating our sin or in making atonement. It is this objective and provisional aspect of the Atonement that is generally referred to as "the finished work of Christ." In agreement with all the major interpreters of this letter, Wiley writes,

> We must understand, therefore, that the word "sanctify" as used here refers primarily to the objective work of Christ in the expiation of sin—the Atonement which finds its ultimate issue in the divine declaration that "the blood of Jesus Christ his Son cleanseth us from all sin" (1 John 1:7 [KJV]). It denotes the total act by which Christ separates His people from a life in sin and places them in the sphere of a new life which rests upon His atoning death and His resurrection unto life.[23]

Yet this is not the full sense of the word "sanctification," since it also has a subjective aspect. Jesus has indeed, by His death, provided an atonement *for* us; His blood, however, also effects a change *within* us. "Purification is the basis of sanctification," David Peterson explains. "By his sovereign action in Christ, God sets apart and binds to himself those who have been purified from the defilement of sin. This objective, consecrating work of God has profound implications for the attitude and behaviour of those who believe."[24] The "sanctified" are those who have had their conscience purified "from dead works to worship the living God" (9:14) and in whose hearts and minds, under the new covenant, the law of God has been written, enabling them to know and serve

---

22. Ibid.

23. Ibid., 84.

24. David Peterson, *Possessed by God: A New Testament Theology of Sanctification and Holiness*, in *New Studies in Biblical Theology*, ed. D. A. Carson (Grand Rapids: Wm. B. Eerdmans Publishing Co., 1995), 34.

Him in the power of a new life (10:10-18). Richard S. Taylor writes, "Jesus, the God-man, by the Incarnation, now shares with man the fatherhood of God as Creator; by sanctifying His own disciples He shares with them the holiness of the Father. A family likeness is thereby established. This likeness to God through sanctification is the deeper meaning of sonship in the NT."[25]

"For this reason," we read, "Jesus is not ashamed to call [us] brothers and sisters" (2:11). Despite the infinite, qualitative difference between Jesus as "the Father's only Son" (John 1:14, margin) and us as His children by rebirth and adoption, He considered it no disparagement of himself to call us His "brothers and sisters," since through His atoning death He has made us like himself. "It is very evident therefore," says Wiley, "that He who leads many sons to glory does so by sanctifying them, and that the only way to glory for the sons of God is through sanctification."[26] "Sanctification is glory begun," Bruce observes, "and glory is sanctification completed."[27]

THE REST OF FAITH (3:1—4:11)

The New Testament bears repeated witness to the Christian understanding of Christ's redemptive work as the new exodus. Jesus is seen in Luke as speaking of "his [exodos], which he was about to accomplish at Jerusalem" (9:31) by His death. In 1 Corinthians Paul speaks of "our paschal lamb, Christ, [who] has been sacrificed" (5:7), of Israel's passage through the Red Sea as prefiguring Christian baptism, and of their eating of manna and drinking from the rock in the wilderness as anticipating our partaking of Christ in the Lord's Supper (10:1-4). The passage before us now takes the Exodus typology one step farther: As God's deliverance of ancient Israel from Egypt prefigured the new exodus, His promise of bringing them into the land of Canaan foreshadows the rest of faith remaining for the people of God (4:1-11).

In Jude we read that "the Lord, having saved the people out of the land of Egypt, afterward destroyed those who did not believe" (v. 5, NKJV). This solemn fact provides the starting point for

25. Richard S. Taylor, *The Epistle to the Hebrews, Beacon Bible Commentary* (Kansas City: Beacon Hill Press of Kansas City, 1967), 10:37.

26. Wiley, *Hebrews*, 82.

27. Bruce, *Hebrews*, 45.

our author's warning to his hearers that they not miss God's promised rest (3:7-11). Quoting Ps. 95, he urges, "Today, if you hear his voice, do not harden your hearts as in the rebellion" (3:15). The immediate reference here is to Num. 14. Another passage in Deuteronomy, however, is pertinent. We are told there that on the border of the land Moses instructed the people what to say to their children when they asked the reason they must observe the Law. They were to tell them, "We were Pharaoh's slaves in Egypt, but the LORD brought us out of Egypt with a mighty hand. . . . *He brought us out from there in order to bring us in, to give us the land that he promised on oath to our ancestors*" (6:21, 23, emphasis added).

Accordingly, after entering into covenant with the Lord at Sinai, Israel set out immediately, under Moses' leadership, for the land of Canaan. Arriving at the border of the Promised Land, Moses sent out men from the 12 tribes "to spy out the land of Canaan" (Num. 13:1-24). When the majority brought back an unfavorable report (vv. 32-33), the people revolted against the leadership of Moses and even threatened to choose a new leader and return to Egypt (14:1-10). "And the LORD said to Moses, 'How long will this people despise me? And how long will they refuse to believe in me, in spite of all the signs that I have done among them?'" (v. 11). In response to Moses' intercession on their behalf, the Lord graciously forgave them (vv. 13-25); but He said, "None of the people who have seen my glory and the signs that I did in Egypt and in the wilderness, and yet have tested me these ten times and have not obeyed my voice, shall see the land that I swore to give to their ancestors; none of those who despised me shall see it" (vv. 22-23). Just the same, over Moses' protest these rebels "presumed to go up to the heights of the hill country, even though the ark of the covenant of the LORD, and Moses, had not left the camp" (v. 44). The result was predictable: they were utterly routed and scattered by the Amalekites and Canaanites (v. 45). As a consequence, they wandered around Kadesh-barnea for 38 years, "until the entire generation of warriors had perished from the camp, as the LORD had sworn concerning them" (Deut. 2:14). Of those who were already full-grown men when they left Egypt, none except Caleb and Joshua survived to enter Canaan.

In a majestic call to worship and obedience, the psalmist some 500 years later warns his contemporaries not to harden their hearts, lest disaster also overtake *them*, as it did their ancestors (Ps. 95). And now the author of Hebrews warns *his* generation, after another span of centuries, "Take care, brothers and sisters, that none of you may have an evil, unbelieving heart that turns away from the living God . . . so that none of you may be hardened by the deceitfulness of sin. For we have become partners of Christ, if only we hold our first confidence firm to the end" (3:12-14). "The rebels in Moses' day missed the promised blessing of entry into an earthly Canaan," writes Bruce, "but latter-day rebellion would forfeit the greater blessings of the new-age."[28]

We are now in a position to consider 4:1-11. "Therefore," the author now reminds his hearers—and all who are in the day of Christ, as we shall see—"while the promise of entering his rest is still open, let us take care that none of you should seem to have failed to reach it. For indeed the good news came to us just as to them; but the message they heard did not benefit them, *because it did not meet with faith in those who listened*" (vv. 1-2, NRSV margin).

This chapter marks a new stage of the author's argument. His purpose is to show that the promised rest was not limited to the land of Canaan. In so doing, he returns to the introduction of this section (3:1-6), in which he affirms the superiority of Jesus, "the apostle and high priest of our confession" (v. 1), to Moses. Jesus, he says here, is superior to Moses in His *person:* Moses was a servant of God; Jesus is the Son of God. Now, in the passage before us, he argues the superiority of Jesus to Moses in His *work.* The weakness of Moses' work was twofold: *(a)* It imparted no power for its fulfill-ment, and therefore Moses could not bring Israel into the promised rest; and *(b)* the rest into which Israel was later brought was an earthly rest and only typical of the true rest of God. Christ is supe-rior to Moses on both these counts: *(a)* He is able through the Spirit actually to bring us into the promised spiritual rest (4:3-6); and *(b)* this rest is real and substantial, for by faith we "today" may enter the Sabbath rest of God (vv. 7-11).[29] Our author tells us,

---

28. Ibid., 66. "For those who had never been illuminated by God's final revela-tion of Himself in Christ," Bruce qualifies here, "Judaism provided a means of access to God—shadowy and imperfect as it might be [10:1]. But for those who had received the illumination of the gospel to renounce it in favor of the old order which the gospel had superseded was the irretrievable sin—the sin against light [6:4-6]."

29. Wiley, *Hebrews*, 130-31.

For we who have believed enter that rest, just as God has said, "As in my anger I swore, 'They shall not enter my rest,'" though his works were finished at the foundation of the world. For in one place it speaks about the seventh day as follows, "And God rested on the seventh day from all his works." And again in this place it says, "They shall not enter my rest." Since therefore it remains open for some to enter it, and those who formerly received the good news failed to enter because of disobedience, again he sets a certain day—"today"—saying through David much later, in the words already quoted, "Today, if you hear his voice, do not harden your hearts" (vv. 3-7).

The psalmist's "today," that is, offers a fresh opportunity to all who will believe to enter into the rest of God. The author is still comparing Moses and Christ. Wiley writes, "Since no mention is made of a new promise to Joshua, or any acceptance of it by David's generation, we may well conclude that the writer has in mind two generations only, that of Moses and that of Christ. Moses failed because there was no faith mixed with the word; Christ succeeds because He ministers the Spirit. It is the presence of the Holy Spirit that brings us into the supreme spiritual rest which is the heritage of every child of God."[30]

Ancient Israel, therefore, did not enter the "rest" of God; that rest is rather reserved for us "who have believed" the message of the gospel (v. 3). "The new day of 'Today' had dawned in Christ (v. 7)," Rordorf writes, continuing, "On this new day it is possible to enter into the rest, and yet more: on this new day this rest has become a reality for those who believe. . . . The distinction between the present time and the time of the generation in the wilderness is clearly marked by the fact that it is now possible to enter into the rest."[31]

---

30. Ibid., 131.
31. Rordorf, *Sunday*, 112. "Despite this" (that the new day of rest is for those who believe), Rordorf says in the above quote, "the passage goes on to say (v. 11) that we should make efforts to enter that rest. This orientation towards the future does, however, correspond to and may even be caused by the way the Epistle to the Hebrews gives expression to that which is the core of the Christian life—namely the tension of living in a situation between the times; this situation is marked by knowledge of the fulfillment which has already taken place and also by a longing for the visible consummation [cf. Heb. 11:1] which has yet to take place."

"We who have believed," our author declares, "enter that rest." He then proceeds to define that "rest" as the rest *of God.* "But in what sense does God speak of 'my rest'?" Bruce asks. Does it simply mean "the rest which I bestow" or does it also mean "the rest which I myself enjoy"? "It means the latter," he writes:

> The "rest" which God promises to His people is a share in that rest which He himself enjoys. Here, then, our author proceeds to bring out the underlying meaning of the reference to God's "rest" in Ps. 95:11 by relating it to Gen. 2:2f., where God is said to have "rested on the seventh day from all his work which he had made" in the course of the preceding six days. . . .
>
> It was not because the "rest" of God was not yet available that the wilderness generation of Israelites failed to enter into it; it had been available ever since creation's work was ended.[32]

Gen. 2:2 ("God . . . rested on the seventh day from all the work that he had done") must be interpreted in light of Jesus' statement in John: "My Father is still working, and I also am working" (5:17). Justin comments on this statement: "God directs the government on this day, equally as on all others." Clement of Alexandria concurs: "God's resting is not, then, as some conceive, that God ceased from doing. For, being good, if he should ever cease from doing good, then would he cease from being God."[33] Genesis simply means that God *began* to rest on the seventh day. "The fact that He is never said to have completed His rest, and resumed His work of creation," says Bruce, "implies that His rest continues still, and may be shared by those who respond to His overtures with faith and obedience."[34]

Here, however, we must part with Bruce, who believes the promised rest of God speaks of the final perfection and rest of *heaven.* He bases his understanding on Heb. 11:39—12:29. This extended passage begins with a statement concerning the Old Testament worthies of whom the author has just written. "Yet all these," he says, "though they were commended for their faith, did

---

32. Bruce, *Hebrews*, 73-74.
33. Both citations from Rordorf, *Sunday*, 83.
34. Bruce, *Hebrews*, 74.

not receive what was promised, since God had provided something better so that they would not, apart from us, be made perfect" (vv. 39-40). It concludes with an imaginative depiction of
Mount Zion and the heavenly Jerusalem, the visible consummation that is awaiting "the spirits of the righteous made perfect"
(12:23). To this heavenly Jerusalem, in the author's vision, God's
people have finally come. There they stand before "God the judge
of all" in the presence of "Jesus, the mediator of a new covenant,"
whose sprinkled blood "speaks a better word than the blood of
Abel" (see 12:23-24). In this vision, the "things hoped for . . . [but]
not seen" (11:1) have at last become visible for those who in faith
and obedience have persevered to the end (see 11:1, 8-16).[35]

These two passages, however, should be seen as constituting
the introduction and conclusion of the author's final plea in 12:1-
17 for Christians not to miss heaven by failing to pursue "the *holiness* without which no one will see the Lord" (emphasis added).

Heaven is indeed the final "rest" remaining for the people,
but the writer declares that "we who have believed enter that
rest" here and now (4:3)—*the rest from sin, preparing us for heaven.*
Here in Hebrews, as everywhere in the New Testament, we find
the tension that characterizes the Christian ethic: between the fulfillment that has already taken place (sanctification) and the consummation that is yet to come (glorification). To be sanctified by
the blood of Christ is to "have tasted the heavenly gift, and [to]
have shared in the Holy Spirit, and [to] have *tasted . . . the powers of
the age to come*" (6:4-5, emphasis added; see 6:1-6; cf. 10:26-31).
When Christ "sets up his throne in our hearts," says Wesley, "they
are instantly filled with this 'righteousness, and peace, and joy in
the Holy Ghost.'" For this reason "the kingdom of God" is spoken
of in the Gospels also as "the kingdom of heaven," "because it is
(in a degree) heaven opened in the soul. For whosoever they are
that experience this . . . can aver before angels and men,

> *Everlasting life is won,*
> *Glory is on earth begun."*[36]

---

35. The vision of the *heavenly* Jerusalem, "the city . . . whose architect and maker is
God" (11:10) replaces the hope of ancient Israel for the promised *land* of Canaan. Here, as
throughout the New Testament, God's promise of *land* is spiritualized (cf. Gal. 4:26).

36. John Wesley, "The Way to the Kingdom," in *Works*, 5:81.

These persons enjoy "that love to God which is both the earnest and the beginning of heaven" and therefore can sing,

Oh, what a blessed hope is ours!
While here on earth we stay,
We more than taste the heavenly powers,
And antedate that day.
We feel the resurrection near,
Our life in Christ concealed,
And with his glorious presence here
Our earthen vessels filled.

—Charles Wesley

"So then, a sabbath rest still remains for the people of God" (Heb. 4:9). This promised rest is the *eschatological sabbath* that began at Pentecost to continue until Christ returns (Acts 2:17-21). It is rest in God, a participation in the Creator's own Sabbath, a never-ending *sabbatismos*—a perpetual day of rest, obedience, and worship—for all who believe. We may therefore confidently assert with John Wesley,

Lord, I believe a rest remains,
To all thy people known;
A rest where pure enjoyment reigns,
And thou art loved alone;

A rest where all our soul's desire
Is fix'd on things above;
Where doubt and pain and fear expire,
Cast out by perfect love.
. . . .

O that I now the rest might know,
Believe, and enter in!
Now, Saviour, now the power bestow,
And let me cease from sin![37]

"Let us therefore make every effort to enter that rest" (v. 11). In this exhortation we encounter once more the New Testament imperative that arises from the gospel indicative. In view of the promised Sabbath rest, we must consecrate every day

---

37. Wesley, "Plain Account of Christian Perfection," in *Works*, 11:382.

and every moment of our life to God—while resting solely in His promise; "for those who enter God's rest also cease from their labors as God did from his" (v. 10). The promised rest is "the rest of faith."

FROM SALVATION TO SANCTIFICATION (5:1—13:21)

We have now come to the heart of the Epistle. The task at hand is to explore the book's central theme—"From Salvation to Sanctification."[38] While the subjects to be explored are treated in chapters 5 to 13 inclusive, "it is difficult to offer a fixed outline," as Wiley notes, since "the subjects shade off and merge into one another."[39] The following outline is offered as a possible approach: (1) Christ, our High Priest, the Guarantor of Sanctification; (2) the New Covenant, the Meaning of Sanctification; and (3) the Pursuit of Holiness, the Imperative of Sanctification.

Christ, Our High Priest, the Guarantor of Sanctification

In treating this topic we must examine, first, the *nature* of Christ's priesthood ("according to the order of Melchizedek," 5:10) and, second, the *efficacy* of Christ's priesthood ("to save to the uttermost those who come to God through Him," 7:25, NKJV).

The Nature of Christ's Priesthood

"Although he was a Son," our author tells us of Jesus, "he learned obedience through what he suffered; and having been made perfect, he became the source of eternal salvation for all who obey him, having been designated by God a high priest according to the order of Melchizedek" (5:8-10).

The writer is drawing from what the psalmist had said in 110:4—that God's Priest-King, when He came, would belong to the order of Melchizedek and not to that of the Levitical priesthood.[40] As he launches out on this theme in chapter 7, he begins by stating the facts found in Gen. 14; he then proceeds to develop and expand the facts by etymology and allegory.

---

38. The title suggested by Chilton and Neusner; see above.
39. Wiley, *Hebrews*, 153.
40. Following both Jesus and the apostle Peter, who found in Ps. 110:1 the prophecy of our Lord's *deity,* the author finds in the same psalm the prophecy of Jesus' eternal priesthood (v. 4). The Messiah was to be God's Priest-King, according to the psalmist. In developing this truth, the author of Hebrews is building upon an Old Testament prophecy recognized as such by the rabbinic teachers of that day; his treatment also is rabbinic (see introduction to chapter).

First, he takes the name "Melchizedek" itself and points out that it means "'king of righteousness'; next he is also king of Salem, that is, 'king of peace'" (v. 2). Then, in verse 3, our author makes a remarkable argument from silence. He notes that nothing is said in Genesis of Melchizedek's parentage. There is no reference to his father or mother, nor to the beginning or the end of his life—to his birth or to his death. Therefore, "resembling the Son of God, he remains a priest forever." As the king of righteousness and peace, Melchizedek foreshadows Jesus' Kingship; the predictions of Isa. 9:7 and Luke 2:14 and all the works of Jesus' life identify Him as King of righteousness and peace. And being without human origin and remaining "a priest forever," Melchizedek foreshadows Jesus' priesthood as One born without a human father and who "continues forever" as our heavenly Intercessor (vv. 23-24). Here is our Guarantor of sanctification: Jesus Christ, who by His incarnation entered completely into our human situation (sin only excepted; 4:14-16), and who now lives as one of us, to intercede "for all time" before God in our behalf (7:25)!

The Efficacy of Christ's Priesthood

When Jesus came into this world, Hebrews tells us, He took upon himself the task of fulfilling the plan of God as described in Ps. 40:6-8: "Sacrifices and offering you have not desired, but a body you have prepared for me; in burnt offerings and sin offerings you have taken no pleasure" (10:5-6).[41]

Four technical terms are used here to describe the several types of sacrifice commanded by the Mosaic Law. Peterson provides a fruitful interpretation of the psalmist's idea: "According to the psalmist, the whole system was designed to encourage and make possible *the willing self-offering of the people to God,* as indicated by the words, 'but a body you have prepared me.' Israel failed to realize this ideal of obedience and consecration to God. In the body 'prepared' for him, however, the Son of God lived a life of

---

41. This quotation, like most in Hebrews, is from the LXX. The NRSV translates the Hebrew, "you have given me an open ear" (v. 6). The thought is that of a receptive ear representative of a life dedicated to God (cf. Rom. 1:5; 16:26, "the obedience of faith," in which *hupakoē* ["obedience"] carries the above Hebrew idea). The Greek represents the underlying idea more clearly by the expression "a *body* you have prepared for me" (emphasis added). In quoting this psalm, which rejects burnt and sin offerings as not pleasing to the Lord, Hebrews (with Jesus, Matt. 9:13; 12:7) expresses the prophetic tradition (cf. Hos. 6:6; Amos 5:21-24; Mic. 6:6-8; and so on) as in fact the entire Epistle implies.

perfect obedience to the Father, culminating in his death as an unblemished sacrifice for sins (cf. 4:15; 7:26-27; 9:14)."[42]

As the Suffering Servant of Yahweh who fulfilled the divinely intended mission of God's chosen people, Jesus came to set aside the sacrificial system of Israel by expressing the obedience that had been the divine intention behind its rituals (see 10:8-9). Finding the Father's will in the psalmist's statement "'See, God, I have come to do your will, O God' (in the scroll of the book it is written of me)" (v. 7), Jesus' self-consecration to God brought about His death, making possible the consecration of God's people to Him, as it had not occurred before (see Isa. 52:13—53:12). Peterson goes to the heart of the matter when he writes,

> By the will of the Father, revealed in Scripture and carried out by the Son, Hebrews proclaims that "we have been sanctified through the offering of the body of Jesus Christ once for all" (10:10). Believers are sanctified because of his definitive sanctification, "once for all" (Gk. *epaphas*) in death. Jesus is "the sanctifier" of the people of the New Covenant (2:11, Gk. *ho hagiazon*), because he was perfected "through sufferings" (2:10). As such, he fulfills the role of the God of Israel under the Old Covenant (*e.g.* Ex. 31:13; Lv. 20:8; 21:15; 22:9, 16, 32).[43]

"For by a single offering," we are told, "he has perfected for all time those who are sanctified" (10:14). In verse 10 the Greek perfect tense is used, describing a state of affairs completed and enduring to the time; in verse 14 it is the present tense (literally, "being sanctified" or "made holy," NIV), which is probably "iterative and means 'those who from age to age receive sanctification.'"[44] Of the relationship of perfection to sanctification in verse 14, Oscar Cullmann writes, "Just as the High Priest concept applied to Jesus is so fulfilled that the purely cultic in general must be raised to a higher level, so must the purely cultic concept

---

42. Peterson, *Possessed by God*, 33-34 (emphasis Peterson's).

43. Ibid., 34.

44. Thomas Hewitt, *The Epistle to the Hebrews*, in *Tyndale New Testament Commentaries* (Grand Rapids: Wm. B. Eerdmans Publishing Co., 1960), 159. Although it would be attractive to see progressive sanctification in this verse, such an interpretation does not seem to fit this context; progressive sanctification, however, does seem to be indicated in 12:14 (a text to which we will give attention when we consider the pursuit of holiness).

teleioun ['to make perfect'] applied to him necessarily include also the sense of making morally perfect. This happens in a really human life—in Jesus the High Priest, who was made perfect, and in the brothers, the sanctified, who are made perfect in him (Heb. 2:11; [cf. 7:26-28])."[45]

If under the Aaronic priesthood "the blood of goats and bulls, with the sprinkling of the ashes of a heifer, sanctifies" externally, "how much more will the blood of Christ, who through the eternal Spirit offered himself without blemish to God, purify our conscience from dead works to worship the living God!" (9:13-14). It is the *internal* sanctification of this passage that Jesus made possible for us when He suffered outside the city gate (13:13). Now raised at the Father's right hand, "he continues forever" (7:24). For this reason "he is able for all time to save those who approach God through him, since he always lives to make intercession for them" (v. 25). The marginal reading of the NRSV, "he is able to save completely," indicates another possible meaning of the Greek phrase *eis to panteles*. As our High Priest who "continues forever," Christ is able to save "for all time"; as the appointed One who has "offered for all time a single sacrifice for sins" and has now "sat down at the right hand of God" (10:12), He is able also to save "to the uttermost" (7:25, NKJV) of their moral and spiritual needs, all those who come to God through Him (see vv. 26-28).

The New Covenant, the Meaning of Sanctification

After having established the superiority of the High Priesthood of Christ (in 7:11-28), the author now proceeds to relate His High Priesthood to the themes of the new covenant. As the Aaronic priesthood gives place to that of the order of Melchizedek, so the old covenant gives place to the new, the earthly sanctuary to the heavenly, and the sacrifices that were but temporary foreshadowings give place to the one perfect sacrifice of Christ (8:1-5). After making the foregoing point, the author can then say, "But Jesus has now obtained a more excellent ministry, and to that degree he is the mediator of a better covenant, which has been enacted through better promises. For if that first covenant had been faultless, there would have been no need to look for a second one" (vv.

45. Oscar Cullmann, *The Christology of the New Testament*, trans. Shirley C. Guthrie and Charles A. M. Hall (Philadelphia: Westminster Press, 1959), 93.

6-7). What the better promises are, on which this better covenant is established, are seen in the quotation from Jer. 31:31-34:

> The days are surely coming, says the Lord, when I will establish a new covenant with the house of Israel and with the house of Judah; not like the covenant that I made with their ancestors, on the day when I took them by the hand to lead them out of the land of Egypt; for they did not continue in my covenant, and so I had no concern for them, says the Lord. This is the covenant that I will make with the house of Israel after those days, says the Lord: I will put my laws in their minds, and write them on their hearts, and I will be their God, and they will be my people. And they shall not teach one another or say to each other, "Know the Lord," for they shall all know me, from the least of them to the greatest. For I will be merciful toward their iniquities, and I will remember their sins no more *(vv. 8-12)*.

The better promises of the new covenant are of a new relationship to God that involve three things in particular: (1) the implanting of God's law within their hearts, (2) the knowledge of God as a matter of personal experience, and (3) the blotting out of their sins forever. When the work of Christ is summarized in this Epistle, as elsewhere in the New Testament, the expiation of sin is the *all-inclusive* provision of the new covenant (1:3; 10:12-14). Accordingly, this exposition will begin with the promise of the blotting out of our sins forever through Jesus' blood.

At the Last Supper with His disciples Jesus "took a cup, . . . saying . . . this is my blood of the new covenant, which is poured out for many for the forgiveness of sins" (Matt. 26:27-28, NRSV margin). What the sacrifices of the old covenant could never do—take away sin—the blood of Christ does: it purifies our conscience from dead works to serve the living God (9:13-14). This once-for-all pardon is God's gift to us, as long as we "walk in the light as he himself is in the light" (1 John 1:7; Heb. 10:10, 26-31; cf. 6:4-6). "Pardoning love is at the root of it all" (Wesley).

In the pardon of our sins through Jesus' blood we are given an *experiential* knowledge of God. Under the Mosaic covenant Israel had simply a *national* acknowledgment of God. But under the new covenant every individual member of the covenant community comes to a *personal* knowledge of God. "And they shall not teach one another or say to each other, 'Know the Lord,' for they shall all know me, from the least of them to the greatest" (8:11). When we trust Christ for the pardon of our sins, that moment "the Spirit Himself bears witness with our spirit that we are children of God" (Rom. 8:16, NKJV).

Furthermore, when God pardons our sins, He implants the Law within our hearts. "I will put my Torah within them" is the original wording of Jer. 31:33. As we have seen in our Old Testament study, Torah implies more than statutory law; it embraces the idea of guidance, instruction, and direction. Under the new covenant, God promises to internalize Torah (Rom. 8:1-17). The implanting of Torah is more than committing it to memory; it is the promise of Jeremiah's younger contemporary Ezekiel: "I will give them one heart, and put a new spirit within them; I will remove the heart of stone from their flesh and give them a heart of flesh, so that they may follow my statutes and keep my ordinances and obey them. Then they shall be my people, and I will be their God" (11:19-20).

The new covenant was to be a new one because it could impart a new heart. It was not new with reference to its substance. "I will be their God, and they shall be my people," quoted here from Jer. 31:33, was the substance of the Mosaic covenant. But while the "formula" is that of the old covenant, it is capable of being filled with fresh meaning to the extent that it can be spoken of as the *new* covenant. "I will be their God" takes on fresh, fuller meaning with the further revelation of the character of God in Christ. Its final meaning is found in Revelation, when a new heaven and a new earth come into being and God's dwelling place is established with mortals in the New Jerusalem (21:3-4; cf. Heb. 12:22-24).

The Pursuit of Holiness, the Imperative of Sanctification

We come now to the all-inclusive exhortation of the Book of Hebrews: the *pursuit* of holiness. "Pursue peace with everyone, and the holiness without which no one will see the Lord" (12:14). This pursuit is the imperative of sanctification. The text must be understood, however, in the broader context of this chapter, in which we are told that holiness is the working of God in us through disciplinary sufferings we endure as His children. In submitting to these disciplinary measures, we become partakers of *His* holiness (v. 10). Holiness, that is, is both God's gift and our pursuit.

The 12th chapter begins with the reminder that Christians are involved in the same struggle Jesus himself endured. "Let us also lay aside every weight," we are exhorted, "and the sin that clings so closely, and let us run with perseverance the race that is set before us, looking to Jesus the pioneer and perfecter of our faith, who for the sake of the joy that was set before him endured the cross, disregarding its shame, and has taken his seat at the right hand of the throne of God" (vv. 1-2).

As runners in the divine Olympiad, we must strip for the race. We must lay aside *anything* (any practice, habit, or secret sin) that would weigh us down or impede us in our race—"and the sin that clings so closely" (Gk. *euperistaton,* literally "besetting"). Adam Clarke says of this passage:

> Some understand it of *original* sin, as that by which we are enveloped in body, soul, and spirit. Whatever it may be, the word gives us to understand that it is what meets us at every turn; that it is always presenting itself to us; that as a pair of compasses describe a circle by the revolution of one leg, while the other is at rest in the centre, so this . . . surrounds us in every place; we are *bounded* by it, and often hemmed in on every side; it is a circular, well fortified wall, over which we must leap, or through which we must break.[46]

However it may manifest itself in our condition, temperament, or circumstance, *the sin* itself *(tēn hamartian)* must be put away promptly—"do it and have done with it" by an act of total surrender and faith.[47] Then "let us run with perseverance the race that is set before us, looking to Jesus the pioneer and perfecter of our faith." It is our confidence "that he who hath begun this good work in you will perfect it until the day of Jesus Christ" (Phil. 1:6, Wesley).

Such commitment to God and the doing of His will may involve physical suffering, social ostracism, and abuse from others. It did for the Hebrews (cf. 10:32-34). Such hardship does not mean that God has abandoned His people. It is rather the expression of fatherly *discipline* (Gk. *paideia*). "We tend to think of discipline mainly in terms of chastisement and correction," says Peterson,

46. Clarke, *Commentary,* 6:777.
47. Wiley, *Hebrews,* 343.

"but Scripture shows that in its widest sense discipline involves positive encouragement and training. Applied to God, it refers to the whole nurturing process by which he 'brings up' his children and shapes them in the way he wants them to go."[48] It is here that verse 10 illuminates the author's point, as Peterson goes on to show: "A rare Greek term for holiness here denotes the sanctity of God's character and life. To share God's holiness is to enjoy life in his presence (cf. 12:9), transformed into his likeness (cf. 1 Jn. 3:2). In the final analysis it is the same as being brought 'to glory' through Christ (2:10). But even now, by faith, we experience some of the blessing of the age to come in anticipation (cf. 6:4-5; 12:22-24)."[49]

So what the writer is saying is that as we learn to submit to God's fatherly disciplines, something of His holiness is reflected in our lives. Trials and suffering are necessary for the development of holy character, as we learn also from other New Testament passages (cf. Rom. 5:3-4; James 1:2-4; 1 Pet. 1:6-9). But they are also necessary to keep us firm and faithful to the end, when by God's grace we will fully share His holiness.[50]

The exhortation to "pursue peace with everyone, and the holiness without which no one will see the Lord" (12:14) is of vital importance to the argument of this chapter. Again Peterson is helpful in pointing out,

> [12:14] picks up the note of "peace" from 12:11 and the challenge of 12:12-13 to move *together* in the direction set by God. This prepares for the warning of 12:15-17 to care for any member of the church who may be in danger of committing apostasy. Although a different Greek word is used in 12:14, the note of "holiness" from 12:10 is also picked up. The wonderful prospect of seeing God, which is another way of speaking about life in his presence, is highlighted. This motif is elaborated in 12:18-24, as the basis for a final challenge not to forfeit the grace of God and the blessings of the coming kingdom (12:25-29).[51]

The Hebrews are urged to seek holiness as a practical expression of the sanctification (*ton hagiasmon*, v. 14) they enjoyed

---

48. Peterson, *Possessed by God*, 71.
49. Ibid., 72.
50. Ibid.
51. Ibid., 73-74.

in Christ, while at the same time keeping in mind the promise that God is disciplining them as His children so that they might share His holiness (*hagiotēs*, v. 10). From this perspective, since we are "holy partners in a heavenly calling" (3:1), we can expect God to be continually at work in us to manifest His holiness in our lives. By perseverance and submission to His discipline, we pursue a pathway to the transformation into godlikeness that God himself has prescribed. But in all this we recognize that the ultimate expression of holiness awaits us in His presence in "Mount Zion and . . . the city of the living God, the heavenly Jerusalem" (12:22).[52] *Soli Deo gloria.*

---

52. Ibid., 75.

10

The Sermon on the Mount

The Sermon on the Mount is of paramount importance for the purpose of this study. It has been reserved for this chapter since it beautifully summarizes the core of *Jesus'* teaching on the subject, treating as it does what Mr. Wesley spoke of as the "substance" of holiness: loving God and others with a perfect heart. "You shall be perfect," our Lord says in this sermon, "just as your Father in heaven is perfect" (Matt. 5:48, NKJV).

But how shall we understand the perfection Jesus enjoins? Is our Lord the new Moses setting forth a "New Law"? Is His a *perfectionist* ethic—enjoining us to keep every "jot and tittle" of His commands (cf. v. 18, KJV)? Or is Jesus holding up an *impossible ideal*—shattering self-reliance, reducing us to despair? Or is He commanding an *interim ethic*—calling for repentance and moral decision in view of the impending apocalypse? Each of these views has been advanced by serious students of the sermon, along with a *futurist ethic* concept that relegates it to the millennial Kingdom, after the Second Advent.

How *shall* we understand the Sermon on the Mount?

To answer this question, we must go back beyond the sermon to that which preceded it. Let us start with the baptism of Jesus in the Jordan, where He heard the voice of His Father saying, "You are My beloved Son, in whom I am well pleased" (Mark 1:11, NKJV). The Spirit then descended upon Him, anointing Him as Savior and Lord.

After His baptism and temptations, Jesus appeared in Galilee proclaiming the good news of the Kingdom: "The time is fulfilled, and the kingdom of God is at hand; repent, and believe in the gospel" (Mark 1:15, RSV). C. H. Dodd insists that the translation should be, "The kingdom of God *has come.*" Frederick C. Grant explains, "The kingdom was so near at hand that one could truly describe it as being present."[1] The long-expected reign of God had projected itself into history. The promised age of salvation was dawning. God was visiting and redeeming His people—in Jesus His Son. "If it is by the Spirit of God that I cast out demons," Jesus says in Matthew, "then the kingdom of God has come to you (12:28)." Again, in Luke He announces, "The kingdom of God is not coming with things that can be observed; nor will they say, 'Look, here it is!' . . . For, in fact, the kingdom of God is among you" (17:20-21; cf. Matt. 13). In Jesus himself and His works, the promised Kingdom was in their very midst!

The Sermon on the Mount, therefore, must be placed in its Gospel setting. Its every word was preceded by something else, as Jeremias says:

> It was preceded by the preaching of the kingdom of God. It was preceded by the granting of sonship to the disciples (Matt. 5:16; 5:45; 5:48, etc.). It was preceded by Jesus' witness to himself in word and deed. . . .
>
> To each of these sayings belongs the message: the old aeon is passing away. Through the proclamation of the gospel and through discipleship you are transferred into the new aeon of God. . . . This is what the life of those who stand in the salvation-time of God is like, of those who are freed from the power of Satan and in whom the wonder of discipleship is consummated.[2]

---

1. Frederick C. Grant, "Biblical Studies: Views and Reviews," *Theology Today* 14 (April 1957): 50.

2. Joachim Jeremias, *The Sermon on the Mount,* trans. Norman Perrin, in *Biblical Series*—2, ed. John Reumann (Philadelphia: Fortress Press, 1961), 30-31. The sayings of Jesus that Matthew gathers here in this first major discourse of his Gospel were certainly uttered on many different occasions (cf. Luke's "Sermons on the Plain," 6:20-49). Jesus would have followed the method of a Jewish rabbi, who would discourse to his disciples on some topic; then the results of that discourse would be summed up in easily remembered propositions. "The method of the Jewish religious teachers," A. C. Deane explains, "was to compress into a few succinct and pointed sentences the expression of any truth they deemed of special importance. Then the teacher would repeat the sentences many times with his disciples, until they knew them by heart. There is every reason to suppose that Jesus used this accustomed method of teaching by repetition. The pointed gnomic sentences of which the Sermon on the Mount consists are exactly suited to this purpose" (Archibald M. Hunter, *A Pattern for Life: An Exposition of the Sermon on the Mount* [Philadelphia: Westminster Press, 1953], 11).

The sayings of the Sermon on the Mount are not intended to lay a legal yoke upon Jesus' disciples in the sense "You must do all these things in order that you may be blessed" (the perfectionist idea); nor in the sense "You ought to have done all these things—see what poor creatures you are" (the theory of an impossible ideal); nor in the sense "Bend every effort to be perfect—the final victory is at hand" (the interim-ethic theory); nor is Jesus saying, "This is how you will live after I return and set up My millennial reign" (the early American dispensationalist view). Rather, these sayings of Jesus delineate lived faith in the *present* kingdom of heaven. "They say," Jeremias writes, "You are forgiven, you are a child of God, you belong to his kingdom. The sun of righteousness has risen over your life. You no longer belong to yourself; rather, you belong to the city of God, the light of which shines in the darkness. Now you may experience it: out of the thankfulness of a redeemed child of God a new life is growing. This is the meaning of the Sermon on the Mount."[3]

THE BEATITUDES (5:3-12)

It is not too much to claim that the Sermon on the Mount is the essence of the Christian life. Therefore, says Barclay, it is not too much to say that the Beatitudes are "the essence of the essence of the Christian way of life."[4]

There is no Greek verb in any of the Beatitudes. They are thus to be taken as exclamations: "O the bliss of . . . !" (cf. Pss. 1:1; 32:2; 94:12). They speak of a blessedness to be enjoyed even here and now, but a blessedness that will not reach its completion until we experience the Beatific Vision.

The Greek adjective *makarios* means "happy," "privileged," "well-off." In a religious sense it means "blessed" (by God). In the Pastoral Epistles we read of "the glorious gospel of the *blessed* God," who is "the *blessed* and only Sovereign, the King of kings and Lord of lords" (1 Tim. 1:11; 6:15, emphases added). The promised bliss is therefore nothing less than the blessedness of God. "Happiness" has its root in "hap," which means "chance";

---

3. Jeremias, *Sermon on the Mount*, 35.
4. William Barclay, *The Beatitudes and The Lord's Prayer for Everyman* (New York: Harper and Row, 1968), 11.

but Christian bliss is the blessedness of the life of God, the joy, therefore, that no one can take from us. It is not a surprise, then, that the Beatitudes are startling contradictions of the world's standards. They are an amazement to anyone who does not know God. "They are not quiet stars," says Deissmann, "but flashes of lightning, followed by a thunder of surprise and amazement."[5] The objective "blessed" is therefore the correct translation, instead of subjective "happy." The opposite of "blessed" is not "unhappy," but "cursed" (cf. Matt. 25:31-46; Luke 6:24-26).[6]

The Beatitudes, moreover, have an ethical dimension. The life of those pronounced blessed is elaborated in 5:17—7:12, the major section of the sermon that spells out the ethical obligations of the "greater righteousness" (see 5:20) of the Kingdom. The Beatitudes thus constitute the indicative mode for the commands of the imperative mode; they are gospel, therefore, not law, the kerygmatic base of the teaching core of the sermon.[7]

Understood as prophetic announcements, the truth claims of the Beatitudes are dependent on the character of the Speaker. Boring observes, "The many allusions to Isa 61:1-11 in the beatitudes relate them to prophetic speech, and indirectly cast Jesus in the role of the 'anointed one' of Isa 61:1. In the narrative context of the Sermon on the Mount, the speaker is more than a prophet, he is the Son of God and Lord of the church, already seen from the post-Easter perspective."[8]

Finally, the nine beatitudes are nine declarations about the blessedness, contrary to all appearances, of those who have entered the kingdom of God. When looked at carefully, we see that the nine are very closely interwoven into a threefold bliss.

The first three describe the blessedness of those who discover their own spiritual poverty; who become painfully aware of their sin and the sin and suffering of the world; and who have committed themselves entirely to God as their Defender in hope of the final triumph of the Kingdom (vv. 3-5).

The next three beatitudes describe the blessedness of those who, famishing and thirsting for a righteousness not their own,

5. Ibid., 18.
6. Boring, *New Interpreter's Bible*, 8:177.
7. Ibid.
8. Ibid.

are filled; who, having obtained mercy, are merciful to others; and who have found purity of heart (vv. 6-8).

The final three beatitudes depict the blessedness of the peacemakers, who, living at cross grains with the world, rejoice in confident hope as they suffer for Christ and the gospel (vv. 9-12).

"Blessed are the poor in spirit, for theirs is the kingdom of heaven" (v. 3). The Greek word for "poor" here is *ptōchos*, which does not describe the simply poor, but those who are completely destitute. The Latin Vulgate has "Blessed are the *pauperes.*" Tertullian alters it to "Blessed are the *mindici*," that is, the beggars. *Ptōchos* represents the Old Testament word *ani*, which had come to mean the poor, humble, faithful person whose trust was in God alone. This is the sense in which *ani* is used in the Psalms. "This poor man [*ani*] cried, and the LORD heard him, and saved him out of all his troubles" (34:6, KJV). The first beatitude speaks of "the poor" of Isa. 61:1, to whom the Servant of the Lord is anointed to preach (cf. Luke 4:18). These are those who feel their spiritual poverty, who confess their moral bankruptcy before God. "We are all beggars," said the dying Luther. And as John Wesley lay dying, he whispered, "What have I to trust to for salvation? I can see nothing that I have done or suffered, that will bear looking at. I have no other plea than this:—

'I the chief of sinners am
But Jesus died for me.'"[9]

From first to last our salvation is by the mercy of God.

This first beatitude is Jesus' doctrine of justification (cf. Luke 19:8-10).

"Blessed are those who mourn, for they will be comforted" (v. 4). The word translated "mourn" *(penthein)* is one of the strongest in the Greek language. It is the sorrow that pierces the heart and is visible on the countenance. "Blessed are those who are moved to bitter sorrow over their sin," Jesus means. The nearer we come to Christ, the more clearly we see the Christlikeness by which we must judge ourselves. "'Blessed' therefore 'are they that' thus 'mourn,'" Wesley says,

---

9. W. H. Fitchett, *Wesley and His Century* (Cincinnati: Jennings and Graham, 1908), 510-11.

who "follow on to know the Lord," and steadily refuse all other comfort. They shall be comforted by a fresh manifestation of his love; by such a witness of his accepting them in the Beloved as shall never more be taken away from them. This "full assurance of faith" swallows up all doubt, as well as tormenting fear. . . .

But although this mourning is at an end, is lost in holy joy, by the return of the Comforter, yet is there another, and a blessed mourning it is, which abides in the children of God. They will mourn for the sins and miseries of mankind: they "weep with those that weep."[10]

The mourning of which our Lord speaks, therefore, is a twofold mourning—for our own sin, and for the world's sin and misery. Hunter writes, "The mourners are those 'to whom the evil that is in the world is a continual grief,' those who mourn the apparent eclipse of God's people and cause, and long for a Savior to arise upon the earth. (The 'Comforter' was one of Messiah's names.) *They shall be comforted.* These words are a veiled claim to Messiahship. It is as if Jesus said, 'Yes, and I will be their comforter.'"[11]

"Blessed are the meek, for they will inherit the earth" (v. 5). Meekness is not weakness; it is humility. It is that fine temper of spirit that yields itself trustfully to the will of God and is not easily provoked in the face of hurts and hatred. It is that spirit and quality of life that was incarnate in Jesus, who was "meek and lowly in heart" (Matt. 11:29, KJV).[12] "When he was abused, he did not return abuse; when he suffered, he did not threaten; but he entrusted himself to the one who judges justly" (1 Pet. 2:23). "Meekness," says Myron Augsburger, "is the greatness of spirit that looks beyond one's self, beyond the immediate. Meekness is patience, gentleness, forbearance, yielding as a greater good. . . . A meek person would rather die than sin, would rather die than ruin another for whom Christ died."[13]

10. John Wesley, "Sermon on the Mount, I," in *Sermons I, 1-33*, vol. 1 in *The Bicentennial Edition of the Works of John Wesley*, ed. Albert Outler (Nashville: Abingdon Press, 1984), 485-86.

11. Hunter, *Pattern*, 31.

12. Ibid.

13. Myron Augsburger, *The Expanded Life* (Nashville and New York: Abingdon Press, 1972), 49-50.

The meek, Jesus promises, "will inherit the earth." This is an eschatological promise, signifying all the good things that come with the messianic kingdom. So Paul can speak of Christians as "joint heirs with Christ" and inheritors of the glory yet to be revealed (Rom. 8:17 ff.), and Peter can apply the language of ancient "Canaan" to our Christian inheritance in heaven (1 Pet. 1:4).[14]

"Blessed are those who hunger and thirst for righteousness, for they will be filled" (v. 6). This saying would mean something quite different to a Palestinian audience in the time of Christ from what it would mean to us today. In that ancient world, hunger was not something that could be satisfied by a passing snack. The same was true of thirst. Travelers whose waterskins had gone dry as they walked the desert would immediately get the picture. So Jesus is saying, "Blessed are those who long for righteousness as a starving person for food, and as a person perishing for thirst longs for water."[15]

The hunger and thirst for righteousness of which Jesus speaks is "the dire need of a right relationship with God and others."[16] It is famishing and thirsting for the righteousness that God makes possible for us through Christ. "God has acted to establish a new relationship between himself and his own," Guelich writes, "and offers the basis for a new relationship among his own that expresses itself in the conduct of 5:21—7:12, the 'greater righteousness.' This conduct comes from a 'wholeness' (5:48) that bespeaks the total commitment of the whole person to God through Jesus Messiah (cf. 19:16-22)."[17]

Wesley therefore seems justified in equating *righteousness* here with *holiness:* "the image of God, the mind which was in Christ Jesus."

It is every holy and heavenly temper in one; springing from as well as terminating in the love of God as our Father and Redeemer, and the love of all men for his sake. "Blessed are they that hunger and thirst after" this. . . . This hunger is in the soul, this thirst after the image of God, is the strongest

14. Hunter, *Pattern,* 33.
15. Barclay, *Beatitudes,* 48-49.
16. Robert A. Guelich, *The Sermon on the Mount: A Foundation for Understanding* (Waco, Tex.: Word Books, 1982), 87. All rights reserved.
17. Ibid., 38.

of all spiritual appetites when it is once awakened in the heart. . . .

"Blessed are they who" thus "hunger and thirst after righteousness; for they shall be filled." They shall be filled, with the thing which they long for, even with righteousness and true holiness.[18]

"Blessed are the merciful, for they will receive mercy" (v. 7). Mercy is an attribute of God himself, and something He requires of us (Mic. 6:8). It is one of the words that Jesus takes over from the Old Testament and makes central to His teaching (cf. 9:13; 12:7). "Be merciful, just as your Father is merciful" (Luke 6:36). It was mercy that the good Samaritan showed (10:37); it is one of the "weightier matters of the law" (Matt. 23:23), the lack of which will disqualify us for God's mercy at the Judgment (18:35).

"If you forgive others their trespasses, your heavenly Father will also forgive you," says Jesus later in this sermon; "but if you do not forgive others, neither will your Father forgive your trespasses" (6:14-15).

General Oglethorpe once remarked to John Wesley, "I never forgive."

"Then, sir," the latter rejoined, "I hope you never sin."

"Blessed are the merciful, *for they will receive mercy*." It is important to understand that this is no "merit" theology. Hunter explains, "To be merciful is the divine way of doing things; and if on Judgment Day the merciful man hears the verdict, 'Come, ye blessed of the Father,' it will not be because he has 'made out, and reckoned on his ways, and bargained for his love,' but because, all unconsciously, he has acted like him of whom it is written, 'as is his majesty, so is his mercy'" (cf. Matt. 25:31-46).[19]

"Blessed are the pure in heart, for they will see God" (v. 8). The Greek word for "pure" *(katharos)* has a wide variety of meanings that have to do with things that are without admixture and without alloy. It was used of pure water, of wine or milk that had not been diluted with water, of grain that had been winnowed from all chaff, of silver or gold that had been refined from all alloy (cf. Mal. 3:2-3).

---

18. John Wesley, "Sermon on the Mount, II," in *Bicentennial Works*, 1:495-97.
19. Hunter, *Pattern*, 35.

"'Purity of heart' is not only the avoidance of 'impure thoughts' (e.g., sexual fantasies)," Boring says in an important paragraph,

> but refers to the single-minded devotion to God appropriate to a monotheistic faith. Having an "undivided heart" (Ps. 86:11) is the corollary of monotheism, and requires that there be something big enough and good enough to merit one's whole devotion, rather than the functional polytheism of parceling oneself out to a number of loyalties. Faith in the *one* God requires that one be devoted to God with *all* one's heart (Deut. 6:4; cf. Matt. 22:37). This corresponds to the "single eye" of 6:22, the one pearl of 13:45-46, to Paul's "this one thing I do" (Phil. 3:13) and Luke's "one thing is needed" (Luke 10:42, NIV)—not one *more* thing. The opposite of a pure heart is a divided heart (James 4:8), attempting to serve two masters (6:24), the "doubt" (*distazō*, lit. "have two minds") of 14:31 and 28:17, and the conduct of the Pharisees (23:25).[20]

"Blessed are the pure in heart, *for they will see God*" (cf. Ps. 24:4). Since "no one has ever seen God" (John 1:18), it is not a matter of optics but of spiritual vision. There are moral conditions for spiritual vision. As Puritan Henry Moore put it quaintly: "If thou beest, thou seest."

The promise is not exhausted in this life. Here "we see in a mirror, dimly, but then we will see face to face" (1 Cor. 13:12). The final reward of the pure in heart is the Beatific Vision.[21]

"Blessed are the peacemakers, for they will be called children of God" (v. 9). The noun "peacemakers" (*eirēnopoioi*) occurs only here in the New Testament. "To make peace" (*eirēnopoiein*) does, however, occur in Col. 1:20, and the phrase *eirēnēn poiein* appears in Eph. 2:15 and James 3:18. Consequently, we must take the term "peacemakers" literally, as the active endeavor to effect reconciliation between opposing parties rather than merely patiently enduring in a posture of nonresistance. God is the Primary Source of *shalom*, but in Isa. 9:6 and Zech. 9:9-10, the Messiah is the Prince of Peace who will effect peace on earth. Guelich writes, "Peace-

---

20. Boring, *New Interpreter's Bible*, 8:179-80.
21. Hunter, *Pattern*, 35-36. "In all things here," Wesley comments; "hereafter in glory" (*Notes*, 29).

making is therefore much more than a passive suffering to main-
tain peace or even 'bridge-building' or reconciling alienated parties. It is the demonstration of God's love through Christ in all its
profundity (John 3:16; Rom. 5:1, 6-11). The *peacemakers* of 5:9 refers
to those who, experiencing the *shalom* of God, become his agents
establishing his peace in the world."[22]

By exhibiting conduct corresponding to that of our Heavenly
Father, we show ourselves to be "children of God." The eschatological divine passive ("will be called children of God") points to
God's claiming the peacemakers as His sons and daughters at the
final Judgment, not to what people say about those who work for
peace in this world.[23]

"**Blessed are those who are persecuted for righteousness'
sake, for theirs is the kingdom of heaven. Blessed are you when
people revile you and persecute you and utter all kinds of evil
against you falsely on my account. Rejoice and be glad, for your
reward is great in heaven, for in the same way they persecuted
the prophets who were before you**" (vv. 10-12).

Jesus here parallels being persecuted "for righteousness'
sake" with "for my sake." This shows that righteousness is not
some abstract quality; it is a Christological affair—a matter of following Christ, of doing the will of God as He defines it (cf. 7:21-
23). But more, we are to *rejoice* in the persecution that may come to
us as a consequence of discipleship. Boring comments here, "The
joy to which the disciples are called is not in spite of persecution,
but because of it. Rejoicing because of persecution is not the expression of a martyr complex, but the joyful acceptance of the
badge of belonging to the eschatological community of faith, the
people of God who are out of step with the value system of this
age. Such people are like the prophets of Israel, who were also
persecuted."[24]

"Your reward is great in heaven," Jesus assures those persecuted and reviled for His sake. This heavenly reward is like the rewards of a happy marriage. "The proper rewards are not simply
tacked on to the activity for which they are given, but are the activity itself in consummation," Hunter quotes C. S. Lewis as say-

22. Guelich, *Sermon on the Mount*, 92.
23. Boring, *New Interpreter's Bible*, 8:180.
24. Ibid.

ing. "The rewards offered to the righteous are simply the inevitable issue of goodness in a world ruled over by a good God."[25]

THE DISCIPLES AS SALT AND LIGHT (5:13-16)

The two metaphors of salt and light define the role that Jesus' disciples, the new Israel, are to play in the world. The life of discipleship is life within a community of faith, a community charged with a mission to the world.

"You are the salt of the earth," Jesus says, "but if salt has lost its taste, how can its saltiness be restored? It is no longer good for anything, but is thrown out and trampled under foot" (v. 13).

This saying is a metaphor rich in symbolism. Salt was a necessary ingredient in sacrifice (Lev. 2:13; Ezek. 43:24); eating together was called "sharing salt," a pledge of loyalty and covenant fidelity (Num. 18:19; Ezra 4:14); salt served as seasoning for bland food (Job 6:6) and also as a purifying agent and preservative. Disciples are to the earth what salt is in this biblical tradition.

Salt loses its "savor," not by some impossible chemical miracle, but by becoming so impure (cf. heart purity, v. 8), so mixed with other elements, that it loses its function. "Earth" here is equivalent of "the world." The world is not evil; it does not belong to Satan. It is God's creation (13:35; 24:21), the scene of the disciples' mission (5:14; 13:38). God's will shall ultimately be done in this world, "as it is in heaven" (6:10). Salt does not exist for itself, nor do the disciples—they exist for the sake of the world.[26]

Jesus then changes the figure: "You are the light of the world. A city built on a hill cannot be hid. No one after lighting a lamp puts it under the bushel basket, but on the lampstand, and it gives light to all in the house. In the same way, let your light shine before others, so that they may see your good works and give glory to your Father in heaven" (vv. 14-16).

Here are two clashing figures put in juxtaposition. The light metaphor declares that disciples are to be illumination for the world. The function of light is not to be seen, but to permit things to be seen as they are. In striking contrast, the figure of a city set on a hill presents the disciples as *being seen* (cf. 6:1-18).

---

25. Hunter, *Pattern*, 39.
26. Boring, *New Interpreter's Bible*, 8:181.

184 WHOLENESS IN CHRIST

The combination of these two metaphors gives force to Jesus' statement, since "light" (to the nations) and "city on a hill" (to which the nations will flow in the messianic future) were both used with reference to Israel's mission to the world (see Isa. 42:6; 49:6; 2:2-5). Since ethnic Israel has failed to carry out this mission as God's people, the new Israel is now charged with the task (28:18-20). "The community that lives by the power of unostentatious prayer in the inner room (6:6)," says Boring, "is not an introverted secret society shielding itself from the world, but is a city set on a hill whose authentic life cannot be concealed."[27]

As a lamp is lit, not to be put under a bushel but on a lampstand, so Christ's disciples are called to let their light shine to all. The metaphor is of the community of faith as "having been lit," as recipients of a light whose source is God. Disciples are to be light for a world in darkness (4:12-17; cf. Isa. 9:2). As Jesus' deeds of mercy did not point to His own glory but to the glory of God (cf. 9:8), so the disciples' acts of piety were to be done for God's glory alone (6:1-18).[28] A lamp does not call attention to itself; it illuminates.

The church *is* mission, we are to understand. In these metaphors the indicative moves into the imperative; but it is still the imperative based on the indicative: Be what you are—salt and light in the world.

THE "GREATER RIGHTEOUSNESS" OF THE KINGDOM (5:17-48)

We come now to the first major teaching section of the sermon, which treats the "greater righteousness" of the Kingdom. From this point to the end of the sermon, the gospel imperative is central—*God's ancient love command redefined by Jesus, addressed to the new people of God coming into being through Him.* This radical reinterpretation of the Torah by our Lord is the topic we must now address.

---

27. Ibid., 182.
28. Ibid.

THE TORAH AND THE
"GREATER RIGHTEOUSNESS"

"Do not think that I have come to abolish the law or the prophets; I have come not to abolish but to fulfill" (v. 17).[29] What *is* the relation of the new aeon of Kingdom to the old aeon of the Law and the prophets? Does the new annul and abolish the old? No, says Jesus, I have come not to "scrap" God's ancient revelation, but to bring about its fulfillment. "To fulfill" *(plērōsai)* means simply "to fill up" and connotes the "completion" of the Law; it signifies "to bring to its final conclusion all that the Law stood for."[30]

"For truly I tell you, until heaven and earth pass away, not one letter, not one stroke of a letter, will pass from the law until all is accomplished" (v. 18). The traditional "jot" and "tittle" of the KJV represent the smallest letter of the Hebrew alphabet and the minute strokes that distinguish one letter from another. It is Jesus' way of affirming the continuing authority of Scripture in its totality as the revelation of God's will. "*Amen* I say to you" was a unique aspect of Jesus' own authoritative speech, affirming but relativizing the Law.[31] "The point is that while the Law has continuing validity, it is not ultimate, in contrast to the word of Jesus, which is ultimately normative and will never pass away."[32]

"Therefore, whoever breaks ["relaxes," RSV] one of the least of these commandments, and teaches others to do the same, will be called least in the kingdom of heaven; but whoever does them and teaches them will be called great in the kingdom of heaven" (v. 19). This statement implies, says Luz, that "'justice, mercy, and faith'—thus indeed the love commandment—are the chief commandment and that commandments like that of tithing (23:23) or

---

29. "'The law or the prophets' forms a literary bracket with 7:12, setting off 5:17—7:12 as the instructional core of the sermon. 'Law' here is the Torah or Pentateuch; 'prophets' comprise both the Former Prophets (Joshua—Kings) and the Latter Prophets (Isaiah—Malachi). This was the central core of the Hebrew Bible of Matthew's day, a functional equivalent of 'the Scripture'" (Boring, *New Interpreter's Bible*, 8:185-86).

30. Guelich, *Sermon*, 139-40. Recognizing the salvation history significance inherent in *pleroō*, Moule writes, "In so far as the Law bears witness to the will of God as an ideal yet to be achieved, and the Prophets held out hope of a time coming when it shall be fulfilled, one who perfectly fulfills the will of God confirms also the predictions of prophecy" (C. F. D. Moule, "Fulfil," in *Interpreter's Dictionary of the Bible*, 2:328).

31. The first of 32 occurrences in Matthew.

32. Boring, *New Interpreter's Bible*, 8:187.

that of the purification of the outside of the cup (23:26) are iotas and little pen strokes. The love commandment stands at the center; the ceremonial laws are of secondary rank. But they also are parts of the law which Jesus fulfills as a whole."[33]

"For I tell you," our Lord then declares, "unless your righteousness exceeds that of the scribes and Pharisees, you will never enter the kingdom of heaven" (v. 20). "For" *(gar)* in this sentence links the "greater righteousness" to the examples that follow; it is not defined as the keeping of "the least of these commandments" in verse 19, but by the demands of the antitheses that follow in 5:21-48. "Greater" *(pleion)* suggests a *quantitative* interpretation: "Unless your righteousness is present in a measurably higher degree than that of the scribes and the Pharisees, you will not enter the kingdom of heaven." On the basis of verses 17-19, it is quantitatively more than observing the Torah. But based on the antitheses, the "greater righteousness" is primarily "a *qualitative* intensification of the life before God—*measured on love*."[34]

In the antitheses that follow in verses 21-48, Jesus contrasts His own pronouncements with those of the old Law, in a manner never done by any rabbi or scribe before Him:

The old Law said, "No murder." I say, "No anger or name-calling."

The old Law said, "No adultery." I say, "No lustful thought."

The old Law said, "Divorce on condition." I say, "No divorce."

The old Law said, "No false swearing." I say, "No swearing at all."

The old Law said, "An eye for an eye." I say, "No retaliation at all."

The old Law said, "Love your neighbor." I say, "Love your enemy."[35]

In these antitheses Jesus first reaffirms the Torah, then He transcends it, then gives it a situational application. His commands do not transgress the Law—they radicalize it; they deal with the inner springs of conduct, which the Law cannot regu-

---

33. Ulrich Luz, *Matthew 1—7: A Commentary*, trans. Wilhelm C. Linss (Minneapolis: Augsburg Fortress, 1989), 269.
34. Ibid., 270 (emphasis added).
35. Hunter, *Pattern*, 44-45.

late.[36] The situational "between the times" applications call for comment. "It is true," George F. Thomas writes,

> that [Jesus'] primary ethical principle takes the form of a commandment: "Thou shalt love thy neighbor as thyself." But this saying . . . commands a practical disposition or attitude which is to manifest itself in many different kinds of acts according to the needs of particular situations. It is also true that more specific kinds of acts are sometimes commanded or prohibited. But these are usually illustrations of kinds of acts that may be required by the practical disposition of love. . . . When we attempt to apply them as rules in a literal fashion, we may easily reduce them to absurdity.[37]

What is even more serious, to take these "focal instances" as *binding* upon Christian conduct is to turn Jesus' ethic into casuistry, into a "New Law."[38] The new aeon has come in Christ, but the old aeon continues, and His disciples must live in the tension between the "now" and the "not yet." This situation "between the times" calls upon Christians to make creative applications of the law of love. Jesus' examples are not casuistic new laws, but models for the disciples to follow as they struggle to discern the will of God in ever-new situations. "All six antitheses are expressions of the Great Commandment (22:34-40), and keep it from being trivialized or sentimentalized."[39]

Five of the antitheses begin with the formula, "You have heard" (vv. 21, 27, 33, 38, 43). This is simply an expression of the common Jewish experience of "hearing" the Law read and expounded in a synagogue or Temple worship setting. In the fifth antithesis, "it was also said" (v. 31) implies a casuistic interpretation of the Law also.

LOVE SHOWS NO HOSTILITY
"You have heard that it was said to those in ancient times, 'You shall not murder'; and 'whoever murders shall be liable to

---

36. "Radicalize" derives from the Latin *radix*, "root."

37. George F. Thomas, *Christian Ethics and Moral Philosophy* (New York: Charles Scribner's Sons, 1955), 39.

38. Robert C. Tannehill coined this phrase. ("The 'Focal Instance' as a Form of New Testament Speech: A Study of Matthew 5:39b-42," *Journal of Religion* 50 [1970]: 379.)

39. Boring, *New Interpreter's Bible*, 8:189.

judgment.' But I say to you that if you are angry with a brother or sister, you will be liable to judgment; and if you insult a brother or sister, you will be liable to the council; and if you say, 'You fool,' you will be liable to the hell of fire" (vv. 21-22).

It is clear that Jesus is addressing an understanding of the Law that was common in His day, namely, as being an integral combination of apodictic commands and legal ordinances.[40] He was cutting through such casuistry by a deliberate use of irony in verse 22, to get at the underlying relationship between persons. The Law outlawed murder; Jesus forbids selfish anger and name-calling. "Whereas the Law had prohibited murder arising from broken relationships which presupposed the reality of evil," Guelich says, "Jesus ultimately demands a relationship between individuals in which there is no alienation."[41] "A brother or sister" speaks of a new relationship established by Jesus among His disciples. The two illustrations that follow (vv. 23-24 and 25-26) are examples of the earliest interpretation of this antithesis. By using the form of legal ordinances, "Jesus called for attitudes and behavior indicative of the presence of the Kingdom—the age of salvation—as seen in restored rather than broken relationships between individuals. Consequently, anything less than restored relationship leaves one culpable before God."[42]

Love not only shows no hostility *but also takes the initiative in the endeavor to restore broken relationships* (cf. Rom. 12:17-21).

LOVE IS NOT PREDATORY

"You have heard that it was said, 'You shall not commit adultery.' But I say to you that everyone who looks at a woman with lust has already committed adultery with her in his heart" (vv. 27-28).

By contrast with the first antithesis, Jesus here quotes the apodictic commandment of Exod. 20:14 with no legal ordinance ensuing.[43] The Law says, "You shall not commit adultery"; Jesus says, "You shall not be guilty of adultery—by looking upon a

---

40. Guelich, *Sermon,* 182-83. "Apodictic commands" are the absolute commands of the Decalogue; "legal ordinances," the rabbinic embellishments of the Law.

41. Ibid., 188-89.

42. Ibid., 241.

43. The penalty for adultery was death to both parties (Lev. 20:10; Deut. 22:22).

woman in order to have her (sexually)." "To lust" in English lacks the accompanying thought of possession inherent in the Greek *epithumēsai* here. Jesus means that the lustful desire to have another man's wife corrupts one's very person (*en tē kardia*, "in the heart"). The two illustrations Jesus now uses are among the most startling in the Gospels (vv. 28-30). "Nowhere is the inwardness of his teaching more evident," Buttrick comments.

The sharpness of the language shows the stringency of the required discipline. Even if the hand should not be amputated, the lustful look should—and the amusement, and the friendship. Even though these be as dear as the right hand and the right eye, they should go. A Christian surrenders what is "lawful" for the sake of a dedicated soul. The fact that Christ speaks in dramatic figure is poor reason for trying to delude or evade his stern truth.

Yet the demand is not repression but fulfillment. Elsewhere (18:8-9) the discipline is levied with the key phrase, "it is better for you to enter life maimed"—than to miss the gate. The purpose of discipline is abundant life.[44]

LOVE IN MARRIAGE

"It was also said, 'Whoever divorces his wife, let him give her a certificate of divorce.' But I say to you that anyone who divorces his wife, except on the ground of unchastity, causes her to commit adultery; and whoever marries a divorced woman commits adultery" (5:31-32).

"Whoever divorces his wife" has no exact verbal parallel in the Old Testament. It represents a summary of Deut. 24:1 expressed in the form of a legal ordinance.[45] Jesus' statement here must be set alongside what He says in 19:3-9 (cf. Mark 10:2-12). The Law permitted divorce because of the reality of sin in human

---

44. Buttrick, *Interpreter's Bible*, 7:297-98.

45. The rabbinic view tended to break down into two schools of rabbinic thought. Rabbi Hillel took the phrase "something objectionable about her" (Deut. 24:1) to cover such matters as speaking disrespectfully about her husband or burning his food. Rabbi Shammai gave a narrower interpretation of the Hebrew term (*'rwh*) to mean "indecency" or behavior contrary to the moral customs of the day, including not only adultery but a woman appearing on the street with her hair down or with uncovered arms or in a slit skirt. The most literal view of all was expressed by Rabbi Akiba who, focusing on the earlier phrase ("does not please him"), allowed divorce when a wife lost her attraction for her husband.

experience, the "hardness of heart" (Mark 10:5) resulting from the Fall. Jesus points back to creation, when God made human beings male and female in order to become "one flesh," to share a oneness in relationship. In other words, as Guelich explains,

> Jesus countered the human experience of sin by calling a married couple to live according to God's intent for creation. Such a demand could only be possible with the overcoming of the "hard heart," an indication of the offer of a "new heart," a "heart of flesh" instead of a "heart of stone" (Ezek. 36:26), characteristic of the age of salvation. Jesus could then apodictically set his demand in marriage in antithesis to the provision of the Law, "What God has joined together, let not man put asunder."[46]

In Matthew's "exception clause" we see the evangelist acting like a "Jesus' theologian," like Paul in 1 Cor. 7:10-16.[47] We must recognize that divorce *was* given by God as part of the Law to protect individuals for whom sin had destroyed the marriage relationship. Divorce itself is not evil, or sin; the evil, the sin is in the broken relationship that divorce legally recognizes. Divorce is but the public acknowledgment of the failure of a given marriage relationship. "Yet over against this reality of broken relationships, Jesus' demand offers hope and wholeness of the age of salvation for the married either by transforming or forgiving one's hardness of heart."[48]

LOVE IS TOTALLY HONEST

"Again, you have heard that it was said to those of ancient times, 'You shall not swear falsely, but carry out the vows you have made to the Lord.' But I say to you, Do not swear at all, either by heaven, for it is the throne of God, or by the earth, for it is his footstool, or by Jerusalem, for it is the city of the great King. And do not swear by your head, for you cannot make one hair white or black. Let your word be 'Yes, Yes,' or 'No, No'; anything more than this comes from the evil one" (vv. 33-37).

---

46. Guelich, *Sermon*, 246.
47. "Except on the ground of unchastity *(porneia)*." The original meaning of *porneia* ("fornication") is ruled out by the fact that a married woman is involved. The most common interpretation is to understand *porneia* as adultery, since this is the most natural meaning of the word in the context.
48. Guelich, *Sermon*, 248.

Jesus' requirement here is radical indeed, since there was no precedent in Judaism for the absolute prohibition of oaths. Judaism continued and elaborated the system of oaths and vows found in the Old Testament to guarantee the truth of one's statement. "Oaths involve communication between two parties, with the name of God (or a valid substitute) invoked as guarantor," Boring explains. "Vows were made directly to God. What was confirmed by an oath had to be true; what was vowed had to be done."[49]

Jesus' antithesis is absolute: "Do not swear at all. . . . Let your word be 'Yes, Yes' or 'No, No.'" This fourth antithesis demands total honesty, just as James 5:12. Taken legalistically, Jesus simply prohibits the use of oaths. But, as in the previous antithesis, His intent is much more radical than simply forbidding the use of oaths. He takes a legal concern drawn from everyday life to express a demand for conduct consistent with the age of salvation—total honesty in completely new human relationships. Anything beyond this "comes from the evil one." Jesus' command implies the overcoming of the evil one in the present day of salvation.

LOVE DOES NOT RETALIATE

"You have heard that it was said, 'An eye for an eye and a tooth for a tooth.' But I say to you, Do not resist an evildoer. But if anyone strikes you on the right cheek, turn the other also; and if anyone wants to sue you and take your coat, give your cloak as well; and if anyone forces you to go one mile, go also the second mile. Give to everyone who begs from you, and do not refuse anyone who wants to borrow from you" (vv. 38-42).

The Old Testament did not command revenge; it sought to curb the tendency to unlimited retaliation, laying down the so-called lex talionis: "eye for eye, tooth for tooth." This law appears three times in the Law (Exod. 21:24; Lev. 24:20; Deut. 19:21), setting limits on private revenge against individuals and their families. It became the keynote of criminal justice in the Jewish law. The law guaranteed an injured person legal justice while protecting the offender from undue penalty.

Jesus not only affirmed the thrust of the Law in opposing unlimited revenge but also called for His disciples to reject absolute-

---

49. Boring, *New Interpreter's Bible,* 8:193.

ly the principle of retaliation in human affairs. The disciple must not oppose an "evildoer" in court (cf. Deut. 19:15-21). This "evildoer" is more than a personal enemy; he represents those who oppose God and His own, "the children of the kingdom" (13:38). The eschatological kingdom of God, already breaking into history in Jesus, embraces the enemy. Thus, Jesus' command not to resist an "evildoer" goes beyond a strategy of passive resistance. It calls for positive action in the interest of the aggressor, as the examples immediately show.

At first glance, the five instances do not seem to fit together. In the first three (being struck in the face, being sued in court, being commandeered for short-term service by the government), one is being victimized by others more powerful than himself or herself, whereas in the last two (beggars and borrowers demanding help), one is being badgered by those who are weaker than himself or herself. The common element in the five illustrations is aggression and pressure from others who interfere with one's selfish pursuits. What Jesus calls for is a response in terms of the good and needs of others, not one's own rights.[50] It is indeed a radical demand.

In the first instance (v. 39) a person is insulted by being struck in the face. The specific reference to the *right* cheek implies that one is slapped with the back of the hand, an act that was particularly degrading to a Jew. Instead of retaliating, the individual is commanded to offer the other cheek.

In the second example (v. 40) a man is being sued for his *coat* (one's basic, form-fitting garment). He is commanded to give up willingly not only his *coat* but his *cloak* (the outer garment that served as a pallet at night) as well. Since the poor fellow would then be standing nude in the courtroom, Jesus' teaching obviously cannot be taken literally. Boring makes the acute observation: "It is a matter of one's being secure enough in one's acceptance by God to enable one not to insist on one's own rights, legal or otherwise, but empowering one to renounce them in the interest of others (cf. 1 Cor. 6:1-11; 8:1—10:33; Rom. 13; 14:1—15:7)."[51]

The third example reflects the Roman practice taken over from the Persians, of commandeering citizens of an occupied

---

50. Ibid., 194.
51. Ibid.

country to give them directions or carry their equipment for a specified distance, as Simon was compelled to carry Jesus' cross (Mark 15:21). Such a request was legally binding, but a follower of Jesus is to go beyond the required mile, to go the "extra mile."

According to the Qumran understanding of the Law, one was expected to keep all the laws of the community, an externally attainable goal that still left operating room for one's own selfish will. By contrast, Jesus' command presupposes a heart blameless before God, the spiritual "wholeness" of the biblical *tamim* (Gen. 17:1; Deut. 18:13), in short, the heart purity of 5:8. Only the love of God poured into our being by the Holy Spirit (Rom. 5:5) can displace the innate selfishness of the heart and provide the *disposition* that fulfills the love command (cf. Rom. 8:2-4).

LOVE IS ALL-INCLUSIVE

"You have heard that it was said, 'You shall love your neighbor and hate your enemy.' But I say to you, Love your enemies and pray for those who persecute you, so that you may be children of your Father in heaven; for he makes his sun rise on the evil and on the good, and sends rain on the righteous and on the unrighteous. For if you love those who love you, what reward do you have? Do not even the tax collectors do the same? And if you greet only your brothers and sisters, what more are you doing than others? Do not even the Gentiles do the same? Be perfect, therefore, as your heavenly Father is perfect" (5:43-48).

It is true that there is no specific command to hate the enemy in the Old Testament. There are statements, however, that God "hate[s] all evildoers" (Ps. 5:5; cf. 31:6), and statements that others do, and should do, the same (Deut. 23:3-7; 30:7; Ps. 139:21-22). This hatred is not personal vindictiveness; primarily it is the religious rejection of others who do not belong to God's people and keep His law.[52] The Qumran writings state explicitly what lies implicitly in the teachings of the rabbis and Old Testament. The Qumran literature distinguishes sharply between two groups of people, those chosen by God and called the "sons of light," and those despised by God and called the "sons of darkness." The

---

52. Ibid., 195.

"hatred" of enemy in 5:43, therefore, stands in continuity with the Old Testament, the rabbis, and the Qumran writings.[53]

Jesus makes the love of God and neighbor the foundational commandment on which all else depends (cf. 22:34-40) and, by contrast to Jewish teaching, the command to love one's *enemies* specific and concrete. He does not base the command on a doctrine of human rights or a strategy to make a friend of an enemy, but on the nature of God as *agapē* (cf. Rom. 5:8). "Be perfect, therefore, as your heavenly Father is perfect" (5:48). Christian perfection is *perfect love*. As our Heavenly Father loves and does good to His enemies as well as His friends, so must we who are called to follow Jesus manifest the same unconditional love. We are called to show the perfection of God's love, which sets no limits on who the neighbor is, which does not draw the line between the good and the evil, the righteous and the unrighteous, the friend and the enemy. "We know it to be *of* but not *from* us," says Thurston, "when, in our desire to follow after Jesus, we can '*do* good to' when we do not '*feel* good toward.' Our perfection begins when, as Paul Tillich translates the phrase, we begin to 'be all-inclusive in our love as [our] heavenly Father is all-inclusive."[54] To be *perfect* is to pray in words ascribed to Francis of Assisi:

> *Lord, make me an instrument of Thy peace:*
> *Where there is hatred, let me sow love;*
> *Where there is injury, pardon;*
> *Where there is doubt, faith;*
> *Where there is despair, hope;*
> *Where there is darkness, light;*
> *Where there is sadness, joy.*
> *O Divine Master, grant that I may not so much seek*
> *To be consoled as to console,*
> *To be understood as to understand,*

---

53. Guelich, *Sermon*, 226. Judaism, however, must not be caricatured as being always narrow and exclusive; there were elements and tendencies toward love for all peoples (Lev. 19:33-34), at times including enemies (Prov. 25:21; Jon. 4:10-11). For other examples see W. D. Davies and Dale C. Allison Jr., *A Critical and Exegetical Commentary on the Gospel According to St. Matthew*, vol. 1 of *International Critical Commentary* (Edinburgh: T. and T. Clark, 1988-91), 551-52.

54. Bonnie Bowman Thurston, "Matthew 5:43-48," *Interpretation* 41 (April 1987): 173.

To be loved as to love;
For it is in giving that we receive;
It is in pardoning that we are pardoned;
It is in dying that we are born to eternal life!

THE PRACTICE OF
RIGHTEOUSNESS BEFORE GOD (6:1-18)

The theme of the preceding section (5:21-48) is the practice of the greater righteousness (*dikaiosunē*, 5:20) toward the neighbor; here it is practicing *dikaiosunē* before *God*. Jesus makes no distinction between devotion to God, expressed in acts of worship, and acts of personal integrity, justice, and love addressed to human beings, *all* of which are called *dikaiosunē*.[55]

As Jesus takes up this third part of the sermon, He has arrived at its center. This is true in respect to both its form and its subject matter. Formally, this third part is preceded by the introduction (5:3-16) and followed by the fourth part (6:19—7:12) and the conclusion (7:13-27). By the same token, the third part itself contains three parts, treating as it does almsgiving, prayer, and fasting. What is more, the center of the middle part, on prayer, is the Lord's Prayer. Formally, therefore, the Lord's Prayer lies at the very heart of the Sermon on the Mount.

With respect to its subject matter, too, this third part constitutes the center of the sermon. Thus far, as we have noted, Jesus has addressed the topic of practicing the greater righteousness as *love toward neighbor;* upon completing this third part, He will speak on practicing the greater righteousness in other areas of life, then conclude the sermon. Here in this part, Jesus concerns himself with the fundamental matter of practicing the greater righteousness as *love toward God.* In the Lord's Prayer, the centerpiece of the sermon, we are indeed at the heart of the sermon. The disciples know God as "Father" (6:9). Through Jesus the Son of God, they are invited to live in the sphere of the eschatological kingdom of God, where they, as children of God, are rightly related to God and know Him as Father.[56] The Lord's Prayer is thus handed

---

55. Boring, *New Interpreter's Bible,* 8:200.
56. Jack Dean Kingsbury, "The Place, Structure, and Meaning of the Sermon on the Mount Within Matthew," *Interpretation* 41 (April 1987): 141-42.

over to the disciples as "the essence of the new truth in which they stand."[57]

"Pray then in this way: Our Father in heaven, hallowed be your name. Your kingdom come, Your will be done, on earth as it is in heaven. Give us this day our daily bread. And forgive us our debts, as we also have forgiven our debtors. And do not bring us to the time of trial, but rescue us from the evil one" (6:9-13).

We should observe that the first petition is *one* prayer expressed in three parallel petitions; "on earth as it is in heaven" modifies all three. When God's name is hallowed by our whole-hearted love, His kingdom is indeed present, and His will is being performed—"on earth as it is in heaven." "'Thy kingdom come,'" Wesley observes,

> has a close connection with the preceding petition. In order that the name of God may be hallowed, we pray that his kingdom, the kingdom of Christ, may come. This kingdom comes in a particular person when he "repents and believes the gospel," when he is taught of God not only to know himself but to know Jesus Christ and him crucified. As "this is life eternal, to know the only true God, and Jesus Christ whom he has sent," so it is the kingdom of God begun below, set up in the believer's heart. The Lord God omnipotent then reigneth, when he is known through Christ Jesus. He taketh unto himself almighty power, that he may subdue all things unto himself. He goeth on in the soul conquering and to conquer, till he hath put all things under his feet, till "every thought" is "brought into captivity to the obedience of Christ."[58]

The Lord's Prayer is indeed a prayer for *personal* holiness, "holiness of heart and life." It is at the same time a prayer for *social* holiness. Wesley—foreseeing the time when "the mountain of the Lord's house," the church of Christ, "shall be established in the top of the mountains," when "the fullness of the Gentiles shall come in, and all Israel shall be saved," when it shall be seen that "the Lord is King, and hath put on glorious apparel," appearing

---

57. Luz, *Matthew 1—7*, 374.
58. John Wesley, "Sermon on the Mount, VI," in *Bicentennial Works*, 1:581-82.

to every soul of man as "King of Kings, and Lord of Lords"—adds immediately,

> It is meet for all those who "love his appearing" to pray that he would hasten the time, that this his kingdom, the kingdom of grace, may come quickly, and swallow up all the kingdoms of the earth; that all mankind receiving him for their king, truly believing in his name, may be filled with righteousness and peace and joy, with holiness and happiness, till they are removed hence into his heavenly kingdom, there to reign with him for ever and ever.
>
> For this also we pray in those words, "Thy kingdom come." We pray for the coming of his everlasting kingdom, the kingdom of glory in heaven, which is the continuation and perfection of the kingdom of grace on earth.[59]

The other petitions of the prayer (vv. 11-13) must be viewed as subordinate to the grand petition for the Kingdom and be kept secondary in disciples' concerns. Although wanting in the most ancient manuscripts, the doxology refocuses the prayer on its central theme: "For thine is the kingdom, and the power, and the glory for ever and ever. Amen" (Wesley's New Testament).

It is in the light of the Lord's Prayer that we are to understand Jesus' instructions on how disciples are to give alms, pray, and fast. They must practice these acts of righteousness *as an expression of their new relationship to God.* Kingsbury explains,

> To give alms is to perform charitable deeds, to pray is to approach God in petition as Father, and to fast is to show contrition. In contemporary Judaism as well as for disciples, these were the three cardinal acts of piety. As Jesus describes the doing of these acts, he contrasts "to be seen by men" (6:1) with "in secret" (6:4, 6, 18). This contrast is manifestly not one between "public" and "private" per se, as though Jesus were denying legitimacy to all public expressions of charitable activity, prayer, and fasting. No, "to be seen by men" expresses intent, and the contrast Jesus draws is between "ostentation" and "proper motivation."[60]

---

59. Ibid., 582. See William M. Greathouse, "John Wesley's View of the Last Things," in *The Second Coming: A Wesleyan Approach to the Doctrine of Last Things,* ed. H. Ray Dunning (Kansas City: Beacon Hill Press of Kansas City, 1995), 139-60.

60. Kingsbury, "Place, Structure, and Meaning," 141.

The hypocrites are those who practice their acts of piety os-
tentatiously so as to gain a *reputation* of piety. The acclaim of others is the only reward they will receive (6:2, 5, 16). Disciples are to
practice their acts of piety "in secret," that is, out of heartfelt devotion to God. Such practice Jesus acknowledges with the promise
of eternal reward at the latter day (6:4, 6, 17-18).[61] Our Lord's
promise of reward here, says Luz, is not to be understood as encouraging the disciples "to calculate simply in a more skillful way
and to live with a more subtle—namely, a religious—form of self-
affirmation." Rather "the reference [is] to the reward given by
God—in actuality—in order to unmask human self-presentation
as the secret goal of good deeds."[62] It is a call for heart purity, a
single-minded devotion, one all-encompassing motive: the glory
of God (cf. 1 Cor. 10:31).

THE EVERYDAY PRACTICE
OF RIGHTEOUSNESS (6:19—7:12)

In this the fourth part of the Sermon on the Mount, Jesus
deals with the practice of righteousness in areas of life not yet
touched on. The key concept of 6:19-34 is the Old Testament idea
of *simplicity*—"the single eye" of verse 22. This phrase has a rich
connotation, which is difficult to capture in English. The literal
KJV translation seems preferable here. "The Greek phrase *(ho oph-
thalmos haplous),*" says Richard Foster, "refers both to a single aim
in life and to a generous unselfish spirit. The two have such a
close connection in the Hebrew mind that they can be expressed
in a single phrase. Singleness of purpose toward God and generosity of spirit are twins. The single eye is contrasted with the
'evil eye,' which is a Semitic expression for a covetous nature."[63]

The concept illuminates the three paragraphs of this section.
To have a single eye is to be free from the greed that stores up
treasure on earth; its treasures are in heaven (vv. 19-21). To have a
single eye is the opposite of attempting to serve two masters (v.
24). Moreover, it is to be free from the anxiety and strivings of
mere worldlings; instead, it is to "strive first for the kingdom of

---

61. Ibid.

62. Luz, *Matthew 1—7*, 358.

63. Richard J. Foster, *The Freedom of Simplicity* (San Francisco: Harper and Row,
1981), 36.

God and his righteousness" and trust the Heavenly Father for whatever else is needed in life (vv. 25-34).

Further, Jesus forbids disciples to judge others, on pain that "with the judgment you pronounce you will be judged" (7:1-5, RSV). In verse 6 (in a prohibition much disputed), Jesus warns disciples against giving what is sacred and precious to persons undeserving, lest they, like swine, "trample them under foot and turn and maul you." In verses 7-11, Jesus suddenly turns from the negative to the positive and urges disciples to be fervent and constant in prayer ("Ask . . . seek . . . knock" [v. 7, RSV]), for they can be sure that "your Father who is in heaven [will] give good things to those who ask him!" (v. 11, RSV). And with the Golden Rule, Jesus brings this part of the sermon to a close by reminding disciples of what He has stressed earlier: Doing the greater righteousness is always, finally, an exercise in love.[64]

INJUNCTIONS ON PRACTICING RIGHTEOUSNESS (7:13-27)

In this concluding part of the Sermon on the Mount, Jesus completes His teaching. In contrast to those who take a lackadaisical attitude toward following the path of righteousness, disciples have chosen the narrow way of radical obedience and discipline that Jesus has enjoined (vv. 13-14). He then drives home an unmistakable point: It is not only the hearing of His words but also the doing of them that counts. Disciples who both hear and do are like the "wise man who built his house on rock" (v. 24). They, unlike the false prophets who will prove themselves to be workers of lawlessness, will at the latter day "enter the kingdom of heaven," for they shall have done "the will of my Father in heaven" (v. 21).

The greater righteousness is indeed the gift of God. The basis of Jesus' demands in this sermon lies in the new relationship God was establishing with His own through Jesus' ministry. Jesus came bringing not a new law, but a new covenant through which God was at work in forgiving sins (e.g., 26:28) and offering reconciliation to and among His own. The conduct, therefore, demanded in the sermon becomes indicative of one's relationship with the Father, the presence of God's sovereign rule in one's life. Like fruit

---

64. Kingsbury, "Place, Structure, and Meaning," 142.

from a "good tree" (vv. 17-18), the conduct was not optional, but inherent to the new relationship with God that Jesus made possible. In one word, the greater righteousness of the Kingdom is both God's *gift* and God's *demand*. Guelich pronounces the last word when he writes, "The greater righteousness represents simultaneously the *product* of the presence of the Kingdom as well as the basis for entrance into the future consummated Kingdom."[65]

---

65. Guelich, *Sermon*, 262.

Appendix

GREEK VOCABULARY TERMS FOR SANCTIFICATION

While the New Testament idea of sanctification cannot be restricted to specific terms, it is important to understand the significant Greek words usually translated in our English version as "holy," "holiness," "sanctification," and "perfection." The words that call for our special attention are the root terms *hagios*, "holy," and *teleios*, "perfect," and their cognates. In formulating the Christian doctrine of sanctification, we must keep in mind that the terms translated as "holiness" and "perfection" are closely related. Both are important to a proper understanding of New Testament thought. While they have their various shades of meaning and singular implications, theologically the two concepts point to the same aspect of the Christian life.[1]

Hagios—"Holy"

Hagios is the Greek root for "holiness" and "sanctification"; it is the equivalent of the Hebrew *qodesh*. Like *qodesh*, *hagios* primarily signifies "separation." This religious significance is always present in *hagios*, just as in *qodesh*. The religious is always the presupposition of the moral. There is no holiness apart from God, "the Holy One." However, *hagios* always carries the further significance of "godlikeness": to belong to God is to be like God (see 1 Pet. 1:13-16). These two ideas, separation and godlikeness, are inseparable. The great prophets of Israel played a major role in deepening the ethical content of *qodesh*, as we have already noted. "The Holy God," Isaiah announced, "shows himself holy in righteousness" (5:16, RSV).

---

1. See Paul M. Bassett and William M. Greathouse, *The Historical Development*, vol. 2 of *Exploring Christian Holiness* (Kansas City: Beacon Hill Press of Kansas City, 1985), 23.

It was Jesus, however, who gave holiness its final expression. Addressing the Pharisees, upset by His disregard of their taboos, Jesus said, "Go and learn what this means, 'I desire mercy, not sacrifice'" (Matt. 9:13; cf. Hos. 6:6). Even more importantly, *the content of Jesus' own character* has gone into *hagios*. Jesus was himself "the Holy One of God" (John 6:69). He was the holiness of God incarnate, *hagios* defined in human personality.

Hagios also means "saint." The term, however, is found only in the plural.[2] The *hagioi* are the *koinōnia* of God, the *fellowship* of those who "mutually participate" in the Spirit who comes from Christ (1 Cor. 12:4-27; Rom. 12:3-8).[3] "There is no holiness," Wesley therefore says, as quoted earlier, "but social holiness."

Hagiōsunē and *Hagiotēs*—"Holiness"

Two Greek nouns, both cognates of *hagios* and translated "holiness," are employed in the Epistles to describe the moral purity and godlikeness characteristic of saints. These are *hagiōsunē* and *hagiotēs*. *Hagiōsunē* is "properly the *quality*" of holiness (Thayer) and is used twice of believers (2 Cor. 7:1; 1 Thess. 3:13). *Hagiotēs* is "properly the *state*" of holiness[4] (Thayer), the *qodesh* of which we become "partakers" through Christ (Heb. 12:10; 2 Cor. 1:12).

Although neither has the importance of *hagiasmos*, they do shed significant light on the meaning of sanctification.

Hagiōsunē occurs three times in Paul's letters (Rom. 1:4; 2 Cor. 7:1; and 1 Thess. 3:13). In Romans *pneuma hagiōsunēs* ("the Spirit of holiness," 1:4, RSV) is taken by most scholars as a Semitism for the Holy Spirit. For our purposes the other two passages are pertinent.

Hagiōsunē occurs first in 2 Cor. 6:14—7:1, in the concluding exhortation of this passage: "Since we have these promises, beloved, let us cleanse ourselves from every defilement of body and of spirit, making holiness perfect in the fear of God" (7:1).

This text clearly implies that there are *degrees* of Christian holiness. The Corinthians are being called upon to "perfect" the holiness that was theirs in Christ, by appropriating God's promises and cleansing themselves from any remaining moral defilement (cf. James 4:8).[5] Grammatically, the aorist subjunctive "cleanse"

---

2. Except Phil. 4:21, where it is "every saint" (see NIV, "all the saints").
3. The meaning of *koinōnia*.
4. Kittel, *Theological Dictionary*, 1:114.
5. Greek participle, *epitelountes*, "bringing to an end," "completing," or "perfecting."

stands in apposition to the perfecting of *hagiōsunē*, as condition and consequence. The sense of Paul's exhortation would then be "Let us cleanse ourselves from every defilement of body and spirit, [thereby] making holiness perfect in the fear of God."[6]

Hagiōsunē is also found in Paul's prayer for the Thessalonians: "And may he so strengthen your hearts in *holiness*, that you may be blameless before our God and Father at the coming of our Lord Jesus with all his saints" (3:13, emphasis added). By implication, *hagiōsunē* (when perfected as in 2 Cor. 7:1) denotes a state of sanctity that would enable his Thessalonian converts to anticipate Christ's return with confident joy (cf. 5:23; 1 John 2:28; 3:2-3; Rev. 22:20).

Hagiotēs, our second term, is found in only one undisputed passage, Heb. 12:10, in which the author reminds us that we as children had human parents to discipline us, and we respected them. "Should we not be even more willing to be subject to the Father of spirits and live? For they disciplined us for a short time as seemed best to them, but he disciplines us for our good, in order that we may share his holiness" (vv. 9-10).

"In the New Testament," Kittel says, "the holiness of God is His essential attribute in which the Christian must share and for which the heavenly Father prepares him by instruction."[7] That is, only God is holy *in himself*; all holiness in humans is *derivative*. We are holy only as we become "partakers of his holiness" (KJV). As F. E. Marsh puts it, "We have no inherent holiness. We are holy as we are possessed by the Holy Presence. We are holy in His holiness, loving in His love, strong in His strength, tender in His tenderness, patient in His patience, calm in His peace, and consecrated in His consecration."[8]

The same idea of sharing God's holiness occurs in 2 Peter, in which the apostle declares that God has given us "his precious and very great promises, so that through them [we] . . . may become *participants of the divine nature*" (1:4, emphasis added). This

6. Some interpreters, however, follow Daniel Steele when he writes, "The duty of perfecting holiness is a progressive work." This is certainly true in regard to the positive growth in holiness as Christlikeness, but 2 Cor. 7:1 addresses the purifying from remaining sin as being enjoined upon the Corinthians. However, the reader is referred to Purkiser, *Exploring Christian Holiness*, 1:161-62.

7. Kittel, *Theological Dictionary*, 1:114.

8. James McGraw, comp., *The Holiness Pulpit No. 2* (Kansas City: Beacon Hill Press of Kansas City, 1974), 16-17.

understanding of holiness as participation in God *(theosis)*, lies at the heart of the Eastern Orthodox tradition. John Wesley reformulated one strand of this tradition in constructing his doctrine of sanctification.[9]

In some ancient manuscripts *hagiotēs* is found also in Paul's personal witness in 2 Cor. 1:12: "For our boast is this, the testimony of our conscience that we have behaved in the world, and still more toward you, with holiness and godly sincerity, not by earthly wisdom but by the grace of God" (RSV).

Kittel speaks of 2 Cor. 1:12 as "a difficult verse," because in some manuscripts we find *haplotēs* ("simplicity," KJV) rather than *hagiotēs* ("holiness"). A cognate of *haploos* ("single"), *haplotēs* signifies "sincerity, purity, or probity of mind," a disposition of "liberality, arising from simplicity and frankness of character."[10] Adopted by the NASB, RSV, and NIV, *hagiotēs* is the well-attested reading. However, since *hagiotēs* denotes a state but *eilikrineia* ("sincerity") a disposition (1 Cor. 5:8; 2 Cor. 2:17), it is probably better to follow the KJV and NRSV reading: *en haplotēti kai eilikrineia*. In either case, 2 Cor. 1:12 may be taken as Paul's testimony to what Wesley spoke of as "entire sanctification" (cf. 1 Thess. 2:10).

Another term, not derived from *hagios* but important in an examination of Christian holiness, is *hosiotēs*, occurring in Ephesians and Luke. In Ephesians Paul writes, "You were taught to put away your former way of life, your old self, corrupt and deluded by its lusts, and to be renewed in the spirit of your minds, and to clothe yourselves with the new self, created according to the likeness of God in true righteousness *[dikaiosunē]* and holiness" (4:22-24).

Luke uses the same two terms but in reverse order. In both passages *dikaiosunē* signifies an ethical lifestyle, while *hosiotēs* denotes "piety toward God." Together the two define a life of moral rectitude that reveals a heart of sincere devotion to God.

Hagiadzein, Hagiasmos—"Sanctify," "Sanctification"

Two other cognates of *hagios* are of special significance in understanding New Testament holiness, the verb *hagiadzein* and the noun *hagiasmos*. Clear evidence is wanting for these two words

---

9. See Michael Christensen, "Theosis and Sanctification: John Wesley's Reformulation of a Patristic Doctrine," *Wesleyan Theological Journal* 31 (fall 1996): 71-94.

10. *Analytical Greek Lexicon* (New York: Harper and Brothers, n.d.).

outside biblical and ecclesiastical writings. According to Moulton and Milligan, the suffix -adzein was as active as our -fy in producing new words, and the abstract -asmos accompanied it as -fication accompanies our words. When biblical writers therefore coined hagiadzein and hagiasmos, the Greeks would understand them to convey the idea of "holifying" or "holy-making."[11]

Hagiasmos is by far the most important term for understanding the nature of New Testament sanctification. It occurs 10 times in the Epistles (Rom. 6:19, 22; 1 Cor. 1:30; 1 Thess. 4:3, 4, 7; 2 Thess. 2:13; 1 Tim. 2:15; Heb. 12:14; and 1 Pet. 1:2). The NASB renders the term "sanctification" in each passage except 1 Pet. 1:2, in which hagiasmō pneumatos is rendered "by the sanctifying work of the Spirit."

In reference to hagiasmos Barclay writes, "Greek nouns which end in -asmos commonly describe a process, and hagiasmos is a process by which we become hagios. Hagiasmos is therefore the road to holiness. Sanctification is therefore more an ongoing process than it is a final state."[12] Hagiasmos, says Kittel, is a nomen actionis (a name denoting action). "Hence it signifies 'sanctifying' rather than 'sanctification.' It is of course conceivable that a nomen actionis might acquire a passive meaning, but philological investigation must begin with the active."[13]

Taking into account the various usages of hagiasmos in the Epistles, Arndt and Gingrich suggest that the word signifies "a process or, more often, its result." Turner concurs, claiming that when translated "holiness," it "connotes a state not native to its subject but as an outcome of action or progress."[14] The standard English versions, apparently agreeing, render the term either "holiness" or "sanctification," depending on its context.

Hagiadzein means literally "to make holy." Thayer's analysis calls for our attention. According to him, hagiadzein means (1) to hallow (God's name, Matt. 6:9; Christ as Lord, 1 Pet. 3:15); (2) to separate from things profane and dedicate to God: (a) things (2 Tim.

11. James Moulton and George Milligan, The Vocabulary of the Greek New Testament (Grand Rapids: Wm. B. Eerdmans Publishing Co., 1930), 4.

12. William Barclay, The New Testament (London: Collins, n.d.), 2:307. Our English "sanctification" (from sanctus, "holy," and facare, "to make") is the exact etymological equivalent of hagiasmos.

13. Kittel, Theological Dictionary, 1:113.

14. Turner, More Excellent Way, 83.

2:21); *(b)* persons (John 17:19); (3) *to purify: (a) to cleanse externally* (Heb. 9:13); *(b) to purify by expiation* (Eph. 5:26; Heb. 10:10, 14, 29); *(c) to purify internally by reformation of soul* (John 17:17, 19; 1 Thess. 5:23; Rom. 15:16). In general, Christians are called *hagiasmenoi,* "as those who, freed from the impurity of wickedness, have been brought near to God by their faith and sanctity" (see Acts 20:32; 26:18; 1 Cor. 6:11).[15]

What Thayer says of the verb *hagiadzein* is equally true of the action noun *hagiasmos,* as an examination of its usage will disclose.

Teleios—"Perfect"

Perhaps the most difficult term with which we must deal is the Greek term *teleios,* "perfect." It is essential, therefore, that the student endeavor to understand the term as used by the New Testament writers rather than certain Greek philosophers.

In the broadest sense, *teleios* denotes something that has arrived at its *telos,* which has actualized its raison d'être. Biologically, *teleios* may thus be rendered "full-grown," "mature," or "adult." Employing this metaphor, Paul admonished the Corinthians who were making a toy of glossolalia: "Do not be children in your thinking; rather, be infants in evil, but in thinking be adults *[teleioi]*" (1 Cor. 14:20).[16]

Of *teleios* Barclay writes, "It has nothing to do with what we might call abstract, philosophical, metaphysical perfection. . . . A thing is perfect if it fully realizes the purpose for which it was planned, and designed, and made. . . . *Teleios* is an adjective formed from the noun *telos.* A thing is *teleios* if it realizes the purpose for which it was planned; a man is perfect if he realizes the purpose for which he was created and sent into the world."[17]

In one word, Christian perfection is *functional,* as will become apparent upon an examination of the passages in the New Testament that employ *teleios* and its cognates.

---

15. Joseph Henry Thayer, *A Greek-English Lexicon of the New Testament* (Edinburgh: T. & T. Clark, 1958), 6.

16. John Wesley understood the "perfect" to be "adult" children of God (Heb. 5:11—6:1) or "fathers" in the faith (1 John 2:12-14).

17. William Barclay, *The Gospel of Matthew,* vol. 1 in *The Daily Study Bible* (Philadelphia: Westminster Press, 1956), 176.

SUBJECT INDEX

Saints, 134
Salt
  metaphor for disciples' role, 183
Sanctification
  in Book of Acts, 70 ff.
  based on Atonement, 156
  as communal, 128-29
  as death to the law, 105
  entire, 104, 132, 136-41, 204
    as spiritual health, 140
  fruit of, 125
  initial, 133-36
  and new covenant, 144-45, 167-69
  promised in OT, 58
  pursuit of, 169-72
  by the Spirit, 114 ff.
  and Torah, 89
  as wholeness, 10
Sedeq, sedeqah, 24-25
Sermon on the Mount, 173 ff.
  in gospel context, 174
  as holiness sermon, 173
  nature of, 11
  not a new legalism, 175
Shema, 55-56, 92, 116
Sin
  as depravity, 46
  and flesh, 115 ff.
  and grace, 48-51
  as *hubris*, 19
  indwelling/inherited, 96, 109
  nature of, 45
  as self-exaltation, 44
  as self-sovereignty, 44, 104

Sonship
  freedom of, 122
Spirit
  fruit of the, 84-85
  in intertestamental period, 66
  life in the, 83
  mind of the, 118
  in the OT, 64-67
Spirit-filled life
  defined by Christ, 63
Spiritual experience
  authentic and unauthentic, 79 ff.
Spiritual gifts (see also Gifts of the
  Spirit)
  test of authenticity, 80
  and love, 81
Tamim, 31-32, 193
Telos, teleios, 144, 206
Temptation
  and the Fall, 42-44
Theological exegesis, 76
Torah, 65, 87-89, 91, 93, 105-9, 115, 149,
  185-87
  internalized, 169
  nature of, 56-57
Total depravity
  and grace, 46
Vows, 191
Vulgate, 177
Westminster Shorter Catechism, 141
Worship
  as service to God, 126

INDEX OF PERSONS

Achtemeier, Paul, 110
Ambriosater, 86
Anderson, Bernhard, 41
Aquinas, Thomas, 68
Arminius, James, 112
Auber, Harriet, 132
Augsburger, Myron, 119, 178
Augustine, 10, 13, 109
Barclay, William, 134, 135, 141, 144, 154,
  175, 205, 206
Barrett, C. K., 83, 103
Barth, Karl, 124
Best, Ernst, 140
Birch, Bruce C., 24, 27, 38, 41, 44, 45, 50,
  55, 56

Bird, Phyllis, 40, 44
Blackman, E. C., 150
Böhler, Peter, 10
Bonhoeffer, Dietrich, 120
Boring, M. Eugene, 61n, 176, 181, 182,
  183, 191, 192
Bruce, F. F., 153, 155, 157, 159, 159n, 161
Brueggemann, Walter, 37
Brunner, Emil, 111
Buber, Martin, 27
Bultmann, Rudolf, 118
Buttrick, George A., 72, 189
Calvin, John, 10, 20, 107, 126
Childs, Brevard S., 56, 147
Chilton, Bruce, 95, 149, 150

SCRIPTURE INDEX

CRIPTURE INDEX

Genesis
1 35 ff.
1:1 36
1:1-2 64
1:21 36
1:26 37
1:26-27 37
1:26-28 36
1:27-28 40
1—15 51
1:28 38, 40, 41
1:29 41
1:31 38
2:2 161
2:2-3 161
2:4 36
2:7 39, 65
2:9 40, 41
2:15 39-40
2:16-17 40, 43, 50
2:17 108
2:24-25 40
2:25 40
3:1 43
3:1-24 42
3:5 45
3:6 43
3:7 44
3:7-13 44
3:8 41
3:8-9 39
3:9 48
3:9-24 48
3:11 49
3:14-19 44, 49
3:15 50
3:20 49
3:21-22 49
3:23-24 49
4:1-16 44
4:4 50
4:15 50
4:25 36, 94
5:1 46
5:1-2 36-37, 54n, 94
5:1-3 36-37
5:3 46
5:24 31
6:5 45, 46
6:9 31
8:20—9:17 50

9:6 37
11:1-9 45
12:1-3 50, 51, 52
14 164
15:5-6 52
17:1 29, 31, 32, 52, 52n, 193

Exodus
1—15 51
15:13 24
19:4-6 53, 105
19:5, 8 58
19:6 52
19:9a 16
19:10-12 16
19:12 16
19:18ab 16
19:18c 15
19:19b 15
19:21 16
19:21-22 16
19:23 16
19:24b 16
20:1-20 105
20:2 ff. 53
20:2-5 54
20:14 188
20:17 108
21:24 191
29:43 19
31:3 65
31:13 166
33:18-23 20
34:6-7 24
35:30-31 65

Leviticus
2:13 183
6:27 17
11:44-45 26
11:45 28
18:5 105, 109
19 16, 105
19:2 26
19:2, 33-34 28
19:33-34 194n
20:8 166
20:10 188n
20:26 26
21:15 166
22:9, 16, 32 166

24:20 191
Numbers
13:1-24 158
13:32-33 158
14 158
14:1-10 158
14:11 158
14:13-25 158
14:22-23 158
14:44 158
14:45 158
18:19 183
Deuteronomy
2:14 158
5:1-21 105
6:4 181
6:4-5 56, 116
6:21, 23 158
7:7-8 55
10:16 59
18:13 193
18:15, 18 148
19:15-21 192
19:21 191
22:22 188n
23:3-7 193
24:1 189, 189n
30:6 59, 116
30:7 193
32:4 31, 31n
34:9 65
Judges
5:11 25
6:34 65
11:29 65
13:25 65
1 Samuel
10:6 65
10:9-10 65
16:13 65
2 Samuel
22:31 31n
1 Kings
8:11 20
8:61 32
2 Kings
2:13 ff. 17
20:3 33
Ezra
4:14 183